# THE SECRET F
## —————— OF ——————
# ALCHEMY

"Written with depth, humor, and wit, *The Secret Fire of Alchemy* is a masterpiece in the field of spiritual alchemy—a link in the shining Golden Chain of the sacred knowledge of spiritual completion and liberation. In the spirit of C. G. Jung, Turner simultaneously explores the time-honored Eastern tradition of self-realization and the Western quest for the lost keys of alchemy. His relentless search across continents and lifetimes opens doors closed for centuries; reveals little-known connections between Hindu, Buddhist, Taoist, and Western esoteric lineages; and bears witness to the wonder of a Pan-Eurasian mystical tradition."

SANKARA BHAGAVADPADA, PH.D., VEDIC ASTROLOGER
AND AUTHOR OF *SELF-REALIZATION THROUGH SELF-KNOWING*

"In this beautifully written book, Kevin Turner uncovers the alchemical Great Work hidden in the inner reaches of Kriya Yoga as well as in Tibetan and Taoist practices. Turner is like a Tibetan *tertön* who rediscovers and reveals hidden spiritual treasures, revelations known as *terma* in Tibetan. His encounters with great teachers in Asia are shared with sincerity and courage, allowing us to participate in his inner journey and deepen our own. A joyful, living book."

GUIDO FERRARI, DIRECTOR OF
*TAO: THE WATERCOURSE WAY AT WU YI MOUNTAIN*

"In this deeply esoteric and well-researched account, Turner recounts his personal odyssey of spiritual evolution, the connection between Eastern mysticism and Western alchemy, and the rediscovery of the inner Stone of the Philosophers. Turner's dream initiation sequences are rare and among the best recorded in the alchemical tradition. Turner also has coined several new terms that I hope will find their way into broader discussions of human consciousness."

SABINE LUCAS, PH.D., JUNGIAN ANALYST AND
AUTHOR OF *PAST LIFE DREAMWORK*

"This book is a generous gift to the world of seekers, worthy of respect and gratitude; there is so much to contemplate here, not only about the path, but the strength of character it takes to walk it."

JACK ELIAS, CHT, AUTHOR OF *FINDING TRUE MAGIC*

"According to Jung, the paradox is 'one of our most precious spiritual possessions,' for 'only the paradox comes anywhere near to comprehending the fullness of life.' Nowhere is the truth of this statement more evident than in the tradition of alchemy, whose links to Kriya Yoga, kundalini, and shamanism are explored by Kevin B. Turner in his new book. Drawing on the author's personal experience over many years, as well as displaying a remarkable erudition of the literature in the field, this richly illustrated study is as fascinating as it is informative and is almost an initiatory experience in itself."

PAUL BISHOP, PROFESSOR AT THE UNIVERSITY OF GLASGOW, UK,
AND AUTHOR OF *THE DIONYSIAN SELF*

"*The Secret Fire of Alchemy* is a fascinating, engaging account of the author's out-of-body experiences, full-blown kundalini activation, telepathic connections, shamanic experiences, and enlightened insights during his courageous pilgrimage across various continents and cultures. Kevin's compelling book inspires us to expand our own understanding and experience of the vastness of human consciousness."

NANCY H. MCMONEAGLE, FORMER PRESIDENT AND
CEO OF THE MONROE INSTITUTE

"Kevin Turner, a curious, intuitive pilgrim of many intertwined paths, engagingly recounts significant encounters and observations along his path to 'becoming.' His inner and outer journeys reveal insights into the esoteric worlds of Eastern mysticism and Western alchemy, and his ouroboric cycle of spiritual successes and humbling defeats makes for an alchemical reading experience like no other."

ROBERT HINSHAW, PH.D., JUNGIAN ANALYST AND
FACULTY OF THE C. G. JUNG INSTITUTE, ZURICH

# THE SECRET FIRE

## OF

# ALCHEMY

### Kriya Yoga, Kundalini, and Shamanism

## KEVIN B. TURNER

Inner Traditions
Rochester, Vermont

Inner Traditions
One Park Street
Rochester, Vermont 05767
www.InnerTraditions.com

Text stock is SFI certified

Cataloging-in-Publication Data for this title is available from the Library of Congress.

ISBN 979-8-88850-069-9 (print)
ISBN 979-8-88850-070-5 (ebook)

Printed and bound in the United States by Lake Book Manufacturing, LLC
The text stock is SFI certified. The Sustainable Forestry Initiative® program promotes
sustainable forest management.

10  9  8  7  6  5  4  3  2  1

Text design by Debbie Glogover and layout by Virginia Scott Bowman
This book was typeset in Garamond Premier Pro, Gill Sans, and Columbia Serial
with The Seasons used as the display typeface.

Image credits are provided in the figure captions; images are in the public domain
unless otherwise noted. Figure 43.3 is licensed under CC BY 4.0.

To send correspondence to the author of this book, mail a first-class letter to the
author c/o Inner Traditions • Bear & Company, One Park Street, Rochester, VT
05767, and we will forward the communication, or contact the author directly at
**shamanism-asia.com.**

Scan the QR code and save 25% at InnerTraditions.com.
Browse over 2,000 titles on spirituality, the occult, ancient
mysteries, new science, holistic health, and natural medicine.

*Dedicated to*

*Paramahansa Hariharananda and all keepers*
*of the Secret Fire*

⁓◡

*I wish to express my heartfelt gratitude to all my teachers,*
*students, friends, and family who encouraged me*
*over the past many years to gather this record*
*for publication and assisted in the process.*

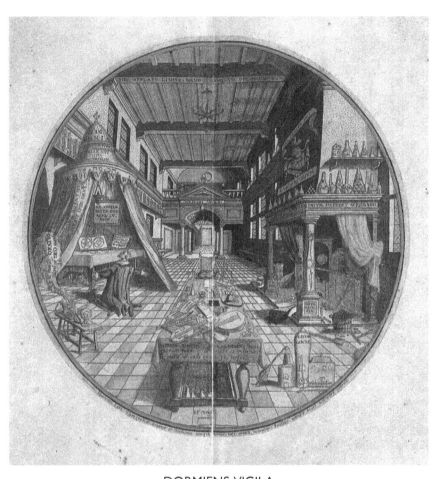

DORMIENS VIGILA
"While sleeping, be vigilant."
From the portico's architrave in Khunrath's
*Amphitheatrum Sapientiæ Æternæ*, 1595.

# Contents

# Introduction

*E MILLIBUS VIX UNI*

The testament of an alchemical novice herein was originally to be shared only within a focused circle of initiates. Pythagoras required initiates to remain silent for five years before they were allowed to enter his mystery school. The keys had to be earned. However, the time of secrecy is passing, and there is a greater need. The evolution of the soul is a human potential accessible to all of us. The goal of alchemy is the transformation of one's ordinary leaden consciousness into the gold of cosmic consciousness. I may not be the wisest link in the *Golden Chain*, but may this personal account be offered in service to the *All That Is*. The quotations from alchemical tradition are accurate and invite measured thought and meditation.

1

*Those for whom the knowledge of Alchemy is intended, will be able, in course of time and study, to understand even the most obscure of Alchemistic treatises . . . you will find the coveted knowledge.*

PETRUS BONUS, *THE NEW PEARL OF GREAT PRICE*, 1338

# 1

# Cave of Fire

*Work therefore with . . .*
*the secret, hidden and invisible fire.*

ARTEPHIUS, TWELFTH-CENTURY ALCHEMIST, *THE*
*SECRET BOOK OF ARTEPHIUS*, PART 6

That I did not deserve to die could not save me. As I attempt to write down all that has happened, be forewarned—if you are comfortable with your current worldview, read no further. Death marks not an end but a beginning. I shake as I grip my pen, *If this must be written in blood, so be it . . .*

In my twenty-first year, by chance, by fate, by intention, I'm drawn into a continuity of awareness in deep sleep to a series of initiations for which I can only find correlations in alchemy. With each inhalation, the bellows bring cool air in, and on exhalation warm air moves out. I seek to extend the time of each of the four phases: inhalation, pause, exhalation, and pause again. In time, I pass directly into dreams without losing a continuity of consciousness. These aren't common dreams but ones of unusual lucidity and power. The first initiation came in the form of repeating, progressive dreams:

*I descend steps hewn from stone to a cave with inner chambers. I walk until I find a room where I see a freestanding stone pillar upon a raised platform. From the top of this stone pillar pours a blazing magma. I'm fascinated, held entranced and cannot turn away. Behind me, a male and a female seal me into the chamber. As the room fills with burning lava, I'm alarmed—surely, I'll soon be burned to ashes! I awaken before the molten fires reach me . . .*

Fig. 1.1. Portal of Eternal Wisdom,
plate 3 from Heinrich Khunrath's *Amphitheatrum Sapientiae*, 1601.
Courtesy of Science History Institute

*VITRIOLVM: Visita Interiora Terrae Rectificando
Invenie Occultum Lapidem Veram Medicinam*
Visit the interior of the earth and by rectifying [purifying/refining], you will find the hidden stone which is the true medicine.

ALCHEMICAL AXIOM, FIRST NOTED IN BASILIO
VALENTINO'S *AZOTH*, 1613

Despite the increasing rigors of architectural studies at the university, I'm again and again drawn in my deep sleep to descend to the underground chamber, to my inner stone room of rumbling fiery magma emerging from the earth. Night after night, I'm entombed by the pair to face my impending death alone, yet always I awaken before the lava reaches me (only later did I research and discover the alchemical quotations and illustrations seen throughout this account).

Lightning . . . gave to the flames of the volcano a bloodlike appearance . . . Vesuvius [volcano] roars. . . . Wrapped in darkness, I seemed to descend into an abyss. I know not how long I remained in that situation.

THE MOST HOLY TRINOSOPHIA[1]

Weeks pass before a new stage unfolds. I'm yet again led by an unseen power to descend into the cave to the pillar of exuberating fire. I'm again sealed in by the pair, but this time I say an inner farewell to all I know in this life, and decisively gather my courage to stare down the primal magma: *The only way out of this is through!* I wade barefoot directly into the burning lava spreading over the stone cave floor.

Curiously, the molten fury offers no pain, and I feel only the rise of a dry heat within me. The room fills to the ceiling with the glowing lava. I calmly surrender as I'm incinerated into ashen embers. Slowly, this dark ash cools into stone, and I become heavy black stone— timeless, deeply at peace. This repeated over several nights until I awoke one morning with a fresh mind of clear light, full of curiosity.

A lake of fire presented itself to my sight. Sulphur and bitumen rolled in flaming waves. I trembled. A loud voice commanded me to pass through the flames. I obeyed, and the flames seemed to have lost their power. For a long time I walked within the conflagration.

THE MOST HOLY TRINOSOPHIA[2]

A new plateau of remembrance is reached, and though the dream stages continued, I no longer found them frightening. I look forward

Fig. 1.2. Detail from the Ripley Scroll, 1590. Note ascending white
feathers and descending red drops into a sea of red below;
a pair of angels stand behind the initiate.
From Princeton University Library Special Collections

to being sealed in, swallowed into my nightly fiery deaths and stony,
cataleptic rest, as I feel more myself each time it occurs. I'm calcified
and dissolved over and again until finally came the *Separation of the
White from the Black*:

> *Humming within the immobile stone of the physical body, I feel and
> know myself to be like a thin skeleton of highly vibrating white light.
> I am the wavering filament of pure luminescence. The fixed is now
> volatile, and like an electric wisp I'm now as slippery and translucent
> as light through a window. Lifting away from the stone, I am free! I
> vibrate and float around the room as a filament of white lightning.
> An indescribable joy fills me; I am utterly myself. I soon find myself
> standing down on the street before my home, light shimmering*

*everywhere off the wet surfaces after an evening rain shower. A gentle peace fills my soul, and I roam my neighborhood in delight.*

> *Solvite Corpora et Coagulata Spiritus*
> Dissolve the body and coagulate the spirit.
>
> THE OUROBORIC CYCLE,
>
> AN AXIOM OF MEDIEVAL ALCHEMY

> *We dissolve the living body with Apollo's fire—*
> *So that what was before a Stone may become a Spirit.*
>
> EPIGRAM CONCERNING THE PHILOSOPHERS' STONE BY
> ALEXANDER DE S. TO GULIEMUS BLANCUS, FROM
> *A GOLDEN AND BLESSED CASKET OF NATURE'S MARVELS*
> BY BENEDICTUS FIGULUS, 1608

Fig. I.3. The "dark fire" of the black sun divides
spirit and soul from the putrefied body.
Daniel Stoltzius von Stoltzenberg, *Viridarium Chymicum*, Frankfurt, 1624.

The midnight forays away from my home became more frequent. Nightly now, I allow my body to drop into the cement-like heaviness, soon reidentifying as the white filament of light. I will myself away from my tomb of stone, released from the heavy, dark ballast of the physical body. The joy of such freedom almost made returning to my fleshy body a burden, feeling encased in a primate form, but in time I learned to balance these two ways of being.

> The symbol of chemistry is drawn by the creation of its adepts, who cleanse and save the divine soul bound in the elements, and who free the divine spirit from its mixture with the flesh.*
>
> ZOSIMOS OF PANOPOLIS[3]

---

*Alternative translation by C. G. Jung: For those who rescue and purify the divine soul imprisoned in the elements, and especially for those who separate the divine spirit from the flesh in which it is entangled . . .

# 2

# Pineal Portal

*In the Sounding of the Trumpet:*
*"Mercury contains all that the Sages seek . . .*
*It dissolves, softens, and extracts the soul from the body."*

EDWARD KELLY, *STONE OF THE PHILOSOPHERS*

That spring of 1982 a three-year process of profound inner initiations commenced in my deep sleep, leading me to eventually abandon my familiar land to roam over the world in search of the sacred key, the *Stone* all philosophers seek, "the quintessence of the Sages, the living mercury which has in itself the heavenly spirit, the most precious of all treasures" (*Sophic Hydrolith*, part 4, 1678).[1]

Weeks after these dream initiations began, the cave of fire was no longer required. Melting into ashen stone while still remaining awake, conscious of the silvery tendril of soul now released, I enjoyed a certain freedom in my local neighborhood for some weeks. Then one evening a new development occurred:

*As my body lay in a heavy stonelike catalepsy, I again reindentify as a long silvery wisp of electricity. However, this time I, the silvery wisp, am drawn upward into a tiny point of liquid metal light at the center of my head. I hear a high-pitched siren growing into a thundering freight train or a heavy waterfall, then becoming many bells struck all around me—now emanating from the center of my head. Louder and louder it becomes until I can no longer bear it. Immersed in intense fear, the process ends.*

Every few nights this repeats: my silvery, electric-light self is inexorably pulled upward through my spine, condensing into a point in the center of my head with the terrifying, piercing sound of metal bells, a high-pitched air-raid siren, or at other times the deeper and more terrifying sound—that of a great rumbling train with its deafening whistle blowing. Time and time again this came, but intense fear arrested the process, such that I would fall into an oblivion of unconsciousness.

Until one has become accustomed to it, the actual process of passing through the "Door" in the pineal gland produces an effect of extreme mental confusion and a terrible fear. Indeed, one feels that one is heading straight for death or insanity.

OLIVER FOX[2]

Nightly now, within my cooling body of stone, I'm withdrawn into my charged spine—an inner pillar of power, then drawn upward, approaching the terrifying rumble at the center of my brain. One evening I simply could not stem the flow into the center of my head. Again, I know the only escape is in and through, so I surrender to the inevitable and with all my courage I focus and fall into the roar as it reaches a ringing crescendo, collapsing into a silvery point at the center of my skull. *Pop!* As only a point of awareness, I'm pulled up and out the top of my head, away from my body. . . .

Led by the blazing star, the candidate throws himself into the midst of the waves. With his lamp upon the crown of his head (the spirit fire lifted into the pineal gland) he struggles for mastery over the currents of the etheric world.

MANLY P. HALL[3]

Fig. 2.1. *Trinosophia*, page 10 of *La Très Sainte Trinosophie*, alchemical text attributed to the Comte de Saint-Germain, 1855.

MS 2400, Bibliotheque de Troyes, France

I struck a terrific blow upon the neck of the serpent. The sword rebounded and the blow re-echoed as if I had struck on a brass bell. No sooner had I obeyed the voice than the altar disappeared and the columns vanished in boundless space. The sound which I had heard when striking the altar repeated itself as if a thousand blows had been struck at the same time. A hand seized me by the hair and lifted me toward the vault which opened to let me through.

THE MOST HOLY TRINOSOPHIA[4]

*The room is lit by a diffuse, shimmering light, as I move about the room now as only a point of awareness thrilled with glorious freedom! I pass out my window calmly observing the trees, houses, and streets of my neighborhood. I'm able to perceive a different quality of color in this state that is not apparent in the usual nighttime physical perception. Calm and quiet at this hour, I hover by trees and homes with a clarity I'd never known before.*

I told nothing of my adventures to my family or friends. An inner voice advised me, "You needn't speak of these things—everyone inwardly knows."

Fig. 2.2. Hermes suggests discretion. Achilles Bocchius, *Symbolicarum quaestionum.* Bologna, 1555.

Despite the intensity of architectural studies, I day by day gently passed into a ceaseless altered state of consciousness, a continuum where everyone and every event felt connected. Time had little meaning; memories of yesterday and those of years ago were equally as clear. I recalled the first time I felt this way:

Andrew and I became immediate friends on that warm first day of primary school in September. The old limestone-and-brick school building was so close I could walk the few blocks there along the stone walls that held back the hilly grasses, common in southern Indiana. After a week or so, I learned our houses both backed an alley overgrown with tall green grasses and vine. Andrew invited me to visit his home one early evening, and I gladly accepted. We walked together down the long alley between our homes, jumping on stones and picking up sticks.

Entering the backdoor of his home, a wave of dreamy nostalgia poured over me. The smells of a familiar dish wafted from the kitchen, as his mother emerged in a simple European dress. His father sat in the living room, his feet upon a great stuffed elephant foot stump, reading a newspaper. He looked up and his eyes shone with a foreign, yet familiar intensity. He leaned forward to his son and said something like, *Wie war die Schule heute, mein Sohn?* Andrew replied to his father that his school day was fine, and quickly turned to explain to me that he and his family were from Germany. His father had come to lecture at the university. They greeted me cordially. His parents had strong accents, but Andrew had none.

"*Gott* is everywhere and everything, even in this cookie," explained Andrew, as we chewed fresh-baked cookies in his backyard after dinner. I had no religious upbringing so this concept was not only new but mind-stretching. One of the finest gifts I ever received from my parents was the freedom to experience spiritual life in my own way. We attended no church, and I was not indoctrinated into any belief system. (That my first best friend should be a young German philosopher now seems wholly befitting.) This talk of God was new; I asked, "God is everything, and in everything, you say? So then, who is this God?" Andrew paused for a moment, perhaps to think of how to reply in English, "Gott created everything, and He created all of us—so He is us!"

My six-year-old world paused to imagine a knowing that was *everywhere* and *everyone* in the universe. I was speechless, reeling backward. I silently returned home where I turned deeply inward. For days I floated in a formless spaciousness, my first introduction to what Tibetans call the *All-Pervading Awareness*.

# 3

# Dominus Liminis

Fig. 3.1. Detail of *Dweller on the Threshold*.
Painting by Reginald W. Machell (1854–1927).

*Niemand ist mehr Sklave,*
*als der sich für frei hält, ohne es zu sein.*
None are more hopelessly enslaved than those who falsely
believe they are free.

J. W. VON GOETHE,
DIE WAHLVERWANDTSCHAFTEN

Despite my relative astral freedom and recovered sense of the All-Pervading Awareness, I was not entirely free and I found boundaries to my explorations. Thus, I was prepared for another initiation in the form of a repeating astral challenge:

*Collapsing into my body of stone, I become the silvery filament of electric intensity. I lift out and away as usual, only this time I'm thunderstruck to encounter a great menace darkening my doorsill! I had avoided shadowy forms in my astral excursions before, so I turn away and attempt to exit the window. This time I'm invisibly held and firmly instructed by a higher knowing to leave only through my door. The enormous black peril stands at the threshold, neither entering nor departing. The sheer malevolence of this being sends a shivering chill to the center of my being, and I'm frozen in unspeakable terror. I return to my body.*

The process repeated several evenings in a row. As soon as I lift away from my body, the dweller is there, his shifting form varying between a hooded figure of intensely dark malice, and a colossal shadowy beast in a silent, seething rage. I felt soul-sick just to be in its presence. I remain terrified to the center of my being, and all my attempts to exit my room fail time and again. Night after night, the Dweller bars my door, his sheer malevolence paralyzing me. I could not understand why this etheric beast did not devour me, but for some reason it did not or could not enter. *Perhaps it's not as powerful as it looks?* In time it felt familiar, even a bit pathetic, as if he contained long forgotten episodes, pitiful mistakes, and failures of character. I even sensed a certain pain in it, and a sympathetic kinship developed. I played with light in my room while my menace stood at the door.

Memory haunts me from age to age, and passion leads me by the hand—evil have I done, and with sorrow have I made acquaintance from age to age, and from age to age evil shall I do, and sorrow shall I know till my redemption comes.

H. RIDER HAGGARD, *SHE*[1]

For weeks this continued. Whenever I sought to exit my door, he blocked it. I solaced myself by watching from my window astral lights dance in the streets below. The dark peril never budged, held at the threshold by some invisible force. Night after night he stood like a sentinel until I could bear it no longer! *I demand to pass this door!* I scream-beamed at him, but he stood firm, growing more powerful as he gathered up shadows of dark pasts I could not fathom. After further attempts, impossibly brief visions of other times and places danced before my inner gaze; negative emotions had been long ago concentrated into an abysmal pit of desolation. I know this shadow, and recognize its familiar darkness—a radiation of dark greed and hidden fears from an unknown past—*perhaps my own?*

> Yet my Threshold is fashioned out of all the timidity that remains in thee, out of all the dread of the strength needed to take full responsibility for all thy thoughts and actions. As long as there remains in thee a trace of fear of becoming thyself the guide of thine own destiny, just so long will this Threshold lack what still remains to be built into it.
>
> RUDOLF STEINER[2]

Finally, one astral evening I decided nothing would deny me freedom. *I would make use of the power of the very fear that kept me in my room to push this menace back, or I would die!* I ploughed into the black horror with all the *Force of my Will.* . . . He vanished, and I found myself floating down the stairwell. An ancient ballast fell away, light emerged, and I came to know a greater freedom than ever before.

# 4

# Temple

*Initiation into the Mysteries was defined by the ancient philosophers as life's supreme adventure and as the greatest good that can be conferred upon the human soul during its terrestrial sojourn.*

MANLY P. HALL, *NOTES & COMMENTARIES TO THE MOST HOLY TRINOSOPHIA*

Local restrictions on astral travel now lifted, I am drawn in the deep of night to a mountain forest temple far over a wide sea. This sacred keep became a regular destination for weeks:

*I'm seated upon a red carpet on the floor before a low, black table covered in golden ritual instruments. On either side are walls of golden lanterns lit from within. Oriental designs appear on some of the lanterns. The temple space is clearly in the Far East. Ahead of me, beyond the large low table, where there would normally be an altar of some kind, there is instead only a large window looking out to a forested scene. I am, or someone is, performing an elaborate ritual with fire, water, incense, bells, and chanting . . . I alternate between being the performer of the ritual and only observing the ritual. I'm enchanted by the peace, power, and serenity emanating from the temple.*

*The complexity of the ritual was offset by the simplicity of the remote mountain setting. Night after night I sit before this black table of ritual instruments before, not an altar, but the open window to a mountain wall. A small ceremonial fire burns before me, and I'm enveloped in a soft glow by walls of yellow paper lanterns. Awareness continues to drift between being the performer of the ritual and watching him from a distance as a roaming point of awareness. The peace and presence of the place is unlike any I've ever known.*

*A shadow in the round mirror in the tower of a*
 *millionaire,*
*Or a silhouette in the square mirror in the palace of the*
 *Emperor of Chin:*
*Who knows from where they have come?*

   KUKAI (KOBO DAISHI) "SINGING IMAGE OF A
    SHADOW IN A MIRROR," CIRCA 820

Each time I visit I sense the creation of an astral structure of remembrance, but I recall few details of how this is occurring, only that the halls and doors of childhood dreams are now brought into a totality of circles within squares, within yet greater circles, discovering more halls of golden lanterns on each return. After weeks of nightly journeys to this remote mountain fastness, a sense of completion is reached and I visit no more. That I would come to live longer in Asia than in the country of my birth did not occur to me at this time. It was simply fait accompli.

Through "hypnotic Visions or dream-Revelations" the soul can Undertake to "understand and explain the secrets of the whole created Universe . . . , to be united with good Spirits; to recount things past, contemplate Present Events, [and] presage those to come."

   HEINRICH KHUNRATH[1]

With these new inner structures now in place, the question from where we came before birth and where we are going after death that had never left me since childhood was reawakened. Days later I set my intention before sleep: *I want to know the secrets of life and death.* I passed through the cataleptic state quickly and leaned up and away from my body. A goddess-like spirit twirled in the room, her soul's voice, like an angelic choir, lifted and passed into my mind on a thin silver wave, "Come, I will show you . . ." Astonished, I could only nod my astral head:

> *We pass out into the night and upward through the dark sky to what felt like the edge of Earth's atmosphere, gracefully arriving in a formal garden (much like parks I would see in Central European cities years later). She stands aside, and another form guides me through this park. Colors unlike those on earth exude their glowing hues from an unknown inner source through the flowers and trees. We soon come before a man with a dark beard in an 1890s three-piece suit sitting on a park bench, looking around in stark amazement. He has a vaguely Mediterranean appearance and holds himself as though he were an authority, sitting rather stiffly. He is waiting for something, seemingly bewildered. I understand that he has finished his time on earth. I focus on him and perceive his radiating self-reflections, "Is this really what it's like afterward?" He is curiously familiar to me, but I cannot place how I might know him. I feel vague, stirring emotions and a compulsion to talk with him, but the spirit beside me interrupts, "He won't understand." I have no idea what that means, but I take the hint and we move away. Awareness drifts for weeks or even months, far into vaguely remembered realms.*

The sharp chatter of birds and painful glare of sunlight burst upon my awareness. Utterly disoriented, I at first had no idea where or when I was. Material reality soon made itself known, as I felt cold and wet under the covers. *What the . . . ?* Unable to carry my body to the bathroom in the middle of the night, my bladder had off-loaded its surplus.

It had been a long, far journey.

# 5

# Mirror of Souls

*All that, whereof this world is an earthly mirror, and an earthly parable, is present in the Divine Kingdom in great perfection and in Spiritual Being.*
JACOB BOEHME, *THREEFOLD LIFE OF MAN*, 1620

Architectural projects were due, and weeks of intense material focus were required in the autumn of 1982. Once my professors were supplied with their requirements, I returned inward, breathing deeply each evening before sleep, when came upon me an initiatory dream of power and significance:

*Side by side, a venerable Teacher and I walk, deep in conversation, down a grand European hall of exquisite beauty. Mirrors within high-arched frames are on my left, while on my right are matching high-arched windows looking out to formal gardens. Overhead, a vaulted ceiling with delicate paintings and sculptured cornices stretched the entire length of the magnificent hall. I wondered inwardly where, or perhaps when this place could be? The elderly teacher's inner voice carries across centuries, through varying times and places. So perfect is the merging of our consciousnesses that my questions are answered as I formulate them. He is more than just attuned to me; he seems to know me better than I know myself. I perceive his messages in profound astonishment.*

*The mysterious figure gives a telepathic discourse regarding time, change, and the evolution of human society, culture, and consciousness. Tracts of little-known knowledge regarding historical developments in Europe move as waves between us. Still young, I feel stretched, awestruck, and unable to encompass the scope of this alternate history of humankind unveiled in pure thought between us. Yet another aspect of myself, a mature, wiser self, understands and is replying to the teacher in kind—in thought, as though I already know portions of all this, a topic that has been in continuous discussion over great lengths of time. These two aspects of myself puzzle me. We three continue down the hall: my young Self in awe of this revelation, my mature Self taking it in as a matter of course, and the elderly Teacher. Memories rise from a deep and dormant slumber—one of this teacher's long-term projects had focused its efforts in this very hall.*

*The elderly teacher now turns to face me for the first time, and I'm stunned—his head is only an oval of brilliant light! I become frightened, it's too much for my spiritually immature perception. Panicking, I attempt to grasp at something familiar, anything young Kevin could remember and understand.*

*Knowing I have reached my capacity, he beams with great force into my mind: "You must remember!" I'm jolted as though a crack of lightning had shot through me. In a panic, I know and feel that I must know this man's face; I must remember his face! I focus on the brilliant oval and perceive lightning-white light as wrinkled lines in his craggy, ancient face. There is a statesmanlike familiarity, yet I cannot identify him. The teacher magnetically tries to hold my attention longer, but as my focus falters and fades he shouts a code phrase into my disoriented consciousness. I bury my face in my hands, crushed at the memory of having forgotten his counsel so many times before. I fold inward, and awaken.*

Fig. 5.1. Detail of *The Signing of Peace in the Hall of Mirrors*,
painting by William Orpen.

The dream remains engraved in my memory. My quest had now expanded: in addition to the secrets of life and death, I must also remember and understand this visionary experience, the alternative history, and discover more about this mysterious figure—this mystagogue. *When and who is this man? What was it I had forgotten?* My intentions were now fused together by a new and singular flame: to penetrate this hidden knowledge.

# 6

# Zwei Seelen

*An intelligent man finds almost everything ridiculous, a*
*wise man hardly anything.*

GOETHE, *MAXIMS AND REFLECTIONS*, 1833

As I had no name to go by, I inwardly referred to the teacher with
the face of light as *the one who remembered me,* and wondered
if and when I might meet him again. Since that dream awakening,
alternating light and shadows portending unanswerable questions kept
me awake late at night. *Of what remembrance did this teacher speak?* I
sensed a split in myself, and a soul loneliness spread over me.

I could remedy this only by having a written conversation between
these two selves: *How can I be both a naive youth, and yet also a worldly
adult Self?* Discovering an unused notebook with a green cover in my
piles of notes, I felt compelled to keep a conversational journal that year.
In this written journal I could ask questions of my elder Self, and he
would reply in written word. Chills and streams of tingling power rose
up my spine each time he gave an especially inspiring reply, jolting more
memory. This often frightened me into a soul wakefulness so intense I
could no longer bear it, and I would run from it. Days or weeks later,
I would pick it up and again be thrilled into a half-madness by the

automatic writing. I spoke to no one about the dream, my elder self, or the teacher with the head of light.

> Emanuel Swedenborg, Edgar Cayce, Rudolf Steiner, Don Juan Matus, and James Van Praagh all subscribe to the binary soul doctrine. Besides the physical body, they all agree, human beings are also composed of two other very distinct nonphysical components. Cayce and Steiner use the very same terminology for these two parts, each referring to them simply as the soul and spirit. Meanwhile, Swedenborg calls them the "inward" and "outward" elements of the soul, Matus calls them the tonal and nagual, Daskalos calls them the psychical and noetical bodies, and Van Praagh calls them the astral and mental bodies.
>
> PETER NOVAK[1]

Advanced Humanities I & II, the course descriptions read, and I registered immediately. We read the Upanishads, Kafka, the lives of great composers, and best of all, portions of *Faust* written by Goethe. The professor was an older, kindly, conscientious woman with long gray hair tied back, and would always give the needed overview of the next topic. One afternoon she introduced Goethe's Doctor Faust as a "divided man." I sat up in my seat with a jolt, and my green journal of divided selves immediately called to me from my hidden drawer a mile away. One line caught my attention: *Zwei Seelen wohnen, ach! in meiner Brust.*

> *Alas, two souls dwell within this breast.*
> *And each is fain to leave its brother.*
> *The one, fast clinging, to the world adheres*
> *With clutching organs, in love's sturdy lust;*
> *The other strongly lifts itself from dust*
> *To yonder high, ancestral spheres.*
> *Oh, are there spirits hovering near . . .*
>
> GOETHE, *Faust*

*Yes, he is correct—we have two souls! How did he know this? Perhaps this Goethe is my mysterious teacher from the mirrored hall?* I had first encountered Goethe's work during my high school German studies, culminating in a summer exchange to Augsburg, West Germany, in 1979, a life-altering experience. I rushed to the university library during lunch break to find what books by Goethe they may have, and if there might be a portrait of him. I found a biography, a book of quotes, as well as a volume of selected works in translation—and his portrait. *Sadly, no, Goethe has not my mystagogue's face.* I could only hope my teacher was still alive.

> Rudolf Steiner taught that Goethe had undergone . . . initiation . . . within his soul during sleep, rather than as a physical plane ceremony.
>
> ADRIAN ANDERSON[2]

# 7

# Forgotten Body

*Always know and remember that you are more than your physical body.*

ROBERT A. MONROE, FOUNDER
OF THE MONROE INSTITUTE

The Christmas holidays returned me to my family home for a welcome break from university studies. It hadn't yet snowed, and leaves were now piled and rotting in driveways all over our forested neighborhood. Exhausted from the long semester of external academic demands and internal exploration, I fell asleep one afternoon some days before Christmas Eve:

What am I doing up here? *I calmly hover a dozen meters above a man and a boy raking autumn leaves from a long driveway.* Oh, I'm away from my body! *Months had passed since I was lucid in this state and I'd nearly lost familiarity with it. I immediately spin into wild, impossible aerial maneuvers high over the front yard with a joy that only gymnasts or stunt pilots can know. I pause in midair over the leaf-raking pair and wonder,* Well, this is fun, but where did I leave my body? *In this state, the ordinary linear-time mind is not quite engaged. What day is it? This I could not recall, but I did know:* My body must be around here somewhere . . . *I sweep around the house, scanning the side and back yards. Nothing. I enter the breakfast room, and skim across the ceiling into the family room—again nothing.*

*Passing along the ceiling of the kitchen, I come upon a sudden and chilling scene—a translucent humanoid creature stands at the sink manipulating instruments. The luminescent colors are both fantastic and grotesque, like an anatomical mannequin that has been splayed open, surrounded by strange auric light patterns that wove throughout the tissues. The creature peacefully continues its work, and seems to pose no threat. I feel this was one of those things to be left alone, to be later understood. I carry on in search of my physical frame. I pass into other rooms, still moving along the ceiling. Out through the dining room window, I rise outdoors up to the height of the second floor. Looking into a bedroom window from outside in mid-air, I see the room now from a point of awareness hovering in space, and I'm thunderstruck! There in my bed, lay a sleeping youth!* How could anyone have the brazen insolence to enter our house and take a nap in a stranger's bed—MY bed—in the middle of the afternoon! How DARE he! *I draw closer and study the sleeping young man. Curiously, his sandy-blond hair and cheekbones are familiar. Then, like a magnet, I'm drawn into my body, encased once again in a simian sarcophagus of stone.*

Gently, I move back into sync with the physical frame, stirring my blood for a moment. I take a deep breath and raise my meat marionette up by unseen soul strings. *Wow.* I slowly stand, getting used to gravity again, and look into the small, wood-framed mirror high on the wall. *Why did I not recognize myself? Why did my face appear different from the outside?* Then it dawns: *I have never seen myself, live in real time, with my eyes closed—a view not possible in a mirror, as my eyes are then open. And my hair is parted to my right, not my left, as it appears to be when I see myself in a mirror!*

My nose welcomed the scents of an early dinner rising from the kitchen below. Still a bit unsteady in my bodily frame, I made my way slowly down the stairs. I silently sat on the kitchen stool, watching my mother in her *marionette* at the sink, still posing no threat. Medical clairvoyants have claimed for centuries that they can perceive within the bodies of their clients. Undoubtedly this is the origin of acupuncture; perceiving the invisible lines of force in the human body was the work of the ancient Chinese shamans. I got a taste of this that afternoon, but today I was more interested in dinner than spiritual anatomy. I would learn in time to perceive astral forms and forces, even within my own body. Importantly, I also learned, or rather remembered, that even when away from the body one doesn't truly become lost. We're psychically bound to our body until we're ready to relinquish it. I further pondered the greater question of identity, *If I am both Kevin and Elder Self, and yet not my body, then who am I and what is happening here?* Such questions remained with me, but my young body needed nourishment and this remained my holiday priority.

Days later I watched an old film on late-night television called *Invisible Agent* (1942), wherein a man uses his chemically induced invisibility to spy upon Nazi Germany. The low-budget film was unremarkable, but the intriguing concept affected me profoundly—the use of *invisibility* as a tool to sway battles or even win wars. I immediately thought of my astral adventures and wondered whether this might be viable. Striking also was that at the end of this film a Japanese agent attached to the embassy in Berlin kills a Gestapo officer, supposedly an ally, and then kills himself in front of a Buddhist altar. The dark episode suddenly felt very visceral, even personal, and it upset me greatly. A sensation washed through me that Germany and Japan were, or would be a part of my life, but I had no sense of why.

"Spiritual psychology," said my mother the following day, when I asked about the topic for her Sunday afternoon meeting in our living room. A group of her alternative friends gathered, and she invited me to join, perhaps inwardly intuiting my astral explorations. I was still a rebellious youth and anything of interest to my parents couldn't pos-

*XLII.*

Anima Ho-   Die Seele des
minis.   Menschen.

Fig. 7.1. The Soul of Man.
Comenius, *Orbis Pictus*, 1658, plate 17.

sibly be of any interest to me, so I defiantly kicked a soccer ball about outside instead. After the talk, everyone left and my mother said the speaker had trained at the Monroe Institute.* The spirits must have had a good laugh that day, as I missed my cue for the spiritual science I so desperately sought. I could not have known then that I would become an instructor there twenty years later. Inwardly I was an explorer of spirit worlds, but outwardly I was still an insolent young man, full of unstable hormones—and full of myself.

---

*The Monroe Institute specializes in out-of-body travel, afterlife exploration, psychokinesis, and remote viewing.

# 8

# Spiritual Science

*Bene visit qui bene latuit.*
*One lives best by the hidden life.*

FRANCIS BACON (1561–1626),
*THE ADVANCEMENT OF LEARNING*, 21.2

As I approached my upcoming internship, the study of architecture drew less and less of my interest, while my astral adventures expanded. After the holidays I returned to university and scoured the libraries for information on parapsychology, knowing it might just be my only possible life interest. There I discovered an old book, *Astral Projection*, by Oliver Fox, and in it he mentions the Pineal Doorway at the center of the head. *I use the same—I've found an ally in this world!* This man's accounts from the 1920s were the only ones I had yet found that precisely described my own experiences. Fox writes:

> I concentrated on the attempt to leave my body, and the result was
> most interesting. I felt my incorporeal self rushing towards, and
> being condensed in, the pineal gland—at least, this was the sen-
> sation and at the same time the golden astral light blazed up and

became brilliant; then my body pulled me back, and the astral light died down again, the sensation being precisely the reverse of the previous one, i.e., my incorporeal self rushed back [into the pineal], [expanding] away from the pineal gland . . . until it coincided with the physical body once more. I concentrated again and the same thing happened, but at the third attempt I succeeded in obtaining separation.[1]

Further on, Fox describes the terrifying sounds as one approaches the Pineal Doorway:

[The] incorporeal self, which was coincident with its physical prison, now rushes up his body and becomes condensed in that pineal point within his brain and batters against the door, while the pale golden light increases to a blaze of glory and a veritable inferno of strange sounds assails his ears. . . . It will appear to him that his fluidic self has again subsided within his physical body; but the terrifying sounds and apparitions are no more, and the room is evenly illuminated by the pale golden radiance. There is a blessed sense of calm after a storm, and fear gives place to triumphant exaltation; for the phase of terror, with its suggestions of coming death or madness, is over. He has passed through the Pineal Door.[2]

I found little but medical information about the pineal gland in the libraries, and even that was limited. However, Rene Descartes captured my attention. The seventeenth-century scientist, mathematician, and philosopher is most well-known for *Cogito, ergo sum* (I think, therefore I am) and Cartesian dualism—the separation of the mind and body, or perhaps the soul and the body. Though a scientist, he proposed that the pineal gland is the "seat of the soul." He postulated the body and the spirit meet at the pineal gland and they both affect each other there. In my experiences, as well as in Fox's, the pineal was an entry and exit point of the soul or spirit. *Is there a difference between spirit and soul?* Shaking with excitement I read more about our puppets *made of earth*. Descartes writes: "I suppose the body to be nothing but a statue or machine made of earth, which God forms with the explicit intention of making it as much as possible like us"[3]

Furthermore, Descartes suggests the gland "secretes our thoughts" as they moved through the cerebrospinal fluid to the rest of the brain. Descartes further postulated that the pineal gland is full of animal spirits, describing these spirits as "a very fine wind, or rather a lively and pure flame." I had no idea what this meant, but I was held spellbound, and had to remember to breathe. Descartes proposed that imagination arises in the same way as perception, except that it is not caused by external objects. Descartes wrote: "And note that I say 'imagines or perceives by the senses.'" Now this was beginning to make sense, and I was reminded of my astral journeys that can often feel so imaginary.

Lastly, Descartes theorized that bodily mobility has its origins in the movements of the pineal gland by "the force of the soul," if there is "a soul in the body; or by spirits swirling about in the ventricles." Descartes continued, "And note that if we have an idea about moving a member, that idea—consisting of nothing but the way in which spirits flow from the gland—is the cause of the movement itself." In other words, it is the soul that enlivens a body, breathes into and through a body, perceives through the body, and brings truly new ideas from a larger reality to the conscious personality—this is surely so self-evident that even an empiricist like Descartes stood by this idea.

*I love those who yearn for the impossible.*

GOETHE, *FAUST*, PART 2, ACT 2,
CLASSICAL WALPURGIS NIGHT, 1832

The fascination with the *Secrets of Life and Death* reasserted itself once again, and one afternoon I laid down on my bed one early evening to find out. *I must know the truth of what it's like to die, to take the last breath.* I counted my in-breath up to twelve, held it for twelve

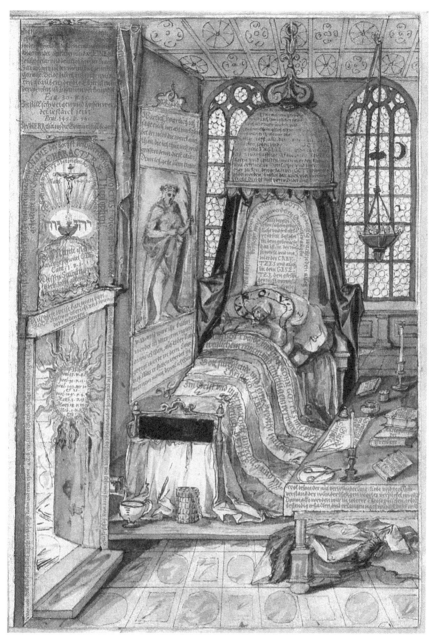

Fig. 8.1. Heinrich Khunrath, *Alchemist in his Bedchamber*,
*Amphitheatre* II, page 116. Note the scrolling revelations
unfurling from remaining awake while the body rests
in the deep sleep state.
British Library archive, MS Sloane 181. British Library, London.

counts, and exhaled over twelve counts, imagining I was dying. I slowly increased the counts to twenty, then forty until I was breathing so slowly it was almost indiscernible. Sinking into a body of stone, I now heard the inner siren both far and near. Pulled up into my skull, I fell inward into the piercing sound of a rumbling freight train at the center of my brain. This time, I did not go through the classic stages of the away-from-the-body experience; instead, consciousness simply shifted directly into another reality:

> I pass into a waking vision and find myself being shown an astonishing alternative history of Earth and the evolution of humankind in 3D holographic format as I float far above. A voice narrates to me the origins of humankind on Earth. Elder Self again takes this in stride, as though it is only a refresher course, but I, Kevin, feel upset—it is not at all the history I've been taught in school. Neither is it any other history I'd been exposed to before. I directly perceive a series of multidimensional factors influencing every stage of physical and social evolution—a grand experiment in time? All traditional concepts of our history disintegrate before my weeping heart/mind. No more please! I cannot bear it now.

I woke up panting and nauseous. Everything I'd been told and taught, the tidy reality package given to me and my peers, was a partial and very limited view. In early 1983 there was no internet chock full of fringe theories, and alternative history books were scarce. Few in my circles so far spoke about reality itself as a manufactured item. To say that I felt off balance would be an understatement—a reality crash was imminent. I told no one. As I prepared for my upcoming spell as an architectural intern, university studies seemed more absurd than ever before.

> *I wonder how the high colleges manage to produce so many high asses.*
>
> PARACELSUS

# 9

# Kundalini Fire

*The shaman, alchemist, and blacksmith all share one surprising and outstanding characteristic: they are all masters of fire.*

T. J. O'NEILL, "THE SUN INVINCIBLE"

"The *serpent fire of kundalini* is licking your brain," the American swami explained, turning in his lounge chair. It was late and I had walked the long distance to his home in the dark of night. The objects in his study swelled and breathed, just as I felt my pulse quicken and relax in turn. Only with great effort could I discern objects in the room. Not because they weren't visible, rather because I was half-submerged in cosmic flux, a state of consciousness that experiences no separation, or "no-thingness." I could neither sleep nor sleepwalk as I had for most of my daytime life. This had previously happened to a lesser degree in Bavaria during a summer high school student exchange program. I was again walking a ceaseless déjà vu, only now it was much stronger and I needed the swami's help.

I accepted an architectural internship position with a small firm in St. Petersburg, Florida, and spent the new year's winter there, very solitary. This proved to be instrumental in the awakening of the kundalini, the innate intelligence of embodied consciousness, referred to by the Hindus in the feminine form as the coiled power at the base of the spine. Friday evening meditations offered by the swami became a weekly medicine. He wasn't a typical renunciate at all—an M.D. and psychiatrist, he drove a flashy sports car, yet wore his ochre Indian renunciate robes to the psychiatric hospital each day. After only a few Friday evening meditations, the swami appeared in a dream, peeling an orange. He offered a piece to me, which I took with gratitude. The following Monday I awoke in the early Florida light and humidity with a subtle feeling of elation, and a strange twitch at the base of my spine, as though my tailbone was humming, vibrating.

I had trouble concentrating at work, but I completed my day at the drafting board. Feeling an overabundance of nervous energy, I rode my bicycle miles to a distant shop to obtain a needed item. Already late when I started my return, a burst tire ended my speedy flight home. I swore, stamped my feet, and shouted aloud at the inconvenience. *Now what?* Florida suburbs are so spread out it would be hours on foot to reach home, and I felt depressed at the thought of the next day, fatigued at the office. I wheeled my hobbled bicycle slowly through the winding streets of outer St. Petersburg under the stars. Despite all my wishes to get home soon for a good night's rest before an early rise, I could not. I laughed. So much of my life I had cursed my lot, but this time I would take a different approach.

Passing a small pond with a large tree next to it, I stopped. *What's the great hurry in your life, Kevin?* I asked, as I sat below the great tree. All my life I'd been trained to push, to accomplish, to hurry. *Tonight, I give up.* I then felt a gentle sinking, as taut muscles deep in my torso were released from long-held beliefs. A state of knowing and perceiving without thought replaced my wishes to be elsewhere. A visible sheen spread over the night, and I fell inward. The center of the universe is right here and now; a silent eternity enveloped me. Light as a feather I stood, noticing a strange glow emanate from my very skin. I had no sense of time and walked the remaining miles home in a state in which I perceived thoughts coming and going, yet I had no wish to change, reject, or amplify them. I was like a young child again, just taking in everything as it was. A subtle joy permeated me to the core.

I didn't bother with the lights when I reached home; instead I sat down in the darkness, absorbed in the simple beauty of surrender. A strange tingling arose from my feet. This slowly passed up my calves and thighs, reaching my hips. I was soon a mere torso floating in space above, with only vibratory waves below. As this reached the base of my hips, the tingling entered my spine and a current sprang to life filling my torso with a powerful vibration. Reaching up into the center of my head, the power transformed into light. Enraptured, I sat for a long while, turning my neck and watching inwardly as my skull was flooded with light, expanding my awareness outward further and further into the night sky. Joy washed over me.

Gleefully I showered, changed, and lay down to sleep, but the inner show was only beginning. I lay astonished at the display of light that rushed up into my head and seemed to expand ever outward into the night air, outside my little home and well into the sky. Exhausted yet exalted I slipped between dreams and the dazzling inner light show the entire night. Morning sunlight poured in through the windows, yet the continuum of consciousness hadn't been broken. *Is this possible? Am I insane?*

"Well, it's about time!" my boss snapped, sparking smiles and snickers around the office. I was late. Smiling sheepishly, I gazed down at my drafting board and saw only a maze of wiggling lines. In my timeless state I couldn't differentiate things as I did before. I smiled and sat down nervously, with no inner reprieve from the *universal light show* that permeated my brain. I could stomach no breakfast or lunch. As opposed to the bliss I felt the night before, I now felt agitated and wracked by irrational fears of persecution.

The day passed while accomplishing very little, and I went home to investigate this phenomenon further. When I reached my single-story Florida apartment, I was vibrating so powerfully I couldn't eat anything save a bit of fruit, fortunately found everywhere in Florida. Pains and sorrows surfaced, and a dance of emotions began. That evening I put slow sitar music on my portable player, and did yoga postures in the dark to release blockages in the flow. Physical pain now appeared wherever there were energetic obstacles in my body. I couldn't stop doing yoga postures or else I felt I might explode. Emotions continued to pour forth, and I felt crippled by them—I could withhold them no longer. I wept bitterly over forgotten hurts and woes. In between such bouts of release, again came glorious light shows in my head, beams of white, orange, and gold soaring out in the sky. My awareness rode these light streams ever outward and I would laugh madly with the sheer joy of it. No worldly distractions compared to what was coursing through me. I felt blessed, and yet also accursedly alone.

Vibrating with energy and unable to sleep, I went out into the night to climb trees and even buildings. There seemed no other way to work off this abundance of energy. I giggled and cried in turn, as old emotional residues were expunged. I was truly a madman now, laughing to myself while sitting in tree branches at midnight staring out at the moon. Astral rings around the moon and planets now made themselves known to me. The radiations of the moon, various planets, and stars took on individual characteristics, as though each had a unique vibratory personality. *This must be how the ancient astrologers started their science, with direct perception of the energetic flows from the heavenly bodies.* I laughed to myself that certainly a straitjacket would be fitted for me should I reveal such perceptions.

I lay down to sleep at 3 a.m., praying for an amnesty from too much bliss, but it was not to be granted. Passing from lucid dreams into out-of-body experiences, I soared through strange realms I'd long forgotten. My unprepared body and weak personality could scarcely contain the power. A wavering sense of dread and failure haunted me; the next moment, joy permeated my every cell.

With no break in the continuum of consciousness, sunlight again fell upon me and I rose to prepare for work. I could hold no food, and my trousers were loose. An inner fire burned in my spine. My metabolism went into hyperdrive and I burned calories more quickly than I could take them in. With a strange combination of paranoia and joy, I sashayed into the office with a smirk and took my seat. This time I decided I would spread only joy. Laughter came from my coworkers; I had come without a necktie and in a pair of blue jeans—this was not okay. I smiled feebly and sat down to try to work. I had the greatest difficulty focusing on hard reality. I could draft for about ten minutes at a time, and I avoided closing my eyes for any more than a blink. If I did, I felt a stream of light pouring up my spine into my head, and I'd find myself a point of awareness out in the sky, gazing over the neighborhood.

"What's up with you, Turner? Are you on this planet or not?" I didn't dare answer my boss, so I sat up straight and strained to take the after-lunch meeting seriously. At that moment, the absurdity of it all hit me: *They're only pretending to take all this seriously. They all know it's not, but are so involved in pretending that they forgot we are pretending!* As I burst out laughing at this inner thought, I felt a strange release in my heart, as though a floodgate of love had opened. Normally, an outburst of laughter in a meeting would have been greeted with guffaws, scowls, and disbelief, but this time was different. A pink light burst from my chest, and immediately everyone else started laughing too! For a full minute we could not contain ourselves and laughed in an otherworldly joy as though we'd heard the curtain call on the *Big Joke*. Our boss then took a deep breath, straightened his meeting papers, coughed, murmured to himself, "What was that all about?" and went on with the meeting.

I passed more nights of tree climbing, lucid dreams, and OBEs, only to find that I was unable to fall back into unconsciousness. *I want a break!* But I was offered none. I got what I asked for and now I had to work with it. Irrational fears and emotions moved me for days, yet I simultaneously vibrated with a joy that passed to others easily. The laughter at work was so contagious that the moment I entered the office, persons would now start to start to dance around with silly smiles on their faces. Laughter ran the office, the kind of joyful laughter that only children can engage in. *Now I've really created a madhouse.*

Fortunately, the weekend arrived and I had time at home to focus on finding a balanced path for this new fountain of life bursting from my inner soul. I spent it all in solitary, only occasionally gazing out at the fruit trees behind my home. Quietly in isolation, the dishonesty of my life now stared at me like a fire-breathing dragon. Despite moments of exaltation, I was disgusted with my own hypocrisy, cruelty, and self-ishness. I was little more than a slug, a parasite in this world. *Have I ever truly loved anyone?* I cried and vomited what little I could eat. I was growing thin at an alarming rate.

A curious phenomenon occurred at this time: my spine began to absorb and pull upward the power in my vibrating testicles up into my spine, which now grew hot for days on end. Simultaneously, inner fantasies beat at the door of my attention, but I held the male elixir within. I also found that my eyesight was improving. I had only recently starting wearing spectacles, but I no longer needed them. I experimented with seeing at a distance with and without them. I found that if I put my focus into my forehead and away from my physical eyes, I could read even the smallest street signs at a great distance. The incongruity of this ability did not strike me until much later; I simply accepted it as part of the Wonderland I had entered.

Fits of depression countered torrents of bliss pouring into my brain through my fiery spine. But something else was unearthed below—something much more powerful than passing emotional residues. Sexual fantasies began to rage through me. I had no moral issue with this; I hadn't been raised in a restrictive atmosphere. However, I sensed that I should withhold my vital fluid during this process. As a young man of twenty-one, this was easier thought than done. Extraordinarily vivid inner visions of women, so unearthly in their beauty I cannot describe them, called to me relentlessly, contorting their bodies into postures of undeniable sexual magnetism. Erections lasted hours at a time, as the ethereal fluid continued to be drawn upward from my testicles up into my spine, and on up into my head in the form of light. I oscillated between two heavens, two kinds of joys. Remaining in a cosmic detach-ment, I came to actually enjoy the stupendous orgies of my inner world, yet I did not succumb. I sensed I could not have done this alone; I had help from an invisible benevolent presence.

Seeking solace in the few books of spirituality I had brought along, I found it impossible to read. Letters danced on the pages, and even when I could manage a few sentences, they seemed trite and inconsequential. I would close my eyes, feel the sky above, and could sense the galaxy as a spiraling whole. While I felt permeated with an inner grace, I also felt forsaken. This world seemed hopelessly mired in greed, cruelty, and fear. *What am I doing here? How could I have been banished to this hell planet?*

Gradually I adjusted to the dual perceptions of grace and exile, but it was not enough. The inner orgies reached a crescendo and the personality of the twenty-one-year-old I was this time around could not dam the flow any longer and the elixir was lost. For a few seconds I was submerged under a numbing, disconsolate bliss of nonexistence, freed from the *Awe*. The inner fire dimmed and the continuum of consciousness came to a close. All magic disappeared. I fell into a dark stupor, and awoke the following morning encased in a sack of rotting meat. Nothing could have prepared me for what I had already lived most of my life. Cosmic soul became a distant memory, and I was again absorbed in my worldly personality. Eight full days had passed, and I had dropped seventeen pounds, an astonishing calorie burn rate of nearly a kilogram a day. I now ate more and could read and work. I was a knuckle-dragging primate again.

The swami assisted with some kind words of encouragement and acknowledgment, but he simply did not have the experience to advise me. *Perhaps something of Cosmic spirit appeared as him in the dream?* I only knew I must find out. I had spiritually matured years in that long week. Architecture would no longer be a viable path, and I knew that I must reach the Himalayas as soon as possible.

When I returned to my coterie of artists and musicians at the university, I learned of a master's degree program in applied linguistics and decided that would be my ticket to Asia, where I would study Sanskrit, Tibetan, and Chinese, to find the answers I sought. Architecture may be a noble art, but it is slow and time-consuming. Painting and sculpture are also soulful expressions, but they won't likely pay the bills. *I must experience the planet as a whole, find the answers I seek, and I cannot wait.* I made plans to complete my undergraduate degree and shift immediately into the graduate linguistics department. I was fortunately accepted on probation and did well enough in my first semester to secure full acceptance. A ticket to an ordinary liberation from my nation and culture was now in the works.

In the meantime, I returned to the university library to read up on kundalini yoga. The only available books there that clearly discussed the kundalini coiled force at the base of the spine were Sir John Woodroffe's books (aka Arthur Avalon). In *Sakti and Sakta* (1918), he describes Kundalini Shakti:

> One may be told that it is a Power or Shakti; that . . . is wakened and goes up through the chakras to the Sahasrara . . . to rouse Kundalini Shakti to enjoy the bliss of union of Shiva and Shakti . . . when once set in movement is drawn to that other static center in the Thousand-petalled Lotus (Sahasrara). When Kundali "sleeps" man is awake to this world. When She "awakes" he sleeps, that is, loses all consciousness of the world and enters his causal body. In Yoga, he passes beyond to formless Consciousness.[1]

And I found here my first clear connection to alchemy and Hermeticism:

> The Nadis on each side called Ida and Pingala are the left and right sympathetic cords crossing the central column from one side to the other, making at the Ajña with the Sushumna a threefold knot called Triveni; which is the spot in the Medulla where the sympathetic cords join together and whence they take their origin, these Nadis together with the two-lobed Ajña and the Sushumna forming the figure of the Caduceus of the God Mercury [Hermes].[2]

Fig. 9.1. Second Key of Basil Valentine, Hermes with caduceus.
Engraving by Matthaeus Merian (1593–1650) from *The Twelve Keys of
Basil Valentine*. Published in *Musaeum hermeticum*, Francofurti:
Apud Hermannum à Sande, 1678.

In the caduceus and the deity Hermes-Mercury, I sensed a connection between the ancient worlds of both the East and West. The caduceus symbolizes latent, innate spiritual power, as well as healing. I sought more information on alchemy and Hermeticism, but these fields proved to be daunting, baffling, even hidden or lost. Knowledge of kundalini obviously existed in Egypt, Greece, and even Europe, but Western esoteric traditions seemed largely inaccessible. I had to shelve this investigation until a later time.

The demands of new graduate courses in linguistics were a welcome relief from the empty rigors of architecture school. I was the only student in the master's program who didn't have a related degree and already speak other languages fluently. I played catch-up and studied with a concentration I'd never applied before. We students were from all over the world, and I was among the youngest and least traveled. I reveled in my classmates' stories of their lives overseas. In late autumn I took a new flat in a once-grand old house downtown, and covered my kitchen walls with world maps on which I scribbled pithy quotes whenever I found them. While the weight of graduate studies opened an outer door to the world, an inner door reluctantly closed to exploration. Thus, the spirits would intervene with a precision strike, an unforgiving and unforgettable awakening.

# 10

# Back through the Bardo

*Only the gaze turned backwards can take us forwards,*
*for the gaze turned forwards leads backwards.*

NOVALIS, *FRAGMENTS–GENERAL DRAFT*

*For myself, rebirth is neither a theory, nor a belief, but an*
*experience.*

LAMA ANAGARIKA GOVINDA,
*THE WAY OF THE WHITE CLOUDS*

This sunny spring afternoon I lay stretched on my carpeted floor, a dry textbook folded over my chest. I fully intend to absorb the volume of historical linguistics for use in my upcoming graduate thesis, but the spirits have another kind of history to reveal in a new and astounding initiation:

*Outward focus shifts to an inward absorption, and I drift in a drowsy, inner reverie. Awareness collapses into a body of heavy immobility. After a moment of cataleptic discomfort, I gradually reidentify with the silvery filament of light, my astral self. Now gently floating as light, I'm drawn upward into a point of focused awareness in the head. As the siren roars louder and louder, I fall into the silvery chasm at the center of my skull.*

*I lean up and away from my body. How good to be out in the full light of day! As I revel in the glory of sunlight's now discernible ethereal qualities, angelic laughter calls to me from above. I turn upward to find a spirit in white flowing robes twirling about, passing down through my ceiling, while emanating a choral song of delight. The combination of a pure youthful joyfulness with a deity-like power is striking and unique in my experience.* "Kevin, we're going to take a little trip," *the spirit beams into my consciousness. I could only nod before such grace, and the floor immediately fell away.*

*I plummet at great speed, as though down a glass elevator shaft, and all thought is drawn out of me. I am purely perception now, while a maelstrom of images 360 degrees around me forms the imaginal walls of this translucent shaft, akin to hundreds of filmstrips streaming upward. The sheer velocity of images is such that none are intelligible. The spirit's voice lifts above the rush of astral winds,* "Focus!"

*I laser attention upon a single strip of images, and in that tunnel of focus, time slows—I see from high up over a sports field the back of a blond boy. Beyond the field I perceive a huge sign on the back of a building—the grocer near my childhood home! This is my local sport field, and that's me! I now clearly perceive the boy; it is myself at the age of eleven years.*

*As fear dissipates, curiosity grows. I laterally scan the other streaming images, slowing the rush with the focus of concentration— they too are scenes of my life, as I grow younger, moving backward in time. I revel in the clarity of these vignettes. Soon childhood passes into scenes of early family and relatives now with youthful appearances; I'm a toddler, learning to walk holding to chairs and sofa, soon back to a cradle covered in white blankets, struggling with the indignity of infant immobility. Then . . . pitch black!*

*Boom, boom, boom, thunders a kettle drum next to my head, as I am thrust into a warm, fluid darkness. I panic for a moment, but the spirit's voice again soothes me. I rest, calmly floating in a dark gel, the rhythm of the booming drum now a comfort. The spirit intones,* "We're now returning to the first heartbeat . . ." *My mother's heartbeat! Returning to when I first heard it as I entered: Boom, boom, boom . . . BOOM . . . and I'm cast out into a silent infinitude.*

*As though skydiving over a galactic expanse, I float over a vastness of swirling bluish smoke. Twinkling fire lights that are not stars spark over the billowing cosmic smoke. After a momentary calm, realm after realm passes before my disembodied view. I move through rings of light and gas until a bright star appears at the end of a tunnel-like mandala. As I approach, the star grows so bright that it burns like the light of a thousand suns. Surely if I'd had physical eyes I would have been blinded, but I was not. As I grow closer, a Power from the innermost core of my essence vibrates, as though every cell of my being is bathed in an unfathomable voltage of light and power. The spirit's voice rings out louder and louder,* "Keep. your focus—hold the Light, hold it with all your strength!"

*The Power becomes the voltage of pure Love and Presence, though a thousand, thousand times greater than any earthly love could ever be. If I had lungs to scream such joy, I felt it would shatter a galaxy. Unable to contain the power of this Luminosity, I lose hold on awareness, dissolving into a timeless oblivion of brilliance.*

*A gentle, cloudy light hovers over a vague image, as I rest in a beingness without thought. The scene gently coalesces into a disoriented view of a room—lamps, furniture, the tops of heads, a bed. I'm looking down from a ceiling. As I become oriented, details slowly come into focus and a memory is jarred,* "Ahhh, I know this room . . . I died here!" *From my ceiling-top view I perceive two men standing at the foot of a bed holding their chins, looking serious. To the side, a woman softly sobs, gazing at someone in the bed below my view. Two long bony legs make impressions under the bedcovers. Then I know—those are my legs. Directly below me, a head is propped up on a pillow.*

Fig. 10.1 Mandala of Bardo Deities.
From *Peaceful & Wrathful Deities of the Bardo,* Tibet, eighteenth century.
Rubin Museum of Art, New York

*A nameless fear shivers through me. I know I must see the face below, but I struggle as one who does not wish to see another self. With all the will I can muster I force my perception to focus directly under me, to the man's head below. Then comes a welcome release— the man's head rests on a thick pillow. His face is that of an elderly European man. Yes, my face as I had known it before. The bygone décor of the room becomes clearer, as memories of my life as a doctor in 1800s Germany well up from within. The spirit sears a name into my mind to assure it is not forgotten. Now with great excitement I wish to move away from my deathbed on a journey of nostalgic reminiscence. I glide across the ceiling toward the door to explore my past, when a loud telephone begins to ring . . .*

*And ring and ring it does, while everyone in the room pretends not to hear the clamor. I find this so annoying that I shout down to them to answer the telephone, "Hey, pick up the phone!" but they don't hear me either. When I see no telephone in the room, I smile to myself and . . .*

I slowly lift a leaden body up into my university flat, dimly lit by late-afternoon daylight. A book slides off my chest and I am disoriented. A phone rings still, to my annoyance. With some difficulty I slide my prone body across the floor, pick up the receiver and put it to my ear— no voice, no dial tone, only a presence on the whisper of a soft wind.

I had been called back.

# 11

# The Quest

*As long as you are unaware of the continual law*
*of Die and Be Again,*
*you are merely a vague guest*
*on a dark Earth.*

J. W. VON GOETHE, "THE HOLY LONGING"

Keys are made to open particular locks, and this key was not to be forgotten. Shaking, I made immediate notes of this important journey, including the given name. Hamlet was amiss when he said death is "the undiscovered country from whose bourn no traveler returns." Rather, I say death is *the briefly forgotten country to whose bourn we all return.* While the remembrance intrigued me, having been someone else also unnerved me. For days I felt split, and I paced my apartment distraught.

Over the following week, each time I passed the university library the memory of the journey back to a previous existence whispered, nudging me to investigate. An inexplicable apprehension turned me away time and again. The weather intervened a week later, and a heavy downpour forced me to pull my bicycle into the lot of the university library. I grudgingly trod into the wide foyer, shaking my wet clothes. Plato defined philosophy as *phaedros melete thanatou*, the practice and preparation for death. I had wanted to know the secrets of life and death. *Where is my courage now?*

Lati Rinpoche's recently published *Death, Intermediate States, and Rebirth* looked back at me with a disquieting mercy. Knowledge of the passage from life into death, through the *Bardo* (between two) after-life states and into rebirth, was apparently well known to the Indian Tantrikas that developed the form of Buddhism that later went to Tibet and was fortunately preserved and developed further there. Here I discover Lama Lati Rinpoche's description of death and dissolution experienced both after death and before subsequent incarnation:

> [At death] the internal sign of the dissolution . . . is the dawning of an appearance called "like smoke," which is like blue puffs of smoke . . . similar to smoke billowing from a chimney in the midst of a mass of smoke. . . .
>
> The [next] internal sign of the dissolution . . . is the arising of an appearance called "like fireflies." It is like burning red sparks seen within puffs of smoke rising from a chimney.[1]

Upon reading these lines I leaned back in my seat and sank into a hidden inner self. All the knowledge of all the libraries in the world suddenly paled compared to this—the secrets of death revealed. I stared up at the ceiling, and a slow fuse lit within. *I need to remember, I must know.* I searched for a copy of *The Tibetan Book of the Dead.* As I held it, I gasped for breath and wished to run. Bolstering my courage, I read on to the Bardo Thodol:

> This mind of yours is inseparable luminosity and emptiness in the form of a great mass of light, it has no birth or death, therefore it is the buddha of Immortal Light. To recognize this is all that is necessary . . . he will recognize his own naked mind as the luminosity . . . and certainly attain liberation.[2]

Upon reading these lines, a calm acceptance settled me. The old doctor had done his service, but he had failed to hold the Luminosity. Thrown from the center of the wheel to the rim once again, I'd been compelled to take rebirth. There could be only one path for me now, and surely the underlying reason I had chosen to study linguistics. I vowed: *I will go to Asia to study Sanskrit and Tibetan, become a Buddhist lama, and this time hold the Immortal Light!*

Another clue remained to be explored—*the name*. I'd never heard the name before, though after the journey back through the Bardo scant memories of the doctor's life remained with me. The spirit had insisted I know the name to the letter, probably attuned to my habitual skepticism. A painful curiosity drove me to search, though I partly hoped there would be no record of him so I could write this off as a likely fantasy. My stomach fell as, indeed, the name existed in the library records. And there was more. Though much younger, the doctor had lived at a time when Goethe still breathed in this world. I felt dizzy and hung my head in a gesture of surrender. Leaning against a wall, I slid artlessly to the floor. Rather than excitement, I felt a dire sense of continuity, a daunting responsibility to complete a *project* unfinished. One might assume it would be fascinating to know and recall a previous existence, yet for me at the time it was a frightful splitting, one I had known since childhood, and a condition that set me uncomfortably apart from my friends and family. My sense of self was suddenly fragile and I felt unprepared. I would tell no one.

Rumbles of thunder and flashes of distant lightning joined the rain outside, and the downpour extended my stay. Inside, I faced the flames of more clues. I discovered the doctor's state of residence in eastern Germany had been a locus of alchemy in earlier centuries. While searching for more, I discovered a volume titled, *Goethe, the Alchemist* (1952). I read like a madman and found these disjointed phrases, noting them down with a shaking hand:

"My mystico-religious chemical pursuits," [Goethe] writes, "had led me into shadowy regions . . ." Goethe's knowledge of alchemical literature must have been very wide indeed. . . . Goethe was devoting himself . . . to Hermetism [Hermeticism]. The degree to which alchemy had established control over Goethe's interests in early manhood can scarcely be over-emphasized. . . . Man must pass through the state of sin, in fact he must be capable of death, in order to be reborn in Christ. To acquire the Philosophers' Stone through "putrefaction" was thus to undergo this death and rebirth . . . the alchemical quest can now be defined a little more closely.

To acquire the Philosophers' Stone was . . . to achieve full knowledge of God. This must now be interpreted as gaining knowledge of the whole universe, an apparently impossible task. It is however precisely the claim of those who have experienced mystic union . . . the inward fire must be kept carefully covered and concealed." . . . Paracelsus called it "a small spark of the eternal invisible fire." . . . The seed of gold, which they connected both with Christ and with the Philosophers' Stone, the All in All, represented the incipient identification with the Divine.[3]

Dusk arrived from a silent horizon, and the rain outside dwindled to a calming sprinkle. I left the library shaken and born into a new life of hidden purpose. Goethe's alchemical quest for the Stone of the Philosophers, and the Indo-Tibetan quest for Liberation by recognition of the Luminosity must be related. *Might Eastern and Western esotericism be a singular human spirituality?* Now set on a course for mystic knowledge, the *Eternal Invisible Fire* is my only quest. Like Parzival, I felt very alone, yet destined to find the secret Grail and return with it.

I never felt more terrifyingly alive.

# 12

# Greater Guardian

*You can measure the depth of a person's awakening by how
they serve others.*

KUKAI (KOBO DAISHI),
ESOTERIC BUDDHIST MASTER, NINTH CENTURY

Further perusal of alchemical texts in my limited free time led to the
feeling that either alchemy is *gibberish*, after the alchemist Geber,
or the secrets are too well hidden, perhaps so well occulted that they
have now been lost. Surely the living esoteric traditions in Asia are a
better choice. My decision was clear, and to preview my journey to Asia
I pasted my studio walls with Sanskrit, Tibetan, Uighur, and Chinese
scripts. The journey back through the Bardo had renewed a fanatical
desire to know hidden realties, but in my spiritual immaturity this also
resulted in a destructive self-absorption.

I fell into my own inner world and paid little heed to my friends'
concerns. A selfish young man bent on his own self-realization, I soaked
myself in mystical literature and held my self-importance like a badge of
honor: *I'm on my way to Enlightenment; I'm better than you sleeping idiots!*
I tolerated no small talk and few courtesies. Though I kept my quest to
myself, I nevertheless became an insufferable spiritual snob. I was a man

on a mission, to get the fastest rocket to enlightenment. *So get the hell outta my way!* I talked down to everyone, even my professors, and blurted loud, inappropriate insolences in the middle of my graduate study classes. I was beyond everyone and I knew it all, or almost anyway. I lost friends and was shunned by others. I became competitive with my few spiritual friends, attempting to one-up them on nearly everything. I became a self-centered monstrosity, fuming with egotism, conceit, and arrogance.

As medicine and healing, three dreams arrived in my Night School:

*A blond boy of about ten years walks toward me smiling, and I see that it is myself at that age. A sudden rage overtakes me, and for no known reason I angrily attempt to strangle him. He only gasps, his eyes bulging with total fear and confusion! I'm torn within—I feel I cannot accept him, but his distress pulls at my heart, and for the first time I feel compassion for him—for myself. I halt my attack and take him in my arms. He melts into me, and I feel an acceptance; a lost childhood joy returns.*

*Floating out in space, I gaze over the entire blue Earth. A great power enters from behind my cerebellum and a hidden reservoir of resentment rears up. Like an angry, spoiled youth I send thunderbolts down to destroy the Earth and all its inhabitants who are so very guilty of not living up to my expectations. Before reaching the planet, the thunderbolt power is immediately withdrawn back into me, and out the back of my cerebellum. I drop my face into my dream hands in shame. I failed a test—I have no real love for anyone. I awoke and vowed to cleanse myself of resentment and disappointment, and be truly kind to everyone.*

*I'm riding in a car with a friend who asks, "Which film would you like to see?" I suggest* Alice in Wonderland. *She replies, "Well, why don't we watch the other one. I think you'll find it interesting." We arrive at a playhouse theater, and my friend leaves me at the door. I enter and sit down alone. The curtain is lifted and there on stage stands a central character with his face in shadow. Soon a great whirlwind of events takes place around him on the great stage. People, places, objects, and events in symbolic form create an elliptical orbit extending several meters out around this central character. This poor, myopic young man perceives only what is within a meter in radius around him and reacts to each event as it comes in his view, but does not realize the larger, evolving picture in which the symbols move from within his immediate perception out into the larger orbit, and later circle back in again. The pathetic figure is in turn sad, angry, happy, depressed, joyful, terrified over the brief passing of these satellite symbols, each a symbol of a person, place, or event in this life. His misery over his inability to control these events is painful to watch, and I feel pity for him. The symbols are Dali-esque, yet I soon recognize the symbols as condensed forms of events in my life! I walk up on stage, and the shadow lifts from the young man's face. It is myself at my current age, in great pain and confusion. A deep compassion swells in my heart for his suffering, and I embrace him.*

> *The life of the psyche may be compared to a great, continuously circling river which is illuminated in only one small area by the sun.*
>
> C. G. CARUS, *PSYCHE*

My friends had been put off by my intense self-absorption, but they had also accepted it with patience and grace. Thanks to them I read and practiced compassion meditations. *Perhaps my liberation is related to the liberation of others too?* I read the Bodhisattva vow, "I'll not depart into Nirvana until every blade of grass has been enlightened." I wasn't ready for that kind of time commitment, but I was getting a glimpse of what compassion was about and realized with gratitude the spirits that had been assisting me. I felt humbled and thankful. *Perhaps we're all in this together? Maybe I can be helpful to others? But in what way?*

> *Be kind, for everyone you meet is fighting a harder battle.*
>
> ATTRIBUTED TO PLATO

In my old house on Elm Street, lost souls visited me now and then, probably because I could perceive them, but I did not yet understand what they wanted, nor how to help them. One such soul was that of a pudgy, freckled boy who wore clothes from the 1950s. When I meditated, he would slowly blow into my ear a cool, ethereal breath. I talked to him a few times, like this: "Hey, this is my apartment. You're not supposed to be here." But that had no meaning for him, though he was amused that I could perceive his wind-like presence. He came so often that he even entered into the dreams of two friends who once spent the night on my carpeted floor. I'd never mentioned the ghost boy, but in the morning they both shared their dreams of the roundish boy with freckles. I wasn't sure what to do about it, but I wasn't upset at the intrusion either. The compassion meditations were working on me. One afternoon weeks later I was resting and withdrew from my body:

*Eerily, I hear a child's nursery rhyme sung in my bathroom. . . . I float into the narrow room to find a young girl of perhaps five or six years old in old-fashioned clothing holding a doll, to whom she is singing. She looks up at me with as much surprise as I was in, and we both dropped our mouths open. Fear overtook me, and I grabbed her shoulders and beamed forcefully to her face, "You're not supposed to be here—this is my bathroom!"*

*At that moment a great pounding thundered on my nearby front door, as if a supernaturally powerful being were beating upon it with all its might. The girl is as shocked and frightened as I am, and I'm overcome by a wish to protect her, to help her, defend her! She shoots out the bathroom window in a flash, and I turn back to the front door to face the great menace alone.*

*The beating is so intense that it appears to be bending the door back off its hinges. This force is far more powerful than the previous Dweller! Gathering every last reserve of courage I had, I push my astral awareness through the wall to know what this thing is. The beating immediately stops, and whatever it was vanished. I return to my bed, lay in catalepsy for a spell, and sit back up in my body.*

I rise, open my door, and asked my neighbor across the hall if he had heard anything. He said, "Yes, I've never heard such a beating on any door! I thought it was my door, but I was too afraid to open it. Shortly after it stopped, I opened my door to peek, but there was no one."

> Hitherto thou hast sought only thine own release, but now, having thyself become free, thou canst go forth as a liberator of thy fellows. . . . [The Greater Guardian of the Threshold's] duty [is] to keep the student away from the supersensible world until he can enter it with the will for selfless collaboration.
>
> RUDOLF STEINER[1]

A new love and caring for others welled up from within me, and I relaxed. I soon met a lovely musician, artist, and former model, and she introduced me to a broader range of consciousness exploration pathways, including Paramahansa Yogananda's *Autobiography of a Yogi*. This book held an extraordinary vibration and I was deeply impressed by not only the miracles but with his humility and service. I felt changed just from reading it. Yogananda and his teachers appeared now and then in dreams, but I was unable to understand their messages.

An expanding new group of artistic and musical friends appeared and I played local gigs with a jazz-folk fusion band. I grew my hair longer, wore headbands and mala beads, read poetry, and expanded my personal library of mysticism. At this time, the band and our friends at the university were mixing and matching loves every few months, romancing each other in a gentle replay of the sixties generation, like much of the music we played. *La Vie Bohème*, an experimental time that I cherished, became a distraction. Another dream teaching was due.

# 13

# Dance of the Incarnationers

After an hour of deep breathing I pass into sleep, then directly into a familiar astral plane where I find myself and many others at an exuberant beau monde party in a stately 1920s Art Deco ballroom:

*A carefree glamour permeates the entire room, as men in tuxedos and women in ballroom gowns dance sensuously within outer circles of standing social cliques. Laughter, heads tossed back, cigarette holders, and cocktail glasses rule—along with seductive eyes and darting glances over new targets of desire. Utterly intrigued, I move closer to a circle to overhear what the conversation topics of such fascination could possibly be. At first, they seemed to be discussing or reminiscing about past adventures in other times and places. I overhear a woman beam with laughter, "Oh, that was when I was your mistress, not your wife, hahaha." Another man leans in and says with glee, "Oh, but we had that week in . . ." Another woman with a comically long cigarette holder cackles, "We were lovers all along, but no one knew that then." I'm astonished at the ribald debauchery being celebrated and laughed about, as it had resulted in jealousies, anguish, and even dark wishes for revenge. Then one woman leaned to another man and said, "Why don't we do another life together where we can have a fling again, shall we?"*

*Stunned and reeling, I turn away and move to another group, where yet again the discussion roils over lost romances, secret dalliances, bold seductions, and unrequited loves, stretching over multiple incarnations. Some faces now appear vaguely familiar and I know, I remember—this group has been mixing and matching romances for centuries! A grand delusion made completely by choice. Most lives discussed seem to have been a weave of European incarnations, yet others spread eastward across Eurasia and others westward to the Americas. The entire crowd is somehow fun-loving, coconspirators in this strange dance of erotic flirtation and romantic ruin, lost in an addiction to inflamed emotions, falling in and out of love, over and again—all in the name of a pained entertainment. Memories flood over me, as I realize I too had been an addict of this dance of romance, just like them.*

*I spot an old soul friend of mine, not from this timeline but from others. He is in a tuxedo and carries an open bottle of bubbly and two glasses. I beam a thought to him and he turns to me with a huge smile, "Wow, isn't this fantastic! Just look at all these dolls!" I beam to him, "Yes, but don't you know this is all a great dream that's holding you." He pauses and looks at me with astonishment and remembrance, but his eyes are immediately cast back to the ladies. "Yes, I know, but, well . . . look, my friend, everyone's having such a good time!" He quickly disappears into a circle of attractive women, and the last I saw of him he was pouring glasses for two women while they made eyes at him, and he returned the compliment.*

Fig. 13.1. *Academie de Danses* from *La Vie Parisienne*.
Drawing by Vald'Es, 1927.

*Then it dawns on me that this is the astral "break room" in between privileged incarnations of never-ending love stories, of elations, romantic chaos, and the subsequent broken hearts, pain, and vengeful wishes holding everyone spellbound, wishing for another chance to do it again and again. I turn and spot a door—I've had quite enough of this. With sadness I say my silent goodbyes to those who I once thought my friends. Thoroughly entranced with each other, they take no notice of my departure.*

"To the Himalayas!" I cried out to Nepalese and Taiwanese friends in our department. "Tribhuvan University in Kathmandu has offered me a teaching position!" I soon learned the grand salary of $8 per month could not possibly buy my flights, pay my student loans, nor even sustain me in Nepal. I begged my family for extra funds, as I knew the Himalayas were where I had to be. With no financing available, I was left with no choice but to decline the position.

Taiwan was my next choice. I had a good friend, Tung Li, a Buddhist from Taiwan. He had clearly attained a certain poise and calm in his spiritual practice there, and I wanted to know more. I also wished to study Chinese language, but I could get no confirmation of work in Taiwan from overseas; by letter they all required me to personally arrive and interview, no promises. Tung suggested I just show up and find work there. I clearly intuited this would be my best choice, but I could not yet trust life to provide. I had been humbled by financial lack much of my life, and fear took hold.

After a week in depression I decided, *Sometimes, one must do things for money*, and so I did. This began a series of poor decisions for money alone that would plague me for years. I was already in debt due to university loans. With much hesitation I accepted a high-paying job in a location I had never considered and had no interest in. My professor kindly said, "Just work this job for a year, and then you can go to Nepal," but it was little consolation.

Voltaire wrote, "To be a good patriot one must become the enemy of the rest of mankind." Now I would become a friend to mankind by becoming an ex-patriot. I would free myself from nationalism and my cultural programming in hopes of becoming an *authentic human being*. I called my father to say goodbye and explain that I was not to become the architect I once hoped to be. He prophetically intoned in a strange voice not his own, "You were never meant to design buildings, Kevin. You will be an architect of mankind." His cryptic and absurdly grandiose words stayed with me, while I felt only dread for what I intuited ahead—nothing short of a personal deconstruction.

The position required me to arrive in Osaka, Japan, in just a few weeks, and my master's thesis wasn't yet complete. I raced madly against time. My professor shook his head, and said, "I don't think you can make it." I burned the midnight oil for days on end. Bleary, unwashed, and exhausted I handed him a better draft. The next day he gave me a nod and smile. The race to finish had few breaks, and on the final night before my flight, I left three copies of my thesis with my friends to be delivered to the dean, the library, and my department chair. At 5 a.m. I drove to my mother's house in a borrowed van, dumped everything I owned on her floor, panic-packed two suitcases, and was delivered to the airport by friends.

Parzival, the fool, set a new foot on the Quest.

# 14

# Mandala

Fig. 14.1. Mandala of the Forms of Manjushri, the Bodhisattva of
Transcendent Wisdom.
The Metropolitan Museum of Art, New York

*The flower's perfume has no form, but it pervades space. Likewise,*
*through a spiral of mandalas formless reality is known.*\*

SARAHA, TEACHER OF NAGARJUNA


Pulling back the morning curtain from my window at the Tokyu
Hands Hotel in Osaka, I gazed out at a concrete jungle that
extended as far as the horizon. Not a single green leaf in the endless city.
My heart sank and I immediately felt I'd made a dire mistake. Hardly
a few days at work confirmed it—Japan is clearly not my cup of tea.
Shivers ran down my spine at the robotic rigidity and blind devotion
to an external idea of perfection. Why Imperial Japan had allied itself
with Nazi Germany was abundantly clear within a few weeks, and I had
doubts whether my spirit could survive a year in this *brave new gulag*.

However, I became fascinated by the traditional arts and architecture in the nearby ancient capitals of Nara and Kyoto, as well as the
hints of mysticism there. Many of the world's oldest wooden temples are preserved in pristine condition, a prime example of Japanese
perfectionism—taking the material realm extremely seriously. In 1985,
many traditional wooden homes still existed in these two cities, as both
had been spared the bombing of the Second World War. I spent a number of weekends alone there, soaking in the atmosphere. Some temples
and shrines vaguely reminded me of the dream journeys to the temple
of golden lanterns, but none were like the one from my visions.

Late one evening while staying in an old guesthouse in Nara, I
dozed and spirit-hovered out of my guesthouse to find myself in the
same location, yet in the Nara of centuries ago. I floated through the
city streets, dimly lit by hanging oil lanterns, astonished at the ancient
beauty of the city. Every detail of architecture and midnight street life
revealed itself to my astral point of awareness. Unlike the polished steel,
concrete, and plastic Japan of today, this ancient city was rough-hewn,

---

\*An alternative translation is: "Likewise, those who [enter] the circle of the mandala,
through the formless nature will know [uninterrupted meditation]."[1]

made of primarily unfinished wood, mud streets, with only a few stone streets and alleys, yet it deeply held a rustic elegance the Japanese now call *wabi-shiku* and *sabi-shiku*. This was the first time I had fully consciously traveled outside my current time period—in the same place, yet in a different time, which will lead to a new term I will coin later in this volume.

Weeks later, after work I went alone to an Osaka theater to take in the new film *The Emerald Forest*, about a boy who had been lost and raised by a tribe in the Amazon jungle. Based on the conflation of two different true events, the film also depicts a striking tribal initiation rite from boy to man: Upon reaching puberty-adolescence, the boy is taken on a long hunting trip with the tribal headman, his adopted father who is also the tribal shaman. On their return from the journey, they spot warriors from a rival tribe in the vicinity. When they arrive back at their village, the men are alerted to keep watch, but the boy, who has brought honey for his mother, runs off to carefree play with the other boys.

This division struck me strongly; there are only men and boys in this society, not the everlasting adolescence of our current society. The film continues:

When the boy soon shows interest in a young female of the tribe, the shaman-chief and the warriors of the tribe appear in fierce tribal battle wear, and announce to him, "It is time for you to die." The mother says, "I'll never see my boy again." He is then taken away to a sacred place where he undergoes a ritual death of the boy to be reborn as a man, and finally a vision quest to find his reason to be. After completion of his quest later in the film, he becomes a shaman himself.

Deeply moved by the film, I lamented the loss of our ancestors' wisdom. What every adolescent boy obviously seeks is no longer found in our spiritually degraded world. A dozen years later I would undergo such an initiation, but until then, if the wisdom of a tribe cannot provide what's needed, the boy seeks to initiate himself, as did I. In the evenings, I trained in martial arts and studied Japanese language on weekends, but soon work took nearly all my time. I became scattered and unfocused. With summer holidays coming up, I registered for a

Buddhist meditation course. Ten days of meditation in silence with purely vegetarian food sounded like an ideal holiday. The retreat proved to be pivotal in my meditation practice and discipline.

The inward journey was more challenging than any outward journey had been so far. At the end of the ten days of meditative silence we could speak freely among ourselves. The mixed group of Japanese and international residents sat outside in the cooling afternoon. In conversation I learned of a Buddhist monastery in Thailand where one could obtain a private hut in the jungle and meditate indefinitely for only a single dollar a day. I made a note of it, looked up to the sky, and was sure I'd seen the clouds smile.

Returning to my home in the northern suburb of Minou, released from deep-seated tensions, I passed my first evening meditating upon a Tibetan mandala I had removed from a large book in German discovered in a used bookstore. I posted it on the wall, and each night I sat before it, focusing on its very center. My newfound concentration after ten days of intensive practice was ideal, though I didn't know what I was doing, nor what I was seeking. I only felt deeply attracted to the vibration in this particular mandala. One evening I was especially focused, and as my attention was held at the central deity with great intention, peripheral vision opened and the many deities in the outer rings of this mandala came alive! They smiled, moved, even danced and performed hand mudras. I was sure I was hallucinating, but each time I refocused at the center, the deities on the outer rings came alive again. *Perhaps this is what is supposed to happen?* I continued late into the night. When too tired to continue, I turned in for the night, and within a dream . . .

*I awake in an astral meadow, lying on my back watching white clouds move across a broad sky. After a brief relaxing spell, all at once, the entire mandala is projected onto the vast expanse of sky in brilliant colors and in a precision far beyond anything possible on a physical canvas. The entire astral sky becomes the living mandala, and I perceive all the same deities in their cosmic fullness, simultaneously—I cannot adequately describe this experience. They are not just animated but conscious, sentient existences—forces of consciousness and intelligence, and they are staring at me with the wild eyes and faces of mad joy!*

*I hear a kind of roaring sound, but I keep my cool and focus on the central deity—immediately a great magnetic force seizes me, sucking me up into the sky, and into the central deity! I become the deity, merging in a silent explosion in which the mandala simultaneously becomes a three-dimensional form. I'm then shot like a rocket through the center of the mandala.*

*In a new realm now, I wander here until I lose consciousness. . . . I find myself back in my flat, standing beside the window watching astral lights move in waves across the sky. A deep calmness is spread through my being. Glancing back at the pathetic ape slumped on my futon, I hesitate to return at all.*

Moments later I find myself cataleptic, held in a body of simian stone. In time I reidentified with the beast, rose, and took a sip of water. Indeed, the mandalas of India and Tibet are maps of consciousness, frequency charts of realms I must know and explore. I hadn't yet reached Nepal.

And it was now time to die.

# 15

# Dying Young

*Dying is a wild night and a new road.*

EMILY DICKINSON, LETTER TO PEREZ COWAN, 1869

*M*oney, *yes—money.* After being a poor, struggling student for nearly six years of university, I now had money—good money, *my* money. I immediately requisitioned from Japan, Inc., an electric guitar; a stereo system powerful enough to lift the roof off my building; a speedy motorcycle; a large set of oil paints, an easel, and canvases galore; giant art books; an expensive Italian suit; and various other pieces of unrequited materialist love—and I found naught but momentary satisfaction in any of it.

The summer meditation intensive was over, and try as I might, I was losing a battle. Already distracted by work, stress, and money, the Japanese tradition of taking life *extremely seriously* sank into me like an infection, resulting in a weakening vision of one of my eyes. An ophthalmologist said only a change in my optical prescription could help me, but I knew it was stress related and I declined the offer of new spectacles. Melancholy cascaded into a savage depression, and I fell ill. Each brief recovery only crumbled into another illness. My Faustian pact for money and pleasure seemed a losing deal. Doctors had no idea what was happening to me, only that my white blood cell count was through the roof.

"You probably have leukemia," said the doctor dryly, casually glancing at his clipboard as though he was just noticing it, "but we'll have to run some more tests to be sure." *What? Terminally ill at twenty-four years old? How can this be?* I was shocked, angry, fearful, and nauseous. I had already run out of both sick days and paid holidays. "Some leukemia patients live several years after initial diagnosis," assured the doctor, as if that would cheer me up. It would be nine long days before the final lab tests were returned, and in 1985 the survival rate was significantly lower than it is now. I said nothing to my colleagues, my family, and friends. I sat with it alone. *How can it be? I'm just starting my life. To die so young?* The secrets of life and death now seemed closer than I had ever wished and all too soon. I meditated like never before. In the late evenings, trembling fears and comforting insights washed over me in alternating waves. Unable to sleep, I stared at the ceiling each night wondering, *If I have only a few months or years to live, what am I to do? What is truly important?*

> *I feared not to die, but to die without illumination.*
>
> La Très Sainte Trinosophie, section 3, p. 45

After days of inner deliberation, *if the tests do confirm I have an incurable malady*, I narrowed my action plan to three options: (1) a criminal joyride of hedonism until I die in a hail of bullets; (2) return to an American hospital, drugged into a stupor, to fearfully wait out the sad and bitter end with wailing relatives; or (3) enter that monastery in Thailand alone, face to the wind, to find the inner Grail, to meditate unto death, to hold the Luminosity and get off the wheel of rebirth.

After a week of sleepless nights, I vowed to meet the Luminosity face-to-face, this time without flinching: *If the tests prove terminal, I WILL enter the monastery in Thailand with only enough medication to keep me sitting in meditation to the very end. I WILL die reaching for liberation, and I WILL succeed in holding the Luminosity.* Opening my eyes, and leaning back against the wall, I whispered a prayer and said my goodbyes to my family, my friends, my entire history. Tears fell, as I would withhold from them that I'd never see any of them again; I could have no distractions from my pilgrimage inward and onward, back to my true home. A lonely exhaustion released me, and on that cool October night I dropped into a dreamless void.

> *At the moment of commitment, the entire universe conspires to assist you.*
> ATTRIBUTED TO JOHANN WOLFGANG VON GOETHE

*Cold, so cold* . . . I reach for my blanket and find it down at my ankles. I pull it up, but moments later, I find it again at my ankles. Puzzled, I pull it back up, turn onto my side, and hold it tightly. Then the blanket is snatched away with force! In shock, I turn upward to an overwhelming blast of golden-orange light, as though from a magnetic, sentient star. The silhouette of an Indian master stands before me, surrounded by an exploding halo of raw sunlight. Enveloped in this electromagnetic force, I'm held breathless in his presence until every cell in my body feels renewed and supercharged. He beams thought-waves into my mind, and I struggle to hold the memory. Overwhelmed and vibrating in a mysterious bliss, I lose consciousness and sleep until morning.

> *The soul is an eye of fire, or a mirror of fire,*
> *Wherein the Godhead has revealed itself.*
> JACOB BOEHME, *THEOSOPHISCHE WERCKE*, 1682

"I hereby resign my position thirty days from today," I typed out at the office that morning. Now obscured from memory, I could recall only that a profound event had happened the previous night. I shuddered inwardly: *Am I mad? Leaving my first full-time job, breaking contract before I even know whether I'm terminally ill or not?* I paused and Elder Self beamed within, *We're all terminal.* I sat, poured a green tea, and knew: *In either case, I shall depart for the Thai monastery as soon as possible.* I booked my flight ticket and made preparations to face the music at the hospital. Days later, the tests came in negative, and I felt great relief that I had more time in this world. Nevertheless, with a weighty portion of unneeded personality now shed, I felt lighter for it. I gladly rid myself of all my newly acquired possessions, cleaned out my flat, and prepared for my flight to Thailand.

> *Death is the midwife of very great things. It brings about the birth and rebirth of forms a thousand times improved. This is the highest mystery of God.*
>
> PARACELSUS, *THE DEVIL'S DOCTOR*, CHAP. 11

An infusion of mental clarity became a natural state for the first time in my brief adult life. *To leave everything—a career, a contract, money, and material ease?* I laughed at myself, but the clarity deepened and all at once I understood for the first time the real meaning of a Faustian pact, which had disturbed me since I read Goethe's *Faust* in school: "Selling one's soul" is a metaphor. More like selling out to the lower self—the weak and greedy, frightened self, the forsaking of the soul's deepest wishes, to follow that which is convenient, easy, and comfortable for the earthly, personality-body complex, one's cultural programming. I would now release myself from this slavery and soar freely over the world to meet an unseen yet soul-felt destiny.

# 16

## The Daishi

*In all chaos there is a cosmos, in all disorder a secret order.*

C. G. JUNG, *ARCHETYPES OF*
*THE COLLECTIVE UNCONSCIOUS*

"Koyasan," suggested my friend Kim, named after Kipling's novel. "That's where I'd go if I were to see only one place before I left Japan. It's a city of temples atop a remote mountain in Wakayama." I had no intention of returning to Japan and wanted to see one last sight of importance. Arrangements were made and I embarked on a long series of trains and cable cars deep into the mountains of Wakayama.

Arriving very late at the monastery high on the forested mountain of Mt. Koya, I woke the monks with my banging. Early November is cool at that elevation. As I listened to the monks inside mumbling and making their way to open the gate, I watched my frosty breaths wavering away on each exhalation. With a lantern down a cool, dim hallway, I was shown to a monastic room with a glittering altar. *They must have run out of rooms, and put me in an altar room*, I wondered. I was served a cold but sumptuous five-tier boxed meal of *shoujinryori kaiseki* (gourmet vegetarian monk's cuisine) in my room, and I quickly fell asleep under a thick futon cover on the floor. After a deep sleep until the wee hours, I inwardly awoke to the inner siren and fell into the abyss at the center of my skull. I lifted out, sat up in my light body upon the futon. Soon, I heard mantras from an ethereal voice in the hallway . . .

*A shimmering monk enters my room through no visible door, holding a tray of ornamental instruments. The room brightens from his presence. He is short in stature with a large round bald head and an exceptionally thick neck. Great power emanates from him. He bows and sits before me in crossed-legged Indian-style (not in* seiza *as would be usual in Japanese tradition). He bows again and I bring my hands together in prayer position. He places golden ritual objects on a tray on the floor—a candle, a bell, small bowls, and some other oddly shaped instruments. He says prayers, offering me a kind of welcome blessing. With hands still in prayer position, I nod my thanks and the apparition fades.*

Realigning my soul with my physical body, I sit up and meditate in the cool darkness until I find myself asleep again in a deep inner hollow of joy. Sunlight reaches me through a previously unnoticed window, and after a sumptuous monk's breakfast I set out to explore the mountain and its scores of temples and monasteries. Not a word of written English, nor even a single Roman letter was anywhere to be found on Mt. Koya at this time, and my Japanese reading proficiency was limited. The monastery in which I stayed was auspiciously located close to an ancient graveyard. Stunned by the light pouring through the mist and giant cypress trees over a thousand years old, I am transported to another time. Deep green mosses cover countless ancient graves of unfathomable age. A spiritual power increases the farther I continue into the sacred forest graveyard, and my body is now vibrating. At the end of the long walk that passes over three small bridges, each over a stream, I reach a modern building, though built in a traditional style. I enter and feel an intense sense of falling within; I rub my eyes in disbelief.

Hundreds of golden lanterns line the walls of multiple chambers;

below are red carpets and black tables on which rest the golden ritual instruments. I come to the central vestibule with golden lanterns lining each side and note a window where there would normally be an altar, exactly as in my repeating astral journeys two years ago. The configuration of the *Torodo*, the Hall of Lanterns, is unique in all the world. *I haven't taken the wrong path; a circle is in progress.*

The original Torodo burned in a fire, and a new concrete exterior has been constructed. However, the inner hall of lanterns is an exact replica of the thousand-year-old original. I circled around the building to find pilgrims lighting candles and saying prayers before an altar set into a mountain wall. The hair on my arms stood on end; I had never before experienced such spiritual power. I meditated silently, enjoying the strange luminosity of the atmosphere, knowing nothing of what was before me. I later walked over the mountain of monasteries for hours and found several paintings of fantastic mandalas that reminded me so much of dreams of passing down formal halls of green carpets and geometrically arranged furnishings, all reminiscent of an esoteric art that I would eventually come to know again. A painting of the thick-necked monk holding the same golden instrument in his hand looked down to me from a high altar, and I thought: *How kind of him to welcome me! He must have been a monk here a long time ago.* I saw his likeness again and again all over the mountain.

Two years later in the Himalayas, I picked up a book called *Japanese Pilgrimage* about a famous pilgrimage route on Shikoku Island. The pilgrims chant and hope for a visit from the *Daishi* (great teacher), who would often appear to devout pilgrims in dreams and visions. Kukai, or *Kobo Daishi*, is the greatest tantric Buddhist master in Japanese history. Koyasan, I then learned at the end of the book, was in fact the Daishi's headquarters, and where most of the esoteric training for his monks occurred. More importantly, the reason for the window instead of an altar in the great Torodo hall of lanterns on Koyasan is because the opening looks out onto the *Gobyo*, the cave of his *mahasamadhi*, his final conscious meditation and exit at death. On March 21 in the year 835, it is said Kukai had himself walled into the cave, merged with *Mahavairocana*, the Buddha of Transcendence, and entered into *mahasamadhi*. The power of this great blessing is still felt all over the mountain, especially here at the very cave, the end of the long walk of the *Okunoin*, the burial place of emperors and great poets, those wishing to be close to the Daishi into the afterlife. His courage to consciously excarnate without flinching inspired me, and I felt nearly breathless with the thought of it. In 921, it is also said, monks opened the stone door to the cave to find Kukai's desiccated body still sitting in eternal samadhi, only his hair had grown long. They trimmed Kukai's hair and beard, changed his holy cloth, and again sealed the cave entrance. It hasn't been opened since.

The Koyasan tradition and the Tibetan tradition have the same source in the great ancient Nalanda University in the state of Bihar, India. If I had come to Japan for no other reason than to see the Torodo, the Hall of Lanterns, then the trip had been worth it. I would appreciate these aspects of Japanese spirituality in the years ahead, and even come to be accepted as a personal student of the *jougo-sama* (chief abbot) of all monasteries on Mt. Koya. For now, I would cash in the chips, pay my student loans a year in advance, and set off as a pilgrim: first stop, Thailand. I would reach that renowned southern monastery, but not before resting on an island beach in the south. With no job, limited funds, and an unknown future, I went to the airport. I entered the stream of spirit.

I let go.

# 17

# Island

*We are like islands in the sea, separate on the surface but connected in the deep.*

WILLIAM JAMES, *THE AMERICAN MAGAZINE* 68 (1909)

The Siamese heat hit me like a welcome balm. My shoulders relaxed, my smile returned, and I felt my heart sing. Bangkok is a riot of spices, traffic, street hawkers, and sensuality. Warm smiles and deep eye contact greeted me all around, the opposite of the cool, pinched, and closed displays I had just left behind. After a few days in the crowded palaces, temples, and shops of Bangkok, I left for the rural south.

After an overnight train, I took a local fishing boat over green ocean waters to a coconut island. From the tiny village port, I hired a rusty Jeep to drive me over the sandy jungle trail to a beach area with no roads or electricity. Dumped before a small guesthouse that offered bamboo huts right on the water for a mere half-dollar a night, I was in heaven.

Like the spirits to a sensitive soul, the waves insist their presence here on the shore of the Gulf of Siam, washing away the stress of a frantic Nippon. I would spend a month on the island before I entered the monastery near Surat Thani for an indefinite period of in-depth meditation. Here on the island, I could hear only waves and the heartbeat of the earth. I spent nearly two weeks just sleeping, meditating, and splashing my feet through the waves until the early hours of the mornings. With such deep rest, the vision in my left eye returned to normal.

The American Thanksgiving holiday of 1985 passed without the traditional turkey dinner for me on that Siamese island. That night I walked the beach until well after a timeless midnight, my feet splashing in the gentle waves, and my spirit open to the dark night winds. In those wee hours a curious sensation appeared. Like a light bulb blinking on above my head, came the face of my aunt! I perceive her holographic form through the top of my head, as if from an eye at the center of my skull looking skyward. She is ecstatic with joy and excitement, and beams to me, "Oh, Kevin, it's all just wonder and joy, and it's perfectly on schedule! I'm just a bit sorry to leave the boys so soon." She continues to giggle in an ecstatic joy. I smile and beam my acknowledgment that her message is received. She vanishes, and I return to my hut to write my father that I'd just met his sister on the beach. As I recall, it was just after 2:30 a.m.

> *The gods conceal from men the happiness of death, that*
> *they may endure life.*
>
> Lucan, Roman poet, *Pharsalia*, book 4, 519–20

I could not at that time explain how I perceived her soul through the top of my head, only that it was so. My aunt had four children: two older daughters, both married and away, and two younger sons, just barely out of their teens. That she was sorry to leave the two younger ones "so soon" made sense. Though quite sure my aunt had left this world, I had no earthly confirmation of this, and felt concern that if I had misunderstood the message my father and family at large might think me mad, and when, *or rather if,* I return for a visit in the future . . . I paused and flashes of a straitjacket and a mental hospital skirted across my inner horizon. Nevertheless, it was time to trust my perceptions. I wrote to my father exactly what his sister had beamed to me, writing the message by candlelight flickering madly in the ocean winds rushing through my bamboo walls. I noted the date and time on the letter, and added the monastery address, my next destination, as my return address. Hours later, my hand shook a bit before I dropped the letter into the wicker basket on the back of the weekly postal scooter. The scooter sped away, sliding over the sands, carrying my letter to the port to begin its long journey over the Pacific.

> *Death is not extinguishing the light;*
> *it is putting out the lamp because dawn has come.*
>
> RABINDRANATH TAGORE,
> *COLLECTED WORKS, THE POEMS*

A year later I would return to the monastery to find a brief letter from my father, explaining that my aunt had died on the afternoon of Thanksgiving Day in Indiana, just as it was early morning here in Thailand the following day. A cancer had spread quickly and there was no time to inform me by letter before I left Japan. I discovered only years later that my father did not inform her children of my letter at the time. A year later, at Thanksgiving dinner, he put my letter in his breast pocket and pondered sharing it with her children. As they sat down to the memorial meal, he thought it might be just too shocking and so decided against it, until her oldest daughter burst out with, "Oh, I forgot to tell you all that I had a dream last year, the day after Mom died!" The table went silent, and the eldest continued, "She was quite joyous, and said that everything was perfectly on schedule, but that she was only a bit sorry to leave the boys so soon." My father nearly fainted. He produced my letter then and there at the dinner table, and from what I hear, it was quite a discussion that night. After this, no one on this side of the family questioned why I pursued my mystical interests. It was the clearest confirmation so far that subtle perception, which can seem so imaginary, is part of a fabric of consciousness on which our souls sail freely.

# 18

# Monastery

*Isolation is the price of greatness.*

SWAMI HARIHARANANDA GIRI

After a torpid month on the coconut island amid green waters, I picked my lazy carcass up off the beach and poured it over the channel back to the mainland for my stay at a large Thai monastery set deep in the jungle. There I met the elderly Buddhapasa, Thailand's greatest living saint, and Aachan Po, the younger master who spoke some English. Aachan (*acharya*, "teacher") Po had incredibly clear, watery eyes and striking poise. I had never met anyone like him. Time seemed to stop in his presence. Once asked if he ever slept, he replied with a quiet power, "Sometimes." I recalled my sleepless week in the midst of the severe kundalini activation last year and reveled in the thought that that could be a permanent state. I was energized now, and felt I'd come to the right place.

Life at the jungle monastery was an easy routine of early morning meditation, quiet study in the day, late afternoon dips in the nearby natural hot spring, and meditation again before a lip-blistering, chili-infused dinner. We few foreigners paid an affordable one dollar per day for food, as we did not go out to beg with the monks each morning. I requested a *guti*, a solitary hut in the jungle, and said that I would like to stay for six months of semi-isolated meditation. One opened after a few days and I settled in for the long sojourn inward to enlightenment. *I don't need illness and the threat of death to encourage me. I'm in charge of my destiny!* A sudden cackle of distant laughter from monks through the forest broke my reverie, and I had to smile at myself.

One late afternoon, meditation in the temple went especially long and I briefly dozed while sitting up. I found myself looking down from the high temple ceiling, wondering for a moment which head below was mine. Sandy locks ahoy, and I was back down into my body with a start. I opened my eyes and looked about to gather my bearings. Aachan Po's wide eyes stared at me with surprise; they narrowed again, and an ambiguous smile spread quietly across his lips. The sit went on—another breath, an inhalation, exhalation, one moment at a time.

"Let's go out to the market for a fresh coconut," suggested a tall Danish man, also staying in the monastery. His light blue eyes were as vacant as the sky. Henrik glowed with spirit, but he usually looked lost, like an innocent child looking for a misplaced toy. I inwardly wondered, *Is this man reality-challenged, or has he truly come to a profound spiritual state?* We walked outside the monastery gates to the village market. Sitting on low stools at a small folding table with our coconuts, Henrik explained that he had worked in Europe as a psychic and was now touring Asia visiting ashrams and monasteries. He paused, sipped his coconut, and then asked, "Are you aware of your previous incarnation?" Surprised, I only nodded and continued to sip my coconut water, as he was now treading in private territory. He looked over my head with cloudy eyes. Looking back and then right through me, he murmured, "Germany." I stopped sipping and held the coconut water in my mouth. He smiled, "And you were a doctor." I gulped and choked. I had never spoken of this to anyone—he had pulled this information out of thin air. "How did you know?" I asked incredulously. He only raised his hands, looked to the sky, and shook his head as though to say: *Silly you, don't you know the universe is an open book!*

I shared that I had been drawn to join a student exchange program in Augsburg, West Germany, at the age of seventeen, and there had undergone an awakening complete with extrasensory and psychokinetic events. The Dane leaned forward and cryptically said, "You've left a project unfinished—there's no escape until you complete it." The truth of his words shook me, and I countered, "But I seek liberation, not karmic debt repayments." I looked at my coconut and back to him, and intoned with grim determination, "I'm remaining here to meditate intensively for at least six months." With his glassy, childlike eyes again looking up and past me, he shook his head as though he didn't believe me, or that I just didn't get it. I felt offended at his flippant attitude toward my spiritual commitment. He parried, "Is *the project* not of importance for others? Where then is your Buddhist compassion?" I had no reply to this and the conversation fell to an uncomfortable silence. As we stood up to pay for our coconuts, he said, "I feel you're being drawn elsewhere." I scoffed at such an idea and thought to myself, *I'm the master of my fate. What do I need with spaced-out spiritual junkies?* Although this fellow was unusually perceptive, I decided he was a distraction and would be no help in holding my feet to the fires of meditation here. I avoided him for the next few days, and then learned he had left the monastery.

I had been accused of being antisocial before, as though it were something undesirable, but here in the monastery it was lauded. I now had freedom from social interaction, an introvert's paradise. In the heat of the jungle in southern Thailand I quickly lost all sense of time or place in the daily rhythms of meditation, food, and more meditation. Yet, after a few weeks I was reminded it would soon be Christmas. A few other Europeans staying in the monastery asked if I'd like to join them for a festive dinner in the nearby city of Surat Thani. Initially interested, I declined, deciding instead to fast and meditate in my hut for forty-eight hours. Rather than the usual gorging and ceaseless chatter, *my holiday this year will be a spartan attempt at union with the enlightened consciousness that perhaps Christmas is supposed to celebrate after all!*

My windowless guti afforded me no view to distractions, and I quickly descended into an altered state in the darkness. Long hours of Vipassana insight meditation passed. When I did take breaks, the hut was so small I was forced to rest diagonally on two reed mats so thin that my hip bones bruised on the hard, wooden floor. By hour twelve my body ached. Soon I was not only hungry but wrought with irrational fears, and feelings that *I'm wasting my life here.* I continued to sit. My father appeared on my inner landscape, imploring me to build a career; then my mother, guilting me for abandoning relatives at home. Christmas songs drifted into my head, along with a vague nostalgia for family and friends. Then Christmas dinner along with all the trimmings—delicious gravy poured over turkey, potatoes, green beans, and desserts, pumpkin pie and the rest. I drooled and moaned in hunger but continued on in my meditations. In the wee hours of the morning, I briefly left my guti to fetch some water from the nearby well. Stars glistened through the jungle canopy. I dumped a bucket of cool water over my head, and returned to my grim discipline, descending into an ever-deepening state. I had moments of stone stillness, coupled with severe agitation. Sunrise came, visible only through the narrow gaps in my simple wooden-board hut. I stretched my sore legs, drank some water, and returned to meditation.

After several more hours, a sudden, irrational paranoia overtook me—*the monks are out to do me in! This is all nonsense—they plan to kill me and take my money!* Inner demons of violence tore at my soul, and I pulled at my hair in a panic. Despite all, I remained glued to my meditation cushion, and a brief calm ensued. Hunger cried from my belly. Day passed into another night, and I lay down to sleep for a spell. An hour later I arose sweating and panting: dancing on the inner horizon of my mind with hyper-clarity came writhing naked phantasms of former girlfriends seductively promising pleasures known and those yet to be explored. Through the night I struggled to hold my vital fluid and my intention, finally falling on my knees in the dark, head to the floor, gasping and begging to survive the second night. After an hour like this, my body contorted into a most unusual position and seemed to lock in place with my head prostrate to the floor, while up on my knees and elbows. I stayed in this odd prayer position for what felt like hours, losing all sense of time.

I felt that dying would be okay, and that a return to spirit would be better than this strange earthly life of endless hopes and subsequent disappointments. My breath became so subtle I couldn't be sure I was breathing anymore. I sank into inner vision—a silent depth, black as a starless night. With no identifiable cerebral train of *me* identification, thoughts ceased and awareness rested in a state of pure perception:

*White clouds appear in a deep blue sky of a vast inner world. A rainbow arcs from the clouds on which emerge a sequence of Buddhist deities, riding along it. The visions are in pure ideal form—no brushstrokes or hand imperfections. Each deity is perfectly formed, varying in specific form, color, and hand mudras; some have geometric forms on their torsos.*

After making careful mental notes of the deities' forms, I felt I had received what was needed. (I later discovered that the odd bowing posture that I'd held for so long had been a Tibetan *Kum Nye* meditation position, one designed to induce profound visions.) I left my dim hut for the canteen and ate in silence. Forty-six hours had passed, just short of my full two-day goal, but it was enough. I rested the next day, journaled a bit, and sat only brief meditations. I slept soundly that evening.

Waking early the next morning to a brilliant sunrise, I was thrust upward from my mat with only one thought screaming from my every cell: *I must go to India immediately!* I handed my guitar to the monks and said that I'd return for it in some months. "What happened to six months of intensive meditation?" Aachan Po asked. Apologetically, I

Fig. 18.1. An angel leads a pilgrim out of the labyrinth of worldly illusion. Hermann Hugo, *Gottselige Begierde*, Augsburg, Germany 1622.

pleaded, "I'm sorry, I only know I must be in India immediately!" He smiled a knowing silence. Within an hour I was on the long train to the capital. The ticket agent in Bangkok asked, "Where in India?"

"I don't know, just get me the fastest, cheapest flight from here to there."

# 19

# Bodhgaya

*If the path before you is clear, you're probably on someone else's.*

ATTRIBUTED TO BOTH JOSEPH CAMPBELL
AND C. G. JUNG

My initial days in Calcutta can only be described in terms of shock. A pair of young travelers and I shared a taxi into the city of twelve million souls with no working traffic lights that day. A sea of humanity crowds every street. In the midst of endless traffic jams, lepers push their fleshy stumps into my face through the broken windows of the taxi, pleading for a few *paise* (pennies). When we arrived in the area of my guesthouse, I was unable to walk on the sidewalks—they were blanketed with the most wretched of the homeless imaginable. Yet, in their sunken eyes was a light and a depth I have never seen in any other country. That they lived so close to edge of life and death frightened and intrigued me. Though I felt powerless, I also felt a painful compassion for them in their suffering, abject poverty, and hopelessness. The crowds and dust, the noise, the cars belching smoke, wandering bloated-belly cows, and beggars leading crippled children through the traffic all sent me back to my guesthouse each time after I ventured out for a few hours. My guesthouse was so full that I slept on the roof under timeless stars. Even atop this decaying building, there was no peace from the cacophony of the city below. Still, I had arrived. I was in India—the mother culture of the world.

Night fell and I stared from my rooftop cot at the stars above: *Different land, same stars. What next? Please prepare me, give me a direction.* An hour later a young Belgian couple, also camped on the rooftop, asked if I needed a train ticket to Gaya, "Our friend decided not to go with us, so we have this extra ticket." I asked, "You mean the Gaya near Bodhgaya, where the Buddha was enlightened?" They both nodded, "That's the one." How appropriate—of course, my first pilgrimage should be to the *Light of Asia.*

The chaos of one's first train ride in India can only be experienced. Waves of humanity undulate around Calcutta's gigantic Howrah Station. Once inside I'm misdirected to half a dozen different unmarked trains until, finally, a whistle blew and the one pulling out had to be it. I dash and leap on board. A conductor confirms its destination and I slump into my second-class seat near a few other Western travelers. We fall into conversation regarding traveling the rails in India and I'm quickly schooled in what to do and what not. Darkness fell along the tracks. While the train faded into a rumbling eternity, I slept gripping my pack tightly.

Loud, rusty screeches from the train's brakes woke me in Gaya, Bihar, at 5 a.m. that cool New Year's morning, and I parted from my traveling companions. It was another 5 kilometers to Bodhgaya (or Buddha-gaya), and I took a bicycle rickshaw all the way so I could watch the sunrise over the countryside in peace. The rickshaw man was only too happy to make a distance fare. Once out of the city of Gaya, we fell back in time. Beyond the narrow path was the India from any possible century—rice fields, palm trees, mud-walled huts in tiny villages. That sunrise hour was one of the most memorable of my life. I felt returned to a pastoral existence I had known, rather we have all likely known, many times before. It seemed little changed since the sixth century BCE when Siddartha Gautama came here to sit under a tree until he entirely pierced *samsara*, the great veil of illusion.

As we approached Bodhgaya, the early sun now blazing, I beheld a site I have never seen before, nor since: a vast plain with countless tents and tens of thousands of Tibetans crowded before a stage far in the distance. A huge white mandala stretched behind a tiny being standing on that stage. I asked a man passing by what was happening. "The Dalai Lama is here doing his first public Kalachakra Initiation, and China for the first time has allowed Tibetans to cross over the pass into India to attend." The crowd forced the rickshaw to a stop at the edge of the village. All was at a standstill—nothing moved, every possible structure was filled to the brim with pilgrims and makeshift tent restaurants serving Tibetan food. The Mahabodhi Temple and Bodhi tree were impossible to reach. What few cafés and shops there were in the village had lines of indistinguishable length. There wasn't a room, a bed, or even a bench available anywhere. *Welcome to the Circus of Enlightenment!*

"There is an Indian Buddhist monastery about one kilometer to the west of here. Perhaps they have space," said a helpful but harried innkeeper, his arms full of blankets. January is quite cool at night and the tiny village was short of everything. I walked through waves of red-robed Tibetan monks to the end of the village and found another bicycle rickshaw for hire. We covered the extra kilometer under an increasingly hot sun.

"Oh, yes, we have space for you. Come right along! I'll show you to your room!" The friendly Indian monk in light saffron robes waved his hands about and shouted at the other monks to make preparations. As I entered the stone monastery with my luggage, I passed a room full of meditating persons; they seemed to be from all nationalities. He showed me to a concrete room with a few hard bunks. "Leave your luggage here and come down for meditation. We'll start in a few minutes," the monk instructed with a big toothy smile, his head bobbing about as though on a loose spring.

*Well, they conduct meditations here! I'll sit for a while and later head out to check out the neighborhood.* I took a cushion and seated myself in the back. I had done Theravada meditation before, so I settled in silently. After some minutes, my knees were already aching, and I was dusty from my journey. I looked forward to getting a shower and chatting with this interesting-looking crowd. The welcoming monk then entered and took a seat, pausing to straighten his robes: "From this moment forward we'll meditate thirteen hours a day, and not speak for nine days," intoned the monk with some solemnity. *Nine days . . . what?* An outward burst of laughter at my predicament wouldn't be appropriate, but inwardly I chuckled at my misfortune—or rather, good fortune. How appropriate that I should sit in silence for nine days of Vipassana meditation where Gautama Siddhartha dropped the whole drama of himself. *Why should I be distracted by great crowds worshipping a tree? I can be my own Bodhi tree right here.* I gathered my resolve for another journey inward. *I can do this.*

Pain. The reality of Buddha's first law *All of life is suffering* was never more apparent than after the first of endless hour-long sits. The monk only rarely spoke, but one evening he intoned, "Pain of the body is only pain of the mind. Do not move, and it will pass." And it did pass. Yet pain came again. "These deeper pains are not physical. They are your *samskaras*—the knots and latent tendencies infused with emotional resistance that you have carried from life to life. They now rest in you," the monk explained. "These are what keep bringing you back to incarnate on the wheel of birth, life, death, and birth again and again." The hours and days went on, and I cringed at memories of when I had hurt others through word or deed, when I had selfishly taken what I wanted without regard for others, and worst of all, the fact, again, that I hadn't truly loved anyone but myself. I burned with regret and promises of reform.

And I got bored—yes, bored even with my own favorite story, *all about me.* Pain punctuated by brief moments of peace and clarity became my daily fare. A slow cleanse was occurring, and deep wounds were released. The insights gained during the nine days could not be described in anything less than a separate volume, but to summarize: thoughts, emotions, and physical sensations come and go, the truth of *Impermanence.* The pain of life is trying to either hold on to them (desire) or push them way (aversion), thus defining an illusory ego, that is, who we think we are, the source of all suffering.

I reawakened to the quest to know the secrets, from where we come before our first breath, and to where we go after our last. The program ended and I returned to the now empty village to circumambulate the Bodhi tree in honor of the Buddha's commitment. In silence, I felt, *Siddhartha went all the way; I'm merely a child.* The Tibetans were gone, and I moved into the Burmese monastery. I sat in my little monk's chamber there, meditating hours a day. Each day after meditation I sat at the long table of a street café in the center of the village drinking chai, watching Indian life wander by. I was in a good space, living moment to moment. I still had no idea why I was in India nor where I was going next, and didn't care. *I might just stay here and die under the Bodhi tree—there is really nothing else to do.* When I gave up my former life that night in Japan, to forgo ever seeing my family and friends again, I became free, no longer bound to a personal history. I was *Dead* to my old life, and like the band, *Gratefully* so.

"Do you need a train ticket to Varanasi?" a traveler stopping at my usual tea stall asked pleadingly, "I no longer need the ticket, and I really need the money." A tiny bell inwardly chimed, and I put down my chai. *Benares, the holiest city in India? Why not! This is where Hindus go to die, to be assured of liberation. More on the secrets of life and death!* Rupees were quickly placed in her waiting hands, and I returned to the monastery to pack my bag. I'm a pilgrim once again.

# 20

# Varanasi

The ancient city of Varanasi on the holy Ganges River is a power-house of spiritual vibrations, and I shook from the sheer voltage of just being there. For over 3,000 years this city has stood at the center of Hindu life. Seeing the dying line the alleys and walkways to the *ghats*, the stairs that lead down to the holy river, I suddenly felt young and very much alive. *I am dying too—true, but not quite yet!* In the day hours I wandered the charming narrow alleys, but spent all my evenings at the burning ghats, where bodies are burned in the open air and the ashes are scattered over the divine river. I stood transfixed, night after night as endless bodies were consumed in the flames. The stench of charred human flesh and the snarls of thin dogs seeking scraps did not dissuade me. Occasionally a foot would roll off the fire, to be either chased by a hungry dog, or fetched and returned to the flames by one of the *Doms*, a special caste that tends funeral pyres. *Death stalks us all. How much time do I have in this body? Where will I go when its expiry date is up?*

One evening, while at the main burning ghat, a festive parade of musicians burst onto the scene and a large group of Indians, all with the red bindi dot upon their foreheads, carried a body wrapped in golden fabric high above their heads, dancing and singing in a gypsylike revelry. Children laughed and smiled, and young boys danced joyfully around the corpse while Brahmin priests tossed colored powders and blessings over the shrouded deceased. *They aren't sad!* Indeed, for many Indians, to die in Benares is true cause for celebration. It is said the vibration here is so powerful that navigating the afterlife from this location is nearly a guarantee of either liberation or at least a fortuitous rebirth. Death in Varanasi is completely out in the open. *Why is there a conspiracy of silence regarding death in so much of the world?* I felt that my culture had failed me, and I was glad to be in India. *Indeed*, I thought, *I shall stay here, become a yogi, merge with the godhead, and breathe my last on these holy ghats.* However, I still couldn't bring myself to bathe in the filthy waters of the Ganges. I wondered how the Hindus could believe such nonsense that any river is holier than any other. I would soon learn.

Late the next evening, after watching a number of pyres perform their duties of bodily dissolution by fire, I walked alone along the dim Dashashwamedh Ghat, a wide dropping array of stairsteps leading down to the Ganges River. When I passed a dark bundle of rags piled there, a disembodied voice called out with a raspy voice. I turned back with a start, not realizing any soul was nearby. The pile of rags stirred with a snort and cough, and there emerged a *sadhu*, a wandering truth seeker clad in dark, draggled robes. He lifted a *chillum* pipe toward me, "Boom Shankar!" I smiled, gave him a large two-rupee coin, and took a deep drag of hashish through my hands (not touching my lips to his pipe). Now, I had been practicing *pranayama* (breath control), and I held in the bittersweet smoke for a long while. Either there was magic in that spot on the Ganges, the sadhu was a real *siddha* yogi, or whatever was in that pipe turned out to be much stronger than expected—in any case, I don't even recall exhaling as I dropped back against the stone steps, falling into a catalepsy. Slipping sideways out of my immobile body, I soared over the Ganges—*freedom!* As a pinpoint of awareness above, I perceived the Ganges not as just a dark river but one flowing with astral tendrils of golden and silvery light! *Ahh, there really is something holy about this river!* I silently floated over the glowing river for a timeless spell and returned to slowly realign with the physical. My body was cold and the bundle of rags was gone. I slowly made my way back to my guesthouse along the midnight ghats with a new appreciation for the holy Ganges.

> *Likewise, in consequence of this divine initiation, we become spectators of entire, simple, immovable and blessed visions in a pure light; and were, ourselves, pure and immaculate and liberated from this surrounding vestment which we denominated body.*
>
> PLATO, *PHAEDRUS*

That night in Varanasi I drifted into an elastic sleep in which came a dream of the same Indian saint who, bathed in the brilliant orange light, had appeared in my flat in Japan:

*A door before me opens inward, and the Master, now dressed in white, invites me to enter. I cross the threshold into a blazing effulgence of white light. I'm also wearing brilliant white, and so are the many souls within. I'm overcome with an inexpressibly wonderous joy. He beams to me, "You were unprepared, so your memory was obscured." Instructions to his ashram appeared in mind. "You may come now."*

# 21

# Kundalini Fire II

*When I ascended into the heavens I saw the holy sons
of God, moving in flames of fire, wearing white clothes,
whose countenances shone like snow.*

ETHIOPIAN BOOK OF ENOCH,
FROM HALEVI, *KABBALAH: THE DIVINE PLAN*

After a series of trains and buses spanning two days I arrived at the town as indicated in the Master's dream invitation. A brief inquiry in the street provided me with the final steps to his ashram. I paused outside the small gate for moment, pondering the path I'd be drawn along. Inside, a painting of him greeted me, confirming his presence. The ashram was a collection of houses that had been connected and combined with passages and courtyards between them. A number of Indians, all in white, milled about; two Westerners were among them. The master was apparently out but was due back soon. I tried to explain why I had come, but the office attendant only waved his hand, smiled, and said with the gentlest humility, "That's okay, I don't need to know. You're here."

In my simple room I unpacked my bag and laughed. *This is insane! How can this be?* I stretched out on my bunk and dozed for an hour. I woke and sat up, feeling a distinct sensation in the atmosphere. I went outside and blinked in disbelief—the sky and the very air around me had the subtlest shade of pink. It wasn't near dusk. I rubbed my eyes again; it was unmistakable. I asked an Indian man about the pink light permeating the atmosphere. He only nodded and said, "The master has returned, of course."

I was led to a courtyard with several Indians already sitting on the ground, crowding before a low platform. An older Indian man leaned toward me and said, "You needn't speak. He already knows your thoughts." Now this I understood, considering my departure from Japan and my arrival at this ashram. A hush came over the room, and many leaned to the side to view someone emerging from behind a post. I cannot adequately describe what I experienced next but I shall try:

As my gaze fell upon this man, I had the sense that I was seeing for the first time a being of the highest order, perhaps the highest frequency of consciousness that could possibly contract into and inhabit a human frame. Above his head I felt the gravity of a galactic center, and yet his feet seemed rooted to the very center of the earth. In him I could detect not the slightest sense of self-consciousness, of wanting to be followed, or accepted, or desirous of anything from anyone in any way. He was simply the most authentic human being I had ever encountered.

His presence was awe-inspiring, yet he was also as genuine and friendly as one's best friend. In him I saw the highest human potentiality. No one spoke. He was more than clairvoyant; he knew our thoughts as we formulated them, answering questions before they were asked, pointing to individuals here and there. Other times he walked about, addressing the group as a whole. The cosmic magnet of his being was such that when he passed closely, my bones would vibrate with an ethereal voltage, as though an entire planet were passing by. Another unique aspect to this teacher was that there was no spiritual program. He instructed each person differently, sometimes outwardly in words or gestures, but usually in inner communications, dreams, and visions. He often didn't speak for days at a time, yet everyone could hear him. I could scarcely believe such a being actually existed. The Indian disciples called him a teacher of teachers, one who only appears briefly in a seeker's life, often sending us to other teachers for individual instruction.

At the next *darshan* (visitation with a saint), he passed close to me, turned, and looked directly into my eyes: I saw there only portals to a vast cosmic realm. Never has that experience been repeated in this life; I had met a genuine master of infinite magnitude. I returned to my ashram cloister and prayed: *I wasn't mature enough in Germany at seventeen, nor in Florida at twenty-one, but I'm now twenty-four and ready for liberation. Please give me full kundalini activation. I'm ready to die to my former self, ready to become a* jivanmukti, *a liberated being!* I rolled over to sleep, utterly oblivious of what I had just requested.

Fig. 21.1. Apollo-Christ (sun/son of fire) with the caduceus of initiation. Detail from Athanasius Kircher, *Ars magna lucis et Umbrae*, Rome, 1665.

Hours later I awoke in the darkness to a tremendous vibration at the base of my spine, as though a power cable had been welded to my tailbone. I quietly sat up to do yoga postures in the dark to relieve the growing pressure I felt throughout my system. I had roommates now, and I didn't wish to wake them. Thin rivulets of power streamed up my spine into my brain, turning both inward and outward perceptions into a bouquet of layered lights. The vibration and magnetic pressure continued to grow; the more I stretched the better I felt, but the more I opened the *nadis* (subtle energy channels) through the yoga postures, the more the stream flowed upward. I was caught between the pain of resistance and a blissful rush of voltage up my spine. An orange light bathed the center of my head, while a roar like a heavy waterfall inwardly resounded.

> *Invisibilem solem plurimis incognitum*
> [In man, there is] an invisible sun unknown to most.
>
> GERHARD DORN, *THEATRUM CHEMICUM*, VOL. 1
> *SPECULATIVAE PHILOSOPHIAE*, 1602

I no longer want what I requested, but on it comes. No matter the extent of my stretching I can neither stem nor soothe the flow of divine energy coursing through me. I pant from the heat as my body hums and vibrates from within. My forehead opens and I perceive the room as though the lights are on. Narrow streams of consciousness pierce the top of my head and rise out into the night sky, offering views over the village. Simultaneously, here in the room something untwists from deep within my sacrum. The serpentine deity undulates up my spine so painfully that I cry out and wake my roommates. My body heat rises dramatically as power moves through my nerves out to the ends of my fingers and toes. Waves of bliss alternate with a depth of both physical pain and a soul pain that I can only describe as the pain of separation from Source—the pain of lifetimes of resistance.

> *The Secret Fire of the alchemists is an electric, fiery, hidden power, the great pristine form which underlies all organic and inorganic matter. It is an electro-spiritual force, a creative power.*
>
> FRANZ HARTMAN (1838–1912), *ALCHEMY*

The inner fire, now alive and burning furiously, rises in waves up my lower back, piercing blockages both painful and blissful beyond measure. I weep and beg Richard in the ashram bunk nearby to massage my spine. He leans up with a sigh at being disturbed, but upon touching my back he exclaims, "Kevin, your spine is red hot—it's nearly burning my hand!" My body now contorts into yoga postures I had never before practiced. From the great river in my spine, streams and tributaries branch off sending divine light and vibration throughout my body. Where the course was clean and pure the flow is unobstructed, but where clogged with emotional sludge and mental rust, great pain arises. An inner stream rising from my hips up one side of my body over the shoulder and up to the back of my eye burns like a rusty wire. From a brief acupuncture study in Japan, I knew it to be along an energetic meridian. The pain grows but I know not how to release it. I shake, weep, and feel close to madness.

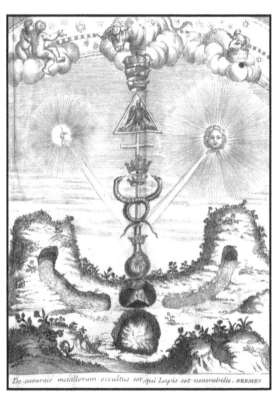

Fig. 21.2. Nepal chakra chart. Nepalese painting, unknown artist, eighteenth century.

Fig. 21.3. The secret fire of kundalini burns at the tailbone of the lower pelvis. *De cavernis metallorum occultus est, qui lapis est venerabilis.* "In the cave of the secret mine [of metals], is the venerable [Philosophers'] Stone." Limojon de Saint Didier and Alexandre Toussaint, *Le Triomphe Hermetique,* Amsterdam, 1689.

A great fiery serpent in my spine, thick as a human arm now, rises halfway up my spine and stops (I later learned this was at the *Vishnu Granthi*, or the knot of self-centeredness). An inner dam blocked this swollen river of burning magma, and I cried out for mercy, *I'm only a foolish child—I'm not ready!* Another guest in the room leapt up and offered me an antidote, "This is holy ash from a saint in southern India; it may help." I took a dash of the gray powder on my tongue and at once something akin to cool, etheric waters poured through me, calming all fires. I passed into a deep, dreamless sleep.

# 22

# Atman Equals Brahman

Brilliant sunlight woke me late in the day. I rose exhausted yet inwardly vibrant, my senses sharper and mind clear. *I'm surely not purified enough for such voltage.* My roommates are gone; I had missed both breakfast and morning darshan. As I stripped off my night clothes to rinse and dress for the day, I heard and felt a painful crinkling, like that of dried paper, from my shoulder and neck. The mirror showed me a perfect red line, like a sunburn, running from the back of my head to the edge of my shoulder. Beneath the red line, under my skin was what looked like a narrow slice of blackened, crispy bacon.

> The trained alchemist learns to separate the various levels of the invisible body of the sun into their refined components and constituents . . . the "Golden Sun" or "Red Sun" represents the pure solar force raised to its highest inherent evolutionary potential.
>
> T. J. O'NEILL, "THE SUN INVINCIBLE"[1]

The kindly German homeopathic doctor shook his head, "You've surely had an electric shock?" I shook my head. "Have you been in any kind of contact with power lines?" I looked away, shaking my head. "I have never seen this before. I don't know how to tell you, but you've been burned from within." He handed me a bottle of small white pills,

"Homeopathy is a vibrational medicine; I believe these will help you." I thanked him and left, offering him no explanation for my condition. I was fortunate to find him working in a neighboring village, a gift of compassion for the India that the doctor admitted had given him so much.

According to alchemical literature, there are two ways to create the Philosophers' Stone: the "Wet Way" and the "Dry Way." The . . . spiritual Dry Way in which the initiate attempts to ascend on a direct path to divine knowledge. The Wet Way works with the "slow, steady fires of nature," while the Dry Way works with the "raging fires. . . ." The rapid spiritual ascent of the Dry Way is very dangerous for unprepared initiates and can result in a loss of personal identity or even madness.

DENNIS HAUK, "THE PHILOSOPHER'S STONE"[2]

*The only worthy goal in life is to prepare myself to embody spirit in form.* Inwardly, I prayed: *I understand now that I'm not ready. Please show me a method, a technique by which I may step-by-step cleanse the rust from my human frame and prepare it to contain the divine in its fullness!* No visions, no instructions, and no dreams came in reply . . . yet. Days passed and I felt forsaken and disenchanted with this whole Hindu guru thing and this potpourri of strange deities and beliefs. My mind drifted back to the Buddhist wisdom I had gained through my own efforts in Japan, Thailand, and at Bodhgaya. The non-guru path of Theravada Buddhism seemed clean, clear, even precise. A traveler had earlier informed me of a place south of Bombay where continuous Theravada Buddhist insight meditation courses are held all year round at subsistence cost. My restlessness and spiritual materialism led my weak mind, and I began to make plans to leave for western India. That night the Master came in an extraordinary dream:

*I walk across a desertlike area of India. I turn and my attention is drawn to the Master sitting in a chair, the back of which is a large golden mandala. I'm immediately pulled to the red bindi point between his eyebrows, and a loving force holds my focus there like a magnet. Then, while his body remains the same size, his eyes grow larger and larger until they fill my entire realm of visual perception. His eyes merge into mine, and indeed his eyes ARE mine; we are one and the same consciousness. "Don't look for me in form; I am not in form," a voice intones. Then, "Atman equals Brahman."*

*The eye by which I see God is the same as the eye by which God sees me. My eye and God's eye are one and the same.*

MEISTER ECKHART, *SERMONS OF MEISTER ECKHART,*
CHAP. 4, CIRCA 1322

I took special note of *Atman equals Brahman*, soon learning from a monk at the ashram the meaning: the individual soul (Atman) and the Cosmic Unity (Brahman) have never been separated. He congratulated me for receiving the blessing of an *Atmic* experience, that is, *all souls are as One*. A drop of water may perceive itself as separate, but this is only a temporary illusion. All rain returns to the ocean.

The following morning a friendly German my age appeared in the ashram, and we became immediate friends. "I was a Native American shaman in a previous life," Reiner boasted, while munching on a piece of raspberry shortbread from a local bakery. "I'm in India because Sri Yukteswar and Yogananda came to me in a dream." Upon hearing these words, I felt a momentary dizziness. Paramahansa Yogananda, author of *Autobiography of a Yogi*, was the first yogi of an ancient order to reveal the inner life of an accomplished master in the West. He had mysteriously appeared to me in dreams, and I was deeply moved by his book. However, the *churchy* atmosphere of the organization he left behind in Los Angeles did not inspire me and so I never sought initiation there. I turned back to Reiner. Swallowing another shortbread with a swig of tea, he added, "I'm soon going to visit the highest living Kriya yogi in Puri, Orissa. He's the last living disciple of Sri Yukteswar." A warmth entered my chest. Reiner added, "Why don't you come with me?"

With steely cold intellect I shook my head and countered, "I prefer the depths of insight meditation to this Hindu guru stuff." I looked up, then away, and crowed proudly, "I'm soon going to a Vipassana center near Bombay to do intensive meditation." Reiner sighed, "Well, suit yourself, but I have the feeling that you'd benefit from this." He continued to follow me around the ashram spouting never-ending stories of one sort or another, and I felt unsure how long I could withstand the verbal siege. It was time for this introvert to escape.

Days later I packed my bags and quietly slipped out of the ashram gate during morning darshan. I made my way through the village and sat down on the bus, sighing in relief. I had been in India over two months now, and the weather was heating up. Time to head west to Bombay, to my destiny, to settle in before the heat made travel even more challenging. The bus jerked forward with a loud, cringe-inducing crunch of grinding gears, moving the hot air about to everyone's relief. We had not passed more than twenty meters when a voice called from the street behind the bus. I turned to see Reiner running after the bus, a mountain of baggage strapped to his back. I dropped my forehead against the seatback in front of me in disbelief. The driver stopped and Reiner stepped on with a big smile. "I'm glad to catch up with you. I know you're going west, but I thought we could travel together part of the way," he cheerfully puffed, trying to catch his breath, as he dropped beside me. I consoled myself: *It is only a matter of time before peace.*

At the railway station we purchased tickets to the central transfer city where we would split—he east to Puri, and I west to Igatpuri. Arriving at the transfer station at three o'clock in the morning, we bought our separate onward tickets and sat waiting for the train in the dark of night, sharing our last travelers' tales, dreams, and insights gleaned. My train arrived first; I was physically unable to stand—a magnet held me to my seat! After a long silent pause came a whistle, and the train chugged away into darkness. Reiner only laughed and laughed. I exchanged my westward ticket for an eastward one and bowed a silent surrender to a larger life. To Puri, we go.

# 23

# Master of Kriya

*This is the noble precious Lapis Philosophorum, the Philosophers' Stone, which the Magi do find . . .*

JACOB BOEHME, IN WAITE,
*THE SECRET TRADITION IN ALCHEMY*

"Rickshaw! Rickshaw?" After a thirty-six-hour string of bus and train catastrophes, Reiner and I arrived in Puri, one of the four holy pilgrimage cities (*Char Dham*) of India, and home of the famed Jagannath Temple. I caught site of the great temple tower at a distance, before turning north to the far beach area guesthouses. I knew little about the temple but had read that the term *juggernaut* derives from the gigantic and enormously heavy carts that carry the temple deities during the summer festival. We took rooms at a seaworn hotel resting on the wide beach with a view over the Bay of Bengal, and that afternoon set off for the ashram. We searched through winding, sandy alleys until finally we found the blue gate of Karar Ashram.

Upon entering the ashram, a calm, nostalgic feeling washed over me, as one feels upon returning to a familiar place. We were led into the courtyard by a young *brahmachari* (celibate) monk in white. An older man, also in white, approached and said, "Swamiji has just returned now, quite unexpectedly." As I look toward the speaker, I see

Fig. 23.1. The Three Deities of Jagannath, Puri, Orissa.
Photo by author of a local postcard, artist unknown, 1986

behind him a man in ochre robes standing farther back near a tree—
*Sri Yukteswar!* The master looks directly at me, turns, and disappears
behind a corner. *What?* I thought to myself. *Can this man, the guru
of Yogananda, still be alive? Why, he must be well over a hundred years
old by now!?* Without saying a word, I brushed by the cordial man and
strode behind a long building in the midst of the garden—there was no
one. I found only flower beds and a path to a stone mandir (shrine). Sri
Yukteswar has a distinct appearance; there was no mistake. I scratched
my head and returned to the main courtyard.

*When the pupil is ready, the teacher appears.*

"You're in luck. Swamiji wishes to see you both," said another man with a mustache, also in white clothing. Reiner and I were instructed to sit and wait on a low garden wall of stone. We glanced around; the ashram was deserted. *How is this so? The world's most advanced living Kriya yogi is here, but the ashram is nearly empty?* Word then came that we should ascend a narrow outdoor stairway leading up to chambers on the second floor. I started up the steps, and my nose nearly struck an older monk descending the stairs. Luminous, watery eyes met mine, and I was frozen in timelessness. I pranam'd (hands folded in prayer position greeting), just gazing into his lustrous eyes. "You have come for God realization?" he asked warmly. I nodded. "Good, come down this way for initiation," replied the bearded Santa, as though an old friend. I turned and moved back down the narrow stairs. In the traditional gesture of respect, the Indians bowed to touch his feet. He only smiled, gently touching them on the head, saying, "God, God, God."

The master waved us all into the hall. "God has come to me today," he said, sitting up on the platform that held a large altar with photos and paintings of the Kriya lineage of teachers: Babaji, Lahiri Mahasaya, Sri Yukteswar, Paramahansa Yogananda, among others. Swami Hariharananda Giri's voice felt like a musical salve upon my battered soul. He was the proverbial wise man, but also Santa Claus or the warmest, kindest grandfather one could only dream of having. Power gently emanated in his voice, "Kriya Yoga is the superhighway to God-realization. God is not only breathing through you; He is breathing you into existence! He is the life that moves you; He is you. Thou art That." That he and my childhood friend Andrew, the German philosopher, should agree on this seemed only natural. Reiner and I were speechless, as if held suspended in a field of electromagnetic power.

With another wave of his hand, flowers were fetched from the garden for our initiation. Swami Hariharananda Giri initiated Reiner first. Then, the master turned to me, looking with a fierce love right through me to the depths of my soul. He put one of his hands on the base of my spine while his other hand pressed on the outer edges of my eyes, now closing. A subtle but tangibly vibrating current moved up my spine. "Do you feel this?" I mumbled and nodded an affirmative, as my spine became ramrod straight. Soon a more powerful vibrating magnetic current seared up my spine to the midpoint of my brain. There at the center of my skull, a scene in white-and-black film negative (the dark and light reversed) clearly formed in minute detail. His fingers still pressing on the outer edges of my eyes, he asked, "Do you see it?" An inner siren grew and drowned out nearly all outer sound. I was now in such shock at the living vision forming in film negative I was unable to reply. He shouted with force, "DO YOU SEE IT?" His arms now shook, as nodes of power holding a powerful current, and I inwardly perceived in living, real time:

*An emaciated, tortured man hangs suspended on a great wood, grotesquely thin from starvation and blood loss. His hair is matted into a single mass, and his wasted body is unimaginably filthy. His head hangs to the right, and his mouth gapes open, his jaw hanging unnaturally low. His bulging, brilliant eyes are turned upward to a dark sky. He is near death—horrific, yet the thundering inner siren in my head trumpets only power and divinity.*

"Yes, I SEE it!" I cried over the siren in my head. The swami then placed his hands over my ears, closing them tightly. "Do you HEAR it?" The *anahata dhwani*, also called the unstruck sound, or *anahata naad*, the first emanation from the holy *Nada Brahma*, the inner sound of creation. This ceaseless inner siren has remained a permanent inner perception since that day. I was unable to speak any further, only absorbed inwardly. Yogananda has written that he was able to give real-time visions of saints and *avatars* (incarnations of God) to others, so perhaps I should not have been surprised.

It is hidden in this world and yet may be had everywhere. "And this Stone is Christ, the Son of the Living God, Which discovereth

Itself in all those that seek and find it." The apostles "went about with this Stone, in power and doing miracles," but it has been persecuted always.

JACOB BOEHME[1]

After the initiation, we were instructed in the technique of Kriya Yoga. Unlike some kundalini yoga systems that stimulate extreme awakenings of the evolutionary power in the spine often leading to severe side effects, Kriya is a graduated system of awakening the kundalini to rise into the cranium, evolving the human brain at an accelerated rate, eventually leading to cosmic consciousness. From that day my nadis were no longer excessively roasted by the fires of *Sri Kundalini*. I'm now connected to a lineage of masters, and the evolutionary force has been tempered for greater overall development. Yogananda further describes Kriya Yoga in his autobiography as a psychophysiological method for transmuting oxygen into life force in the brain and spinal centers. "The advanced yogi transmutes his cells into energy. Elijah, Jesus, Kabir, and other prophets were past masters in the use of Kriya or a similar technique, by which they caused their bodies to materialize and dematerialize at will."[2]

Yogananda relates that this royal yoga was protected by the *rishis* (spiritual masters) until arrival of the materialistic ages. "Then because of priestly secrecy and man's indifference, the sacred lore gradually became inaccessible." According to Yogananda:

> St. Paul knew Kriya Yoga, or a similar technique, by which he could switch life currents to and from the senses. He was therefore able to say . . . "I die daily." In the initial stages of God-communion (savikalpa samadhi) the devotee's consciousness merges in the Cosmic Spirit; his life force is withdrawn from the body, which appears "dead" or motionless and rigid. . . . As he progresses to higher spiritual states (nirvikalpa samadhi), how he communes with God . . . [is] in his ordinary waking consciousness, even in the midst of exacting worldly duties.[3]

Reiner and I gathered our precious notes and sat in the garden drinking chai, stunned by the power and grace of the initiation. A few Indian disciples sat with us, curious about the foreign guests. "You are truly fortunate that Swamiji suddenly changed his plans and returned early. You were both able to take initiation directly from the hands of the greatest living Kriya Yoga master. That's not always possible with the crowds you'll see tomorrow when word spreads that he's returned." Reiner stepped out of the ashram to smoke a *bidi*, a thin, high-nicotine Indian cigarette, and I immediately felt compelled to ask a question of the Indian man with the mustache:

"Good sir," I asked in my increasingly Indian English, setting my chai down on a low garden wall. "When I arrived earlier today I was certain I saw Sri Yukteswar standing by that tree, but he turned, stepped behind the hall and disappeared." He chuckled. "Well, that's not possible. His *mahasamadhi* [final conscious exit from the body] was fifty years ago." He paused and tipped his head to the side. "But then again, perhaps nothing is impossible?" He smiled and raised his eyebrows up and down. "You say he disappeared behind this hall?" I nodded, and he led me behind the meditation hall to the large stone shrine. "This is Sri Yukteswar's mandir; he is buried intact here. In India our saints require no purifying cremations; they are buried as anchors of divine force."

*And it came to pass, as they were burying a man, that, behold, they spied a band of men; and they cast the man into the sepulchre of Elisha [Elias]: and when the man was let down, and touched the bones of Elisha, he revived, and stood up on his feet.*

2 Kings 13:21, King James Version

The deathless master had blessed me with a visitation. *Perhaps the masters are always near, but it is we who do not perceive them?* Thought melted into a profound state of timeless presence, and I fell into an inner silence. Reiner returned from his smoke and we were dispatched to the beachside hotel on a bicycle rickshaw. I slept that night in an ever-expanding dreamworld of *many mansions*. I drifted out to the deep sandy beach, and there I watched lights in the sky—only to find myself again in my bed, soaked in sweat. Several times that night I was again a young child, unable to tell the difference between my dreams, astral travels, and waking states. I felt continuously reborn into an entirely new state of consciousness.

Reiner and I practiced Kriya the next morning, studying our notes as we went through the steps. Now in a permanently altered state, I felt as though time had slowed to a near halt. We managed an Indian breakfast and returned to Karar Ashram, now thronged with a crowd. It seemed everyone in Orissa State knew Swami Hariharananda Giri had returned. At seventy-eight years old, he is the famed "last-living direct disciple of Sri Yukteswar." We couldn't believe our good fortune at having taken initiation personally from him just yesterday in peaceful, spacious surroundings. Only from the far back of the room could we find a space on the floor to sit and hear the master speak. Swamiji was utterly himself that day, and possessed tremendous illuminative power as he spoke to a full house anxious to hear him:

"The Kriya Yoga technique is the essence of the *karma yoga, raja yoga*, and *bhakti yoga* methods. It is the true application of the yogic scriptures; that is why we call it the scientific method of God-realization. This yoga is meant for householders, for your Self-realization. Babaji Maharaj gave the scientific orientation to this yoga. Through his disciple, Lahiri Mahashaya, a householder, he offered this Kriya Yoga for the spiritual advancement of the entire human race, with no sectarian limitations. His disciple Sri Yukteswar transmitted the Kriya Yoga teachings to his students here at Karar Ashram.

"You must practice the six levels of Kriya Yoga with personal initiation and instruction from a qualified Kriya Yoga acharya. In first Kriya, by activating the God-realization process in the spine, you convert your ordinary mind into higher consciousness and experience the triple divine qualities of vibration, inner light, sound. By bowing, touching your head to the ground, and stretching the spine you magnetize the spine and the frontal lobe of the brain and begin to feel the divine light there. The living spirit of God is hiding in the physical body, the jungle of material matter. Through Kriya Yoga, the dormant kundalini is awakened, and we can directly perceive that God is functioning through us.

"Now watch the power of God traveling up and down the seven-story elevator [the seven major chakras of the body], giving power to our brain and Soul. The first five floors are where human ignorance and evil wander about. Floors six and seven are the kingdom of heaven, where God is directly activating everything. The first Kriya draws the Kundalini Shakti, which is the dormant, unevolved divine power from the coccygeal center to the pituitary and above.

"*Mahamudra* [a physical postures portion of Kriya preparation] cultivates the body, thereby charging your vital organs, cardiac, gastrointestinal, and other biological functions. This enables you to gather the spiritual harvest of the entire body and Soul. When your mind, intellect, thought, and ego are calmed, then you can hear the divine sound, the whisper of God. Through practice, you hear this sound continually. This is called *anahata dhwani,* or nonstopping divine sound. In first Kriya the meditator can get *subhechha samadhi* or deep desire for God-realization. Now, everyone practice . . ."

In the dark of evening after meditation, Reiner and I wandered the brightly lit, crowded road to the nearby Jagannath Temple. The moment I came before the towering temple a timeless familiarity overwhelmed me. Only Hindus may enter the inner sanctum, but the temple area is open late into the evening to the great masses of pilgrims from all over India who crowd the Grand Road before the great temple day and night. The current temple dates from the tenth century, but the worship of the wide-eyed Jagannath deity may date back to the Rigveda, which mentions him as far back as 4,000 years ago. Recent Hindu ideas associate Jagannath with Vishnu, Krishna, or even Shiva, but historians estimate that the image is from an aboriginal, perhaps shamanic, past of unknown date or origin. Paintings, statues, and amulets of Jagannath and his companion deities are sold everywhere on the Grand Road before the temple.

Reiner and I continued the practice of Kriya Yoga two or three times daily. The effects of the personal initiation and the practice were astounding. I had never been more present in the here and now since I was perhaps a toddler. Days seemed to last weeks, even months. After a few more of these *days like months*, I became alarmed that my parents might be concerned about me. I could scarcely recall how long I had been away. I couldn't remember their address, but I found it among my belongings. It took an hour to write out a simple postcard note to say I was healthy and safe. I wandered for a day's eternity to find a post office only half a mile down the road. "What year is it please?" I asked the post office teller. Blank stares surrounded me. "Will someone please tell me what year it is?" A schoolboy standing nearby pointed at a Krishna calendar on the wall. *Okay, it's 1986. Good, good. Yes, I can work with this timeline.* I dated the postcard, passed a few rupees across the counter, and with a slam-stamp and toss, my filial duty was complete.

No more jolting, bewildering, and uncontrolled kundalini activations for me. Now I had a direct line to a method to take me home. While amateur yogis like me may unintentionally awaken the full might of the *solar force*; Kriya brings the cooling and mediating *lunar currents* into play, thus balancing the heaty, parching quality of the dry solar way. Reiner and I were in such a timeless state we could scarcely hold conversations—usually only half sentences, broken by laughter. We sat drinking pots of chai and staring out to the Bay of Bengal beyond. We only knew the time of day by the sun and the rumbles in our bellies, and often laughed at our predicament. *How can we possibly function in the world like this?* Younger Self was melting away and I was returning to myself, Elder Self, or perhaps something more? This was paradoxically both blissful and vaguely disconcerting.

We may have held eternity in our proverbial palms, but Orissa was now heating up, and the draw to return to the modern world pulled at me fiercely. Reiner was downing half a dozen lemon sodas per hour in the ghastly heat, driving him finally to depart for high-elevation Nepal, where he was destined to eventually study Tibetan medicine. I counted through my dwindling funds, packed my bags for Calcutta, and set off to make my new fortune in Taiwan. There I planned to live a modern life, with modern amenities, while privately practicing Kriya Yoga. I bowed deeply to Swamiji, and with his blessing departed. I returned to Bangkok and took a train south to the Thai monastery where I picked up my guitar and a yellowed envelope from my father.

In Taiwan I was soon introduced to Tai Chi and Taoist alchemy, topics to be discussed later in this volume. However, I was also swept up into a high-speed world of motorcycles, money, and all the pleasures of the modern world. Consciousness was again pulled down into the heavy densities of material indulgence. I forgot the unforgettable and remembrance needed bolstering. After nearly a year I left my work there, cleaned out my apartment in Taiwan, sold my motorcycle, stored a few boxes of Chinese language study books, and waved farewells to my new friends there. Financially enriched but physically and spiritually spent, I returned to Puri—to the Master of Kriya.

# 24

# Orissa

Upon my return to Orissa, a desire welled up from deep within my doubt: I wanted no less than three confirmations that Hariharananda was truly a master. So weak was my faith in even my own experiences! However, the Kriya master was in another city, not due back for some days or even weeks. As I waited in Puri, I met Helena from Germany. She had met Baba after his first trip outside India (Switzerland) in 1974 and became his devoted disciple. Helena advised, "Spend time with him whenever you can; he is always teaching us in his every word and motion." She also introduced me to Puri city, famously a conch-shell spiral mandala of temples. *Spiralling inward for interiorization!* "When you are born you grow into the extrovert stage, when you return to God you move into the introvert stage," said Hariharananda.

The Konarak Sun Temple, only 3 kilometers from Puri, had just been named a World Heritage Site the year before and the road to the astounding thirteenth-century site is now improved. I stared across an ocean of time at the Sun Temple, a great chariot reaching across the lives of generations, dedicated to the sun god Surya. The entire complex is an astronomical instrument. From the erotic sculptures covering the great temple, it was obvious India has been dealing with the lure of sexuality from the earliest of times. Here it appeared to be positively celebrated. Seven horses (perhaps the seven chakras) pull the chariot on

Fig. 24.1. Konarak Sun Temple, Orissa, India.
Photo by Mayank Choudhary

twenty-four great wheels. At any given time, four of the wheels may be used as sun dials to tell time. *Perhaps the Konarak Sun Temple and its plethora of erotic sculptures point to the power of sublimated and transformed sexuality, rocket fuel to the Sun of liberation?*

*Truly our work is perfectly performed; for that which the heat of the sun is a hundred years in doing . . . our secret fire . . . doth as I have often seen in a very short time.*

ARTEPHIUS, *THE SECRET BOOK OF ARTEPHIUS*,
TWELFTH-CENTURY ALCHEMICAL TRACT

Returning to Puri, I spent the next week in near silence, meditating at Sri Yukteswar's mandir in the day, and attending meditations at Karar Ashram in the evenings with the sincere monks, though it wasn't quite the same without the living thunderbolt of power that was Hariharananda. As the evening meditations were the main event, I had hours of free time throughout the day to practice and read up on Kriya Yoga. Yogananda lays out the spiritual evolution of humankind thus:

> "Kriya Yoga is an instrument through which human evolution can be quickened," Sri Yukteswar explained to his students. . . . The Kriya Yogi mentally directs his life energy to revolve, upward and downward, around the six spinal centers . . . which correspond to the twelve astral signs of the zodiac, the symbolic Cosmic Man. One-half minute of revolution of energy around the sensitive spinal cord of man effects subtle progress in his evolution; that half-minute of Kriya equals one year of natural spiritual unfoldment. . . . The scriptures aver that man requires a million years of normal, diseaseless evolution to perfect his human brain sufficiently to express cosmic consciousness. One thousand Kriya practiced in eight hours gives the yogi, in one day, the equivalent of one thousand years of natural evolution.[1]

Much in the same way, I discovered later, the transformative power of spiritual alchemy performed the same function in the West: "Thus the wise man does that by art [alchemy] in a short time, which nature cannot perform in less than the revolution of a thousand years."[2]

Upon his return, the Kriya master gripped the hair atop my head, and stared into my eyes. "The Self is a deity experiencing divine illumination and the sensation of God. You see a superconscious light above the crown, lighting up the whole universe. The body of the guru will appear dark, with illumination all around it." Without a word from me, his words were precisely my vision of the yogi in silhouette just over a year ago, before departing Japan. First confirmation received.

Not a day later, Baba chatted with a group of students in the meditation hall. His kind eyes spoke to my soul, "I have seen Sri Yukteswarji in Karar Ashram after his death many times. He called me, and brought me to Karar." I felt great relief to receive this second confirmation, as I too had seen a living Sri Yuktewar on my arrival the year before. Sri Yukteswar is now clearly my *paramguru* (my guru's guru).

At this point, I no longer needed a third confirmation and had even forgotten my intention to receive a third. Nevertheless, the next early evening before meditation, Swamiji, Gurudev, or Baba (*father*, as we called him) held a private audience for foreigners in his sitting room. A European visitor asked about Christianity, and Baba replied, "In the Holy Bible, Jesus says that the Kingdom of God dwells within you— that is meditation. Jesus said to first seek the Kingdom of God, is it not? So Kriya Yoga is deeply Christian, and if you meditate deeply, then Jesus, or any one of the many masters, may appear to you."

My eyes became watery and I could not speak. The lineage is truly genuine and original in every sense of the word. I could scarcely fathom the grace I had received so far. Now I had to fulfill my part in this venture—daily practice. As a teacher, he never asked for money, or anything at all, and thus he gained my natural respect. The ashram operated solely on donations. He in fact has never asked anything of me; he only wished for me that state of consciousness he had reached, nirvikalpa samadhi. Such saints are more than rare.

That evening I returned for meditation and found a group of Westerners sitting silently, some bowing for long periods of time, stretching their spines. While sitting on the floor before him I found that my spine was drawn into a straight rod, and yet with no discomfort. He would say to us, "It's good that you have come. You cannot get this Power sitting alone at home. Sit with the teacher. Keep good company, and you'll become good!" But in turn he often shouted, "What are you Europeans doing here in India? Do you expect to find God dancing in the streets? You should be meditating in your home countries!"

*Hasten slowly—for it is of the greatest importance that the influence of the fire should be brought to bear gently and gradually.*

WAITE, *THE HERMETIC MUSEUM*, VOL. 1, *THE SOPHIC HYDROLITH, OR WATER STONE OF THE WISE*, PART 2

After only a year of practice, impatience got the best of me; I wanted initiation into second Kriya. When I asked, Swamiji only laughed. "Kriya will transform you. It is a path of many years; it cannot be rushed." The master soon left for a week's visit to another city, so I read more about the science of yoga. Yogananda explains: "Yogic science . . . enables the devotee to switch off or on, at will, life current from the five sense telephones of sight, sound, smell, taste, and touch. Master of his body and mind, the Kriya Yogi ultimately achieves victory over the 'last enemy,' death."[3]

Yogananda further describes the life of an advanced Kriya yogi, who is "influenced, not by effects of past actions, but solely by directions from the soul. The devotee thus avoids the slow, evolutionary monitors of egoistic actions, good and bad, of common life, cumbrous and snail-like to the eagle hearts. The superior method of soul living frees the yogi who, shorn of his ego-prison, tastes the deep air of omnipresence."[4] Inspired by Yogananda and the living example of Hariharananda, I vowed to practice diligently every day in hopes of being promoted to second Kriya. However, after more idle days on the beach, my mind began to wander, turning to a brilliant woman I'd met in Taiwan shortly before returning to India. I wrote her aerogram letters in my hotel room in my free time, hoping to reconnect upon my return to Taiwan. The master returned, and we all gathered, at least a hundred Indians and a handful of Westerners, in the crowded hall anxious to be with master again. He looked out over the crowd with an intensely serious face, perhaps even displeased. Finding me in the crowd, he shouted at the top of his lungs:

"You!" Pointing a shaking finger at me. "You're writing so many letters to your girl!" He began to sing, "Night and Day, Night and Day, you are thinking of that girl night and day . . ." The crowd laughed nervously and the Indians shifted their positions to distance themselves from the now suspicious foreigner in their midst. I had been utterly exposed. His laser eyes pierced into my soul, and my lower chakras were held in a light-filled state of suspension. He could not possibly have known anything about her, as I hadn't mentioned her to anyone. Truly clairvoyant beyond doubt, he continued to shout and berate me in front of the crowd, while I was unable to move, speak, or even breathe. I had no body sense, and was drawn up into an absorption in the higher chakras. The astonishing humiliation was a blessing. I wanted to weep over my gross failures, lost I was in the material world. He again pointed at me and carried on mercilessly, "You're not getting God. God is spelled G-O-D. You've got it backward—you're getting only D-O-G. Dog!" Everyone laughed, and many looked at me with pity.

The roasting that yet teaches, burned like slow coals within. Any standing I had left in that community seemed lost. The humiliation was one of the most difficult blessings I'd ever received. Inwardly I felt defensive and protested, *Why shout only at me for mere thoughts and letters, when others are hardly celibate, even here in Puri?* He then paused, and continued, "Sex is God, and when you are enjoying sexually God is enjoying through you. But you are here for God realization, and yet you're only thinking of sex then, or sex in the future. Be with God now; know that you are God now!"

Later I would come to understand that he holds an inner ring of students to a different standard to burn away the residue of lifetimes of indulgences. He was even more severe with his monks. I understood his view that "sex is also God," but that we, as he would say, "must feel and perceive God breathing through [us] at each and every moment, in the present moment." It was the mental distraction away from the present that is the so-called sin, which is nothing other than simply missing out on the Presence of God in every moment.

For many of us just starting out, Swamiji was the kindest, gentlest, most loving, grandfatherly St. Nick one could ever wish for, drawing us in with a love so uniquely pure that I cannot compare it to normal human affection. But for those whom he sensed had been on the path for years or even lifetimes, he could be ruthless, cutting at the roots of our egoic minds with the sharpest, hottest flames of fire. This was not only in the light of day, but he even enters the dreams of sincere disciples in order to teach. In the midst of an absorbing dream in my midnight slumber:

*Baba appears lighting matches and throwing the tiny fires at me. They light my pants on fire and I hurriedly try to brush out the flames. The old children's song, "Liar, liar, pants on fire" dances through my mind. Baba smiles with a loving fierceness only he could bestow, "Hold always to the truth!" I awaken and enter meditation until sunrise.*

One evening Baba pulled me aside and said, "Kriya Yoga is the fastest, the simplest, the most complete path for spiritual transformation, but you're not getting enough change!" He knew my inner intentions, impurities, and my divinity too, which he coaxed and encouraged to come out. His mind was attuned to mine, but I was not yet attuned to his. I was young, restless, and emotionally immature. Baba reminded me almost daily now, "Be born again from fire, water, and spirit. Fight with your evils!" He often lifted his arms and mimicked a female Indian dancer. "There are too many distractions dancing in your mind. I know all your hypocrisies!" He leaned close, and whispered, "You will know when you're ready for second Kriya."

Days later I was suddenly afflicted with a terrible pain in one of my shoulders, as if all the anxieties of a lifetime had knotted the muscles there into a stone. I was in great distress and tried everything to rid myself of this but said nothing to anyone. The practice of Kriya in the hall with a large group of meditators offered some relief, but the pain was still intense. At the end of evening meditation, we had the opportunity to bow and offer respect to the teacher in the traditional Indian way. At these occasions he normally only beams love and says a few gentle words to each, sometimes touching us lightly on the head. But this evening, without warning, he brutally slapped his palm upon that very shoulder with a loud clap! The knot and all my pain immediately disappeared, and I felt freed of a great karmic burden, origin unknown.

With smaller groups of students, Baba often talked about the "bindu, the atom point, four inches inside the head from the point between the eyebrows, and three inches deep from the crown of the head—immerse yourself in this dimensionless point of awareness." *This must be related to the inner doorway that I had known in earlier years.* Yogananda wrote that the Kriya yogi knows "his body is a kingdom, governed by Emperor Soul on the throne of the cranium, with subsidiary regents in the six spinal centers or spheres of consciousness."

*[The] Philosophers' Stone is a real entity produced by spiritual generation.*

A. E. WAITE, *THE SECRET TRADITION IN ALCHEMY*, P. 32

Late one night at my beach hotel in Puri, sitting under a new and spacious mosquito net, I set a fierce determination to meditate until sunrise. I repeated Kriya again and again until I was nearly vibrating off my bed. I continued sitting and after a long while passed into a dreamlike state where I found myself standing out on the dark beaches. There I saw both Sri Yukteswar and Hariharananda with a glow of golden light about them, walking up the night beach from the direction of the ashram toward me. Astonished, I attempt to move toward them, but then found myself lying in bed.

In the morning I returned to Karar Ashram. *I must know more about the life of Swami Hariharananda Giri!* Yogacharya Swami Yogeswarananda explained that Hariharananda had been initiated into *Jnanayoga* (yogic path of wisdom) at the age of twelve. His teacher later encouraged him to meet Sri Yukteswar, from whom he received first Kriya initiation in 1932. Three years later he received second Kriya from Paramahansa Yogananda during his visit to Calcutta in 1935, and during this time he was also able to witness Yogananda in samadhi, the breathless pulseless state of cosmic consciousness. In 1940, he mastered the *kechari, bhramari,* and *shambhavi* techniques, and an effulgence of supernatural divine light glowed around his body, witnessed by many. In 1940 and 1941, he learned third Kriya from Swami Satyananda Giri. From 1943 to 1945, he received fourth, fifth, and sixth Kriya initiations from Shrimat Bhupendranath Sanyal, a realized householder disciple of Lahiri Mahasaya. Then a mysterious yogi appeared and gave him additional instruction. From 1946 to 1948, he attained different states of samadhi, culminating in the final stage of nirvikalpa samadhi, a state of permanent Unity Consciousness and the ability to enter the pulseless, breathless state at will. Feeling an indescribable gratitude, I bowed and touched my head to the base of the Kriya lineage altar. A subtle sense of acknowledgment poured into the top of my head, and I spent the rest of the day in silence.

*Kriya itself is a form of fire. Kriya generates inner fire.*
BHUPENDRANATH SANYAL, "THE DIVINE TEACHINGS
OF SANYAL MAHASHAYA," IN *SANYAL MAHASHAYA*

Inefficiency is rife in India. After a few months I felt frustrated and impatient, and I missed the conveniences and pleasures of the industrialized world. One afternoon, I said not a word, but was inwardly feeling especially critical. Baba immediately called me into his room. "You believe you are so intelligent and everyone else is a fool. You should leave, you've learned nothing." I asked once again, but the reply was similar, "No, you cannot practice higher Kriyas! You are full of impurities—there are too many ladies dancing in your mind," Baba raised his hands and again did a mock belly dance. I dropped my head. "If you're immersed in animal qualities, you're just getting D-O-G! Always remember the Infinite." Outside, Swami Yogeswaranda tried to console me. "You'll know when you're ready, but more importantly, Gurudev will know. Don't be discouraged. Gurudev is hardest on those he loves; he's truly trying to teach you."

When the alchemists speak of a long life as one of the endowments of the Philosophers' Stone, . . . it is simply their intention to deny any positive qualities to evil and, by inference, any perpetuity; when they testify that the possession of the Stone is the annihilation of covetousness and of every illicit desire, they mean that all evil affections disappear before the light of the Unveiled Truth.

ARTHUR E. WAITE[5]

What little I could glean from a study of Western alchemy told me that it was concerned with the same process as Kriya—the evolution of the human soul from leaden to golden, and finally into the Philosophers' Stone. The alchemical laboratory was most importantly the alchemist's own body. Here I had a *living Philosophers' Stone* before me, but I was too immature, too unprepared to appreciate him.

Within me were so many powerful contradictions—dark and light mingled. I felt like a rebellious backslider, a hardened ego-nut, too stubborn to crack. I looked at my stack of spiritual books and recalled the old adage, *A donkey piled high with books is still a donkey.* The Orissan heat again became unbearable in April, and I had run into a wall, my limit. My search had been a success, but I had touched something too hot, too divine, and had to drop it. At just twenty-six I wasn't ready to give up Kevin to become the *Self.* My desire for the world suddenly seemed very normal, while this master's lofty standards felt excessively, impossibly puritanical.

The Bardo visions and the quest to become a lama hadn't been forgotten, only submerged. I had new tools this time. I continued to practice Kriya, but the visions of Tibetan Buddhist forms now reemerged and I again felt strongly drawn to the Himalayas. *Perhaps the unexplored avenues among the Tibetans are for me?* Before I left, I went to bow my goodbyes to the master. Swamiji's eyes shone. He drew me close with a look of boundless compassion, and perhaps a touch of sadness too. He said in a low voice, "Don't make too many plans."

I bowed, and he added, "Plans bring only pain."

# 25

# Lama

*Hasten slowly and you shall soon arrive. Renounce all*
*worldly goals, and you shall reach the highest Goal.*

MILAREPA, FROM EVANS-WENTZ,
*TIBET'S GREAT YOGI MILAREPA*

A cosmic siren blares from two or three miles away, and I sit up in
my bed just before sunrise. The anahata dhwani (the unstruck
sound) resounds in the center of my head more loudly than ever
before, varying now between a deep bell within and a siren far away.
*What is happening? I must be in a holy place!* I had arrived in the dead
of night after a harrowing bus ride from India over the first ridge of
the Himalayas into the Kathmandu Valley. I rose, hastily dressed, and
stepped out of my room into the first cool morning in many months.
The purple of the predawn sky is just light enough to make my way
along a forested path to a flight of stone stairs leading high up to temple
gates high upon a hill. The inner siren continues to blare but I know its
purpose now and I'm calm. Monkeys swing and screech in the trees as
I ascend the steps. Atop the great flight of stairs, I stand before a great
stupa with two huge painted eyes. Beside these eyes I turn and look
out over the great valley, and to the northeast I see the towering tips

of snow-capped peaks. Gazing at the holy mountains for the first time, all thought is drawn from me and I watch the sunrise in a new silence of soul. The richness of Nepalese culture is a delight, and within days I'm convinced I would spend the rest of my life here. It offered everything I could want in a spiritual life and more. Compared to the heaty Indians, the Nepalese are cool and patient, like the high mountains that surround them. Nepalese culture is a fusion of Indian influences from the south and Tibeto-Mongolian from the north, the result of a long history of Himalayan migrations and trade. Muslim conquest and destruction did not reach the Kathmandu Valley, so many of the ancient wooden temples and structures are original. The Hindu-Shamanistic-Tantric Buddhist melange of spirituality is unique in the world and extraordinarily beautiful. The magic of Nepal can only be felt, not described. After an austere India, I indulged in the pizza and cake luxuries Kathmandu had to offer. However, even this grew tiresome after a week, and wishing Tibetan contacts I escaped the city to the eastern portion of the greater valley.

A Tibetan monastery of the Gelug school rests beyond the great Stupa of Bodhnath and was known for accepting foreign guests. The lamas and monks there were kind, but I felt no connection, no compulsion to initiate my studies there, instead making use of their wonderful, multilingual library. Still unsure just why I was in Nepal, I knew only that there was an unturned stone regarding the legacy of esoteric Buddhism, one that left India and thrived in Tibet, and was now returning to India/Nepal to escape the destruction in Tibet. The Bardo between-states visionary journey had initiated my quest, leading here me to the Himalayas, *but now what?* I felt like a pilgrim adrift.

A curious clue revealed itself there at the foot of the Himalayas. In the monastery library I discovered that the Chinese scholar who had written a commentary on *The Secret of the Golden Flower*, was in fact Swiss. I'd seen the book in libraries and bookshops over the years, but never got around to reading it. Now as I held Wilhelm's thin volume in my hand, I recalled a Ms. Jung from Singapore when in graduate school. I never made the connection that, in spelling only, the Chinese surname is also a Germanic one, meaning *young*. I searched the library for more, and found a tattered, early version of *The Tibetan Book of the Dead*, also with C. G. Jung's commentary. I take it up, open to the commentary, and leaping at me from the pages, the Swiss psychologist writes, "This knowledge also gives us a hint of how we ought to read the Bardo Thodol, that is, backwards."[1]

With a gasp I took a step back, tripped, and was duly seated on a chair, stunned that Jung advised studying the ancient text *backward*— just as in my journey back through my life, back through the in-between states between death and rebirth! (See chapter 10.) Bardo, or *bar-do*, means "between two." I hungrily read on, discovering that Jung advised studying the text *backward* no less than *four* times! *I've found a brother in the quest.* Even so, as I read through his commentary, I continually felt constrained by Jung's excessively Eurocentric psychological interpretations. The Swiss psychiatrist had left a dried breadcrumb on the trail to an unreached destination, but he seemed bound by a hidden restraint, and any connection to a living spiritual lineage felt vague or missing for him. I left Jung's commentary behind and focused on Dawa-Samdup's translation of the Tibetan text.

My stay at the Gelug monastery had so far been restful, but less than inspiring—until the surprise arrival one morning of my old friend Richard. We laughed together about my "red hot spine" and shared our adventures since our time at the ashram in India the previous year. When he saw the copy of Evans-Wentz's *Tibetan Book of the Dead* I was still reading, he mentioned that Jung had written his esoteric commentaries at his Tower, a small stone castle he built on a lakeside in Switzerland. With mind flashing to Europe, I momentarily felt disoriented, and upon recovery made a mental note to visit there someday if I had the opportunity. After a half-day reunion with endless cups of Tibetan butter tea, Richard the seeker blurted, "By the way, I'm climbing to the monastery high in the hills tomorrow." We stepped outside and he pointed up to monastic structures clinging to the high mountainsides to the north. "Why don't you come with me? We'll offer incense to the lamas and receive their blessings."

In the morning we bought incense and silk scarves in the local market, gathered light packs with lunch and water, and set off on our hike. Life isn't easy for the rural Nepalese, but the rugged land is impossibly beautiful. I expected nothing from the day trip, but within an hour I realized an entrancing beauty in Nepal that I hadn't yet experienced. Those hills remained in my dreams for many years. We hiked several hours past deep green rice terraces, over cool streams, and up rigorous, rocky trails to *Nagi Gompa* (Nagi Monastery), perched high on the edge of the Kathmandu Valley. Bearing gifts to honor a *Rinpoche* (Tibetan: precious jewel), if one was there, we talked with a few monks and were soon led into a private altar room with a rich, deep red Tibetan carpet.

My knees buckled and my hands came to prayer position the moment I saw his noble face. "Sir . . . *Rinpoche*, I must tell you of a vision!" Until that moment the vision received in the Thai guti during my Christmas fast had rested in forgotten recesses of my mind. Richard was stunned and possibly embarrassed by my sudden outburst, but the lama calmly replied, "Yes, tell me." I described the rainbow of deities that had emerged from an inner sky while I held a particular body (*Kum Nye*) position during my fast in Thailand. Each had particular geometric forms on their torsos, colors, and hand positions. The lama raised an eyebrow, and replied in English, "This is an unusual and important vision. Take the Buddhist vows here tomorrow morning— you shall be my personal student."

We offered the incense and silk scarves, and the Rinpoche in turn blessed the scarves and wrapped them around our necks. Richard chatted for a while with him, but I only felt dizzy, quietly falling inward. We were briefly shown around the mountain monastery by another monk, and we left in a daze. Richard turned to me as we started down the mountainside, and asked, almost pleadingly, "But why? You have taken initiation into the sacred Kriya Yoga. What need do you have of a lama's teachings?" Aghast at my spiritual greed, he could only shake his head. I was silent as we bumbled down the mountain, reaching the Gelug monastery at dusk, where I finally replied, "I don't know why, but the journey back through the Bardo came for a reason, and the Tibetanesque visions in Thailand have a purpose. I must see this through." Tibetans refer to a special word, *tendrel*, meaning sacred connections established in a former lifetime, to explain such sudden bonds. The following morning, I packed up for the move from the Gelug to the Kagyu monastery. I made the hike with my heavy pack, but this time the strenuous climb had a known purpose. The *Vajrayana*, the Diamond Vehicle, was revealing itself.

"I take refuge in the Buddha, the Sangha, and the Dharma," I repeated after His Holiness the fourteenth Shamar Rinpoche. He gave me a Tibetan name, and empowered me—a subtle current entered my head and ran down my shoulders, and I relaxed into a presence no thought could invade. After a spell, butter tea was brought and we discussed the Bardo and memories of former lives. "Your Bardo experience and visions are rare, and yet also normal," Rinpoche replied. "To have such clear memories is a sign of previous Dharma practice. There will be a point where you can," he paused to think, "*encompass* all your incarnations, integrate and even unify them. I myself am still in the process of encompassing the many previous incarnations of Shamarpa." I did not understand what this meant at the time, but it felt important and I later made note of it after the evening meal.

The following morning, we walked around the monastery grounds overlooking the Kathmandu Valley, now visible under the rising mist. Holding a book in his hand, Shamarpa said, "Today I'm traveling overseas for about three weeks. Stay here, and when I return we'll start your formal initiations and practice." I nodded, but wondered what I would do for those weeks. "Rinpoche, I have never been into the Himalayas. I should like to trek into the holy mountains in your absence. I'll be sure to return after that." The lama looked over my head and beyond me, appearing to perceive something at a distance. Rinpoche then nodded, handing me a copy of Gampopa's *Jewel Ornament of Liberation* in English, a primary textbook for the study of Mahayana Buddhism in the Kagyu monastic schools and colleges. "Know this by heart in my absence." I bowed and went to pack my bags.

As I was departing, I met a monk who spoke English well. "You're most fortunate!" The monk went on, "Until the return of Karmapa, Kunzig Shamar Rinpoche is the highest ranking in our Kagyu lineage. And he takes few personal students—be sure to return!" *How could I not?* Beside myself with joy, I had waited lifetimes for this. *Now I would know the mysteries of the mandala, the Tibetan Bardo Thodol—the secrets between life, death, and rebirth!* Intentions set strongly with purpose and compassion will reach fruition. Soul trajectories with focus continue onward to their completion, no matter how many incarnations are required.

*The Jewel Ornament of Liberation* is regarded by all Tibetan Buddhist schools as one of the most inspiring and comprehensive works of the tradition. Written by Gampopa in the twelfth century, the primary spiritual son of the great hermit kundalini-yogi Milarepa, this text lays out the stages of the Buddhist path and explains how an enlightened attitude is strengthened by practicing the six perfections of generosity, discipline, patience, exertion, meditation, and knowledge. I carried the book like a treasure into the Himalayas, to meet a jewel of another kind.

# 26

# Synlocality

*It's hard to believe in coincidence, but it's even harder to believe in anything else.*

JOHN GREEN, *WILL GRAYSON, WILL GRAYSON*

"*Ek chai,*" she said, her wide Mediterranean eyes gliding from the Nepalese woman out to the snows higher up. This tiny Himalayan village at 10,000 feet afforded stupendous views, but I looked down to the needed sugar, milk, and caffeine that only a Nepali spiced chai can provide. The young woman turned about and smiled to me. As though looking through a tunnel of time, her eyes fell into mine—she was as familiar as an old friend. "Don't you like the chai?" she asked, with the charming lilt of a Semitic accent. I was momentarily paralyzed, still holding my chai cup up as though to take a sip. "Oh, yes, the chai is good," I sputtered. We immediately became trekking friends, an invisible link forming between us as we walked. Savrina is of Russian descent, born in Israel. She did her stint in the army and a kibbutz and was now circling the globe. We conversed with other trekkers along the way, and she noted, "Your heart isn't open to people, Kevin-ee," as she liked to call me. This struck a wound in me. I'm an introvert who had learned something of the subtle realms, but I had an age-old fear of persecution, and I remained closed and wary of others. That I didn't stop seeking answers to the questions most cast aside seemed to hold me apart from the interests of others.

At the peak of the Langtang trek is a yak butter and cheese producer, and we enjoyed the protein intake while chatting with scores of other trekkers. Being near Savrina I felt my chest massaged, and I smiled more often. At night, temperatures were so low we slept in hats and coats, even within our down sleeping bags. The glory of the snow-capped Himalayas surrounded us by day. My dreams by night were as clear and crisp as the high mountain air.

After days among those snowy peaks, we descended to a village below, the start of the long trek down and back to Kathmandu. Now low enough to wash our hair in the waters rushing down from the snows, we bathed in an icy river for the first time in over week. Night fell again, and hot *dahl baht* (lentil curry and rice) warmed us as we snuggled together around a fire amid a group of trekkers in a small village shack on the edge of the river. Late that night I felt a tremendous pain in the center of my chest and I sat up with a fright. A rusty door over my heart was forcibly pried open, and a flood of emotional pain from years past swiftly flowed out, leaving me in the natural joy of the present. "My heart is open!" I cried. Savrina only giggled sleepily and turned to cuddle closer to me. The world suddenly became a magical place, light danced over the shack, and from the raging river nearby I heard a splashing divine chorus. I couldn't hold a thought and perceived all about me as if from the center of my chest. Utterly unique in my experience, it was a revelation.

> *A man sees in the world what he carries in his heart.*
>
> GOETHE, *FAUST*, PART 1

A shaft of morning sunlight beamed pink on a peak resting in soft clouds, illuminating our little village with gentle light. *I had only to open my heart!* I had never before understood what this meant. We packed up. I kept Gampopa but left two fat books of intellectual philosophy there in the village—heavy ballast, no longer needed, now released. While descending I beamed love from the center of my chest to everyone I met, and received more smiles than I had ever known. After more days of trekking, it grew warm. When Savrina and I arrived in the busy city of Kathmandu, we understood we had been, and still were, in an intensely altered state of consciousness.

For days we wandered the ancient streets, only half in our bodies. One evening we meditated and something opened above our heads; we then saw the faces of former lives appear over our own. We slept and I dreamed we were speaking an archaic dialect, and she was calling me by another name. Many nights we astrally soared together over the valley and the Himalayan foothills. Though enthralled, Savrina soon became precariously ungrounded and she decided to return to Israel. I saw her off at the airport, still relishing this connected open-heart space. The following week in Kathmandu passed like an endless dream. I was so inspired that I bought a large bound journal of traditional Nepalese paper, and filled it with poetry and sketches of mandalas. I enjoyed swapping road tales with the other travelers in darkened, candlelit cafes in the crumbling ancient buildings of Kathmandu. I wanted nothing more than to live the rest of my life in this wisdom of the heart.

In my sleep, astral journeys over the Kathmandu Valley continued, leaving me breathless and in awe in the mornings, unable to speak while journaling over continuous pots of sweet, spiced Nepalese chai. One disturbing dream journey stood out: I soared over the valley leading up to a daytime view of Nagi Gompa where from above I saw pitched battles between shaven-head *punk monks* in black leather jackets and other red-robed monks. I recorded this dream in the morning over yet another pot of sweet, spiced Nepali tea, and felt perplexed by the oddities of such a lucid dream-vision: *Perhaps this isn't literal, but rather symbolic of events to come?* I continued to mill about in Kathmandu, while my vows, *I take refuge in the Buddha, the Dharma, and the Sangha* rang only in my memory. Rinpoche was surely back in Nepal now, but I had little mind for that now. Naively, I felt that if I could just remain in this velvety-divine heart space for the rest of my life, I had little need for other kinds of enlightenment. The Dharma would soon put me on recall.

One late afternoon I followed a free-roaming holy cow on a meandering dirt path over a muddy stream. This led me back to the monkey temple, Swayambhunath, where I had first arrived in Nepal. I climbed the long flight of stone stairs while the sun was gently descending in a clear blue sky and walked about the holy grounds of the *Self-Arisen One*, as the hill is known. The hill was an island in the great lake that was the valley 3,000 years ago. It is said that the Hindu god Shiva drained the valley lake and rested here, though it is now a Tibetan stupa and monastery. Shiva is sometimes referred to as *Swayambhu* or self-existent, not subject to birth and death. The unblinking eyes painted on the great stupa oversee the entire valley.

As I gazed out over the valley, gray clouds gathered in the sky above me, swirling into the strangest formation I had ever seen. These further darkened, and within minutes a stupendous rainstorm commenced! I dashed into a portion of the monastery that was open and sat on the floor near the spinning prayer wheels. Electric power was soon lost and the whole mountain rested in darkness beneath a raging storm. I sat for hours among those butterfat lamps and prayer wheels, while the storm showed no sign of abating. Winds blew so hard that most of the lamps around the prayer wheels were blown out and I shivered in the cool, darkening void.

*We are near waking, when we dream we are dreaming.*
NOVALIS, *MISCELLANEOUS OBSERVATIONS*

*"Aum mani padme hum, aum mani padme hum . . .,"* emanated from a stairwell behind the circle of prayer wheels. A faint light emerged along with the chanting, and an elderly Tibetan monk appeared, blinking, holding a candle. He bid me follow him down the stairs. The stairwell led down, farther and farther down into the still, dark mountain. *Have they tunneled the full depth of this hill?* We arrived in a dungeon-like room with a table and a raised platform next to it, piled high with

rumpled blankets. He lit another candle for me and motioned to me to wait. Shortly later I heard footsteps and he arrived carrying a tray on which sat a large bowl of *thukpa* (Tibetan yak meat and noodle stew). He motioned to the platform with the pile of blankets and made sleeping gestures. I spoke little Tibetan at this time, but thanked him, "*Thu'chiche*" (great compassion). He disappeared into yet another dim stairwell. I ate and soon drifted away in the darkness to dream a dream within a dream.

*I leave our tent for a cool evening walk in a darkened northern forest. Through the trees I perceive shadows moving—the shadows are men. They emerge from the dark forest and their animal heads are revealed. I dash back to our tent to wake Savrina. She leans up and says, "What are we doing here? Didn't we fall asleep somewhere else?" We are momentarily disoriented and then . . .*

*"Do we have something for breakfast?" I yawn and stretch in the desert morning sunlight. Savrina mumbles something about pastries and coffee when I realize that something is not quite right. I look about at the familiar surroundings—and pour a cup of coffee for myself (I'm not a coffee drinker) and come over to her. She sits up and says with a start, "We're not back yet—we're still a level in." This made no sense to me whatsoever until I looked at the cup of coffee my hands . . .*

*Floating in a dark starless void. I eventually feel gravity again, along with coarse sensations about me—squirming furry critters, all over my body. Must be rats! "Are we back now?" murmurs Savrina. "Yes, we're back—to pile of rats!" I cry. Fumbling with the matchbox in the dark, the flame illuminates our faux horror—kittens! We had slept the night away with an entire litter. They must have been in another part of the platform and crawled to us for the warmth. We fortunately hadn't crushed any of them, and I wondered,* Were the tiny souls part of our multi-levels dreams? *We gently moved them to one side of the platform. We compared notes on our dreams within a dream, and confirmed similar perceptions.*

Then I awoke, again, this time alone in the dark—among kittens.
I fumbled in the dark for the candle and a match, and lay there
astonished, petting one of the kittens. Still in my clothes, I put on
my shoes and emerged from the inner cavern into the early morning
light. Thanking the monks, we enjoyed silent smiles and a warm butter tea together. I then slowly descended the great outer stairway to
Kathmandu. The dawning of a particular form of remembrance grew
within me that morning, as I made my way from Swayambhunath to
my guesthouse. Inwardly silent for most of that long walk, I wondered
if I wasn't still in a dream or a dream level. My childhood philosopher
friend's notion that "God created us, so He is us" turned over in my
mind as I pondered:

What if we, as the All-Pervading Awareness, or God, are dreaming a Great Dream in which we are all the dream characters, and we
became so absorbed in it that we not only forgot we were dreaming,
but we dreamed yet another dream within that dream so convincing
that we forgot that we had dreamed this level too? And then we dream-
condensed that dream yet again to make it appear so solid and real that
we were unable to find our way back out of these levels of dreams? This
would imply several levels of dream-densifying, perhaps across eons of
time, requiring great effort to awaken from.

I liked my new term *dream-densification*, and made note of it. I
sat for hours in my room at the decaying Bluebird Hotel, staring out
the window at children playing around an ancient Nepalese shrine.
I recalled Ramana Maharishi's profoundly direct *sadhana* (spiritual
work) that consists solely of deeply meditating upon the question, *Who
am I?* until we peel back all the layers, a *de-densification* of the dream
levels to remember that we are indeed the One as the Many, and the
Many as the One.

Buddhists prefer the impersonal term *All-Pervading Awareness* to
the more personal term *God*, simply two semantic sides of the same
coin. In the Tibetan dream yoga I would later learn, an initiate is to
consider all experiences, including our ordinary consciousness and our
seemingly physical reality, to be just one of the many dream realities. I

felt that I was now walking just one of the dreams within dreams, and I passed another week in Kathmandu experiencing the continuing joy of not quite knowing which dream I was in at any given moment. I surrendered to this dream flow, and the liquid déjà vu realm I had known in Europe as a teen returned.

I recalled another Tibetan master's words: *Void means no reference points; there is no final reality.* Alone with another pot of Nepali chai, I wrote Savrina about the dreams within a dream, but it would be many months before I received the confirmations in her reply that she had indeed experienced a similar dream sequence with me in a tent in a forest with animal-headed human beings, a desert morning with coffee, and a dark cave with kittens far below a temple. Very alone in Kathmandu now, the city began to take a toll on me. In 1987, visitors were incessantly hassled to change money on the black market or buy tourist items. This dream world suddenly felt wicked, infected with greed, fear, and desperation. My heart slowly closed again.

I hid in a tiny guesthouse on Freak Street in Basantapur and took up Gampopa's book for some consolation. The long treatise is for beginners on the path, full of harsh moralizing and every bit as lofty on the ethics as Hariharananda's moral demands. On the short length of one human incarnation, Gampopa writes, "A single human life passes as quickly as an arrow released from a taut bow." *Have I been distracted from the quest?* The heart opening Savrina catalyzed in me was indeed important. Mysteriously, I had been drawn back to Swayambhunath, the temple of All-Pervading Awareness, the place I had first entered upon my first dawn at the foot of the Himalayas, and a power spot for more than three millennia. Tradition has it that even Siddartha Gautama, the Buddha, born in Lumbhini in present-day Nepal, traveled north to the wealthy Newar city of Kathmandu and preached atop the hill of Swayambhunath.

Now late for my return to the lama and the teachings, I hurriedly took a rickety bus out to Boudha and walked all the way up the hill back to Nagi Gompa to seek out the Shamarpa, the Rinpoche, the precious jewel, my teacher. On arrival, a monk recognized and greeted me.

He informed me that Rinpoche was not here, but had just returned from Delhi and was now at Swayambhunath. "Why, I just spent the night there days ago?" He instructed, "Go back to there and ask for him; he's waiting for you there now."

I had no idea that Shamarpa had any relationship to Swayambhunath at all. I made the long trek back across the Valley, and back up the Monkey Temple hill. There a monk spotted me and I was waved to immediately go upstairs inside the monastery building. In a large plush office with another deep red carpet, Shamarpa stood to greet me, "I just arrived back two days ago. This is my head office in Nepal. How do you like it?" he asked with a mischievous grin, as though he were part of an inside joke I had missed. I was atop the very building under which, in that dungeon below, I had emerged from dreams within dreams. I was astonished by the *synlocality* of it.

We speak of synchronicities to describe meaningful coincidences in time. However, I venture to coin a new term here, *synlocality*, that is, *two or more events that occur at the same location, but at different times.* This describes, as I'll show later in this volume, the eternal return or circular nature of relationships and events at different nexus points of time, with a common fixed geographic location. So rather than a co-incidence in time, *synlocality* describes a co-locality in space. Thus, a location in space becomes a nexus point for all the times and events that share the same space, and consciousness can slide over time at this point in space. Certain locations can become charged with so many history-altering events that sensitive persons may perceive such atmospheres. Thus, locations where great historical events occur may become charged with consciousness, pivotal points for individuals, nations, or peoples. On a smaller scale, locations may have a personal significance to individuals or groups of souls that incarnate together over strings of time to perform particular activities.

Many, if not most of us, have experienced the uncanny sense of circling back to a location to *tie a loop in time*. Goethe wrote of an experience similar to *synlocality* when he was twenty-two years old and preparing to return to his home after completing studies in Strasbourg where he had fallen in love with Fredericka. Goethe concluded he wasn't ready to marry and take on the responsibilities of a wife, so he made an emotional visit to Fredericka to advise her of his decision. He later wrote the curious vision he experienced while on horseback riding away from her home in his autobiography *Dichtung und Wahrheit*. "I saw, not with the eyes of the body, but with those of the mind, my own figure coming towards me on horseback, and on the same road, attired in a suit which I had never worn," he wrote. He described the suit as pike gray with gold lace, an item he did not own at the time. "As soon as I shook myself out of this dream, the figure had entirely disappeared." Eight years later, Goethe found himself once more at the same point on the same road, wearing the pike-gray suit with gold lace he had seen in his vision.

# 27

# Vajrayana

*Meditation is a natural antidote—you can be liberated.*

THE FOURTEENTH SHAMAR RINPOCHE
(IN PERSONAL CONVERSATION WITH AUTHOR)

"What have you learned in my absence?" asked Shamarpa, seeing my depressed state. "I've learned that there is no happiness in samsara, the realm of worldly illusion. I'm lost in a dream and I wish to awaken." A broad smile broke over his face. "Good! Tomorrow, we'll return to Nagi Gompa, and you'll take initiation into the *Ngyodrol*, or Four Foundation practices. These will purify and prepare you for the advanced trainings ahead," instructed the lama. I was already unsure of time, space, and the dream at this point. Now the I, or at least who I think I am, is to be entirely deconstructed.

Each of the four practices is to be performed 100,000 times. After a brief calculation, I realized that even at working ten to twelve hours a day, it would be months before completion. The first practice, the *Vajrasattva* purification, involves a complex visualization and a long mantra. Over and again, I practice until it becomes a living reality for me. Weeks pass and my body is now permanently filled with brilliant light, even in my sleep and dream states. After intensive practice until midnight one evening, I lay back in my bunk, drift into a wakeful sleep, and dream:

> *I feel a peculiar tickling in my cheek, so I consult a large, standing mirror. A small hole opens in my cheek and squirming pink worms with black ends emerge. I'm alarmed as more worms are expunged out of my cheek and fall on the ground. Then a deep shaking at my mid-back shudders my entire body. A serpentlike creature with a head like a crocodile dislodges itself from my back and ribs and moves up and out the widening hole in my cheek. I scream as the repulsive reptilian entity, now about 4 feet in length, is expelled out of the hole in my cheek. As it falls to the ground, its hideous face turns back to me, hissing with noxious fury and scorn. It scurries away at speed.*

I awoke with the pure love I had often felt in childhood. A darkness that had been with me for so long was now gone and with it a great weight of hidden avarice. My own resentments and bitterness had attracted this creature, as like attracts like, and it rested within me, feeding off an inner malevolence and increasing it. A first step had been taken. If Tantric Buddhism hadn't already impressed me, I was now awed. Years later I would learn how to shamanically detect and remove such intrusions. For now, the cleansing only increased my drive to complete the Four Foundations. I reported the purification dream to the lama, and he replied, "This is an outstanding sign, and so soon! You'll be initiated into Mahamudra tomorrow morning."

Inwardly I rejoiced, but Kevin again took it as a death sentence. Memories of the faux-terminal illness in Japan peeked from behind my conscious awareness. *Well, I'm getting what I asked for!* The following morning, I took initiation (empowerment: *abhisheka*) into the Kagyu Mahamudra (also known as *Dzogchen*), an advanced practice requiring a high degree of discipline and concentration. Such is the power of the practice that I became dizzy for days and had to inhale the smoke of roasting *tsampa* (barley powder) to relieve what the Tibetans call *lung*, or *winds* (power moving through the spiritual channels due to kundalini activation) to ground me. Too much power was rising in my *shushumna* (spiritual channel in the spine) to the top of my head, and I felt tremendous pressure on the underside of the top of my skull.

The brain and cerebrospinal system require time to adjust to the reopening of the *Secret Fire*, the voltage of awakening from the Cosmic Dream. In my room I carried on a sporadic practice of Kriya Yoga to make the adjustments easier. Vajrayana Buddhism is similar to Kriya Yoga in that the transmission of certain teachings only occurs directly from teacher to student during an empowerment initiation (*shaktipat, diksha,* or *abhiṣeka*). These teachings may be considered "self-secret," that is, without the direct power-current transmission conferred by initiation, mere words or books cannot convey the teaching.

An equilibrium developed and I plumbed new depths of meditation. With Mahamudra practice I discovered levels of emotionality close the core of false self, and it was profoundly frightening. I returned to Four Foundation practices time and again for relief from inner and outer obstacles, doing hundreds of prostrations a day. A loneliness weighed on my heart. At meals I observed the other lamas, monks, and laymen— they seemed quite happy, even carefree. *But this is their culture. Shaving my head, giving it all up? Shall I never live in the West or modern Asia again? Shall I never have a partner, a family?*

I was given a room directly below my Tibetan master in the upper monastery where only high lamas reside—apparently an honor, though I was unaware of this at the time. I only saw the flames of my own funeral pyre burning before my inner eye. Feeling condemned to the gallows of Mahamudra, I rose each morning at 5 a.m. for solitary meditation. No heat warmed the monastery, and here in the foothills of the mighty Himalayas it was often below zero before dawn. Each frozen morning, I felt warm under my thick yak-wool blankets; to rise in this temperature was an arduous test of endurance.

One morning was particularly frigid, and I was sure a touch of frost crackled at the end my whiskers. *I'll just meditate lying down.* Pleased with such a strikingly original idea, I remained nestled in my cozy, yak-wool lair—and promptly fell asleep. Shortly later I felt the vibratory stage overtake me and I leaned up out of my body to the astral sound of an ethereal voice calling me from above. I looked up and beheld Shamarpa leaning through the ceiling in his own astral form, pointing and waving his finger at me, beaming, "Awaken and continue your meditations!" I quickly reidentified with the physical and sat up. I missed no more frosty morning meditations!

A sea of clouds blanketed the valley each morning, so soft and thick that one might just walk out over the valley on them. By noon the clouds would lift into a brilliant blue sky. In the same way, each time a thought-emotion train would carry my attention away in meditation, I step off and watch it chug away into the distance. Awareness remains in the present. Each time I try to grasp at personal agendas, they fade into a spaciousness. Days passed into weeks, and I gradually yet continually return to the moment before thought begins, releasing awareness into indescribable grace. Eternities passed within ordinary hours, and any sense of "I" was disappearing into a state of natural joy.

As current leader of the Kagyu Sect in the Karmapa's absence, Shamarpa had many spiritual and political duties. He flew to Delhi, then to Europe and wasn't due back for a month or two, so I trekked the Annapurna circuit near Pokhara west of Kathmandu. Over the weeks deep in the Himalayas I often hiked off the trail to find a sitting spot for gazing out at the snowcaps, where I practiced becoming the snowy range of mountains, disappearing into them until I felt no cold any longer. Without thought, only pure perception, I rested there.

I met scores of trekkers of varying nationalities in the many villages along the way, but when I came upon a Swiss couple from Basel we immediately felt like family. Bruno, Rosie, and I had heartwarming conversations there high in the Himalayas and all the way back to Pokhara, and even on back to Kathmandu. We hoped to keep in touch and meet up again someday. I mention them here because they will later reenter this account in a most remarkable way.

Back at Nagi Monastery, I passed the days practicing alone and studying Tibetan with the two servant monks who cooked for Rinpoche. Neither spoke English, but one spoke Nepalese and the other spoke

Mandarin. Between them and the Tibetan language study book I procured in Kathmandu, I was steadily learning new phrases and trying to formulate my own each day. Nagi Monastery is quite isolated and offered few distractions in those days. Shamarpa was delayed in Europe, and with next to nothing to do, my mind easily wandered again to worldly pleasures. Dancing in my daydreams, pizza, cakes, and ice cream called to me from Kathmandu. Then came the perfect excuse! My visa would soon expire and I had to return to Kathmandu to extend it. I bid my farewell, explaining that I would return in a week or so. The monks informed me, "Rinpoche is due back next week; be sure to return by Sunday!"

When I arrived in Boudha after the long hike down the edge of the valley I learned that Erik, the Tibetan interpreter, would be translating for a rare teaching given by a visiting lama. I admired Erik and often saw him at Nagi Gompa, sitting straight, copying sutras in perfect Tibetan. He seemed the model disciple, humble yet profoundly capable. I procured an invitation and attended the private meeting with the lama. The Rinpoche was enormous, easily weighing 300 pounds, and so merged with a Wrathful Deity that he shook the entire stage with power. The deity spoke through him in a booming voice of such supernatural force that I was frozen in place with awe. Danish Erik sat focused and unfazed, translating without blinking into his third language, English. I left the meeting absolutely staggered.

Although I knew little about shamanism at this time, I couldn't help but feel the importance of it in Tibet. In fact, the most powerful practices seemed to be of shamanic origin, with only a thin veneer of Buddhist philosophy painted over the top. I certainly wasn't the first to realize this. Many researchers and authors had already made note of Tibet's shamanic origins, and in a few years time Geoffrey Samuels would publish a book on the subject, writing, "The sophisticated body of shamanic practices within Tibetan Buddhism probably constitutes Tibet's most important single contribution to humanity."[1]

The cafés around the Great Stupa of Boudha are a delight. In one of those, over a pot of chai one afternoon, my eyes met those of an older Argentinian nun, clad in the deep red robes of the Tibetan tradition.

We smiled, sat together, and had a wonderful discussion over a second pot. Her eyes shone as she described how she had given up everything to become a hairless, penniless nun, living only by the way of Buddhist Dharma. After a year with no possessions she had become attached to the one cotton-cloth shoulder satchel that Buddhist renunciates are allowed to carry, virtually worthless on its own. As happens in the dusty subcontinent, it became filthy and so she washed it and hung it out to dry; it was stolen. I could see from her wince that she still suffered the loss, yet she also laughed about it. *The earthly personality seeks attachment, and lives by it.*

She then shared an astonishing story: while in India the previous year she had to go to an immigration office for a visa extension to continue her studies with a powerful Tibetan lama, known for his siddhis (spiritual powers). As a nun with a Buddhist passport it should have been easy, but she said, "The officer only shouted, 'Impossible! I'll never grant an extension to you!' Then he suddenly fell silent, and grasping his neck, started to cough and choke, his facing turning red. Unable to breathe, he quickly stamped my passport with a one-year extension, and handed it back to me. Only then could he breathe again, and he scurried away to a back office as quickly as he could!" We laughed, finger flipped tea oblations to the sky, and with wide smiles looked up to the deities.

My visa was also soon extended to a surprising length, and I enjoyed the city for a few more days, eating in every other café and restaurant, savoring the variety of cuisines there. Tibetan food certainly keeps one alive but becomes tedious quickly. Between cinnamon rolls and chocolate cakes, I scoured the remarkable bookstores for Tibetan texts, discovering Lama Anagarika Govinda's book *The Way of the White Clouds*. I poured through the German lama's memoir while downing more pots of sweet Nepali chai. Born Ernst Hoffmann in Saxony to a German father and Bolivian mother, he was later one of the first Westerners (1930s) to become a full lama in the Tibetan tradition. He related a fascinating tale of reincarnation: While studying at the Univerisity of Freibourg in Switzerland prior to going to Asia, he felt compelled to write a story. Upon completion he asked a friend to review it, and the friend immediately recognized the content as being nearly identical to that of an unfinished story by the German mystic poet Novalis (Georg Philipp Friedrich Freiherr von Hardenberg, 1772–1801), who was also born in Saxony. Here it was, now completed in its entirety before his friend's astonished eyes; they both had no idea what to make of it. Furthermore, Novalis never finished it because he died young from the same ailment (tuberculosis) that led Govinda to Ticino, Switzerland, for medical treatment.

Some time later, Govinda encountered a visiting professor at a social gathering in Capri who stared at him as though he'd seen a ghost. The man never spoke with him, but Govinda remained the object of the professor's intense visual scrutiny throughout the gathering. Govinda later inquired about the man and discovered that he was a professor of German Romantic literature and had just completed a large research project on Novalis. The professor told others at the party that Govinda's face was so similar to Novalis (at the same age) that he was unnerved and therefore unable to approach him. Govinda did not pursue the investigation any further, and instead felt that he had simply completed what a former incarnation had not. Rather than becoming infatuated with it, he simply acknowledged the continuity:

No work of importance, that one's heart is bent upon with single-minded devotion, will remain unfinished. This is what Tibet has taught me, where the saints and Siddhas of old kept on returning through ever new incarnations, in ever new forms until the present day—thus confirming what first came to me as a faint remembrance or message from the past and grew in the pursuance of a distant aim into an inner certainty. It is not my ideal to be reborn forever in this world, but neither do I believe that we can abandon it before we have fulfilled our task in it—a task which we may have taken upon ourselves in some remote past, and from which we cannot run away.[2]

I closed Govinda's *White Clouds* renewed, feeling that I also wish to close the book on unfinished works. I later discovered that

Sangharakshita once told Lama Govinda that he "had the impression that his writings were influenced by the German romantics. Lama Govinda said that actually he was not just influenced by these writers; he had certain recollections that led him to believe that he himself was the incarnation of one of them. I later came to understand that he believed that he had been the poet Novalis in a previous lifetime. It is perhaps not too far-fetched to think that artists are working on a story that takes them many lifetimes to write."[3]

Knowledge of the realms between life and death are easily accessed by realized yogis, lamas, and shamans. Kriyananda shared an intriguing story of Yogananda's divinatory precision regarding the whereabouts of a disciple's reborn mother:

A few years after Dr. Lewis lost his mother, [Yogananda] . . . informed him, "She has been reborn. If you go to . . ." he mentioned some address north of Boston, in New England, "you will find her there." Dr. Lewis made the journey, [and met the family]. "It was uncanny," he told me later. "The child was only three years old, but in many of her mannerisms she seemed exactly like my mother. I observed, too, that she took an instantaneous liking to me. It was almost as though she recognized me."[4]

The Tibetans have an intriguing concept in their tradition, the notion of *emanations*. Thus, we are not necessarily individual souls incarnating in a linear fashion but instead are emanations of certain patterns of a Higher Order. The Hindus have a similar concept (*vasanas*), much older, of course. Some reborn lamas, known as tulkus, have two or more simultaneous emanations. The German mystic Jacob Boehme wrote in 1624 how consciousness of this Higher Order connects to and manifests in human bodies:

For the Male and Female, do mutually cast a seed into one another; which is only a Sulphur of the Astrum and four Elements, afterwards it is hatched in the Matrix, and Coagulated to a living Spirit . . .

when the fire is enkindled in the Seed which is sown in the Matrix
. . . as the light from the fire according to the right of the Eternal
nature: And two become manifest in one, viz. a Spiritual body from
the Astrum, and a fleshy body from the four Elements.[5]

*Enough of Kathmandu! If one more tout asks me to change money
or buy stuff* . . . I packed for the return to Nagi Monastery, but first
stopped in Boudha to visit Chokyi Nyima Rinpoche, an important
Kagyu lama. He had always been especially friendly to me and he was
building a new monastery nearby, so I dropped in and asked for him. I
was sent upstairs to the top floor, the largest hall of the new monastery.
As I turned the corner among all the construction works, I saw him
emerge from the great shadowed hall. There I perceived a rare vision—a
rainbow aura radiating out 5 meters around him. He greeted me jovially
and we sat on construction props cracking sunflower seeds in our teeth,
discussing the rising number of building projects around Boudhanath
(large scale construction was just getting started then).

In the Nyingma and Kagyu traditions the Rainbow Body (*jalü*)
is a level of realization, but it can have different manifestations, and
may also involve the breathless, pulseless state. The passage of time
may in fact be altered, yet within the same space. This reminds me of
Australian Aboriginal shamans who can, physically and vibrationally,
walk in the Dreamtime and not be perceived by others in ordinary
reality. Doubts assailed me personally, yet there was no doubt that the
Tibetan tradition was genuine. Erik the interpreter was all in, while I
was not. I remained a doubting Thomas, a half-faith Peter sinking in
the seas of hesitance.

# 28

# Doppelgänger

Shamar Rinpoche was already due back at Nagi Monastery, so the next day I hurriedly made the long hike back up to Nagi Gompa. When I arrived panting in the bright sunshine of midday, I rested for a moment outside the main monastic hall, looking up at the flight of outdoor steps that I would soon climb to the upper portion of the monastery. I asked a monk I knew whether Shamarpa had returned, and he shook his head, "Perhaps he's again at Swayambhu?" Feeling a bit miffed, I lamented, *Oh, chasing this lama about is getting a bit tiresome.* With a sigh of resignation, I mentally prepared to turn around and head back down the mountain when someone up the steps caught my attention:

Shamar Rinpoche stood waving to me from up on the mountain steps with a large, uncharacteristically silly smile on his face. He looked directly at me and continued waving, almost frantically. I waved back and stepped forward to go to him, but he miraculously descended the stairs in a flash and dashed into the kitchen behind the monastery before I could reach him.

I quickly made my way to the kitchen entry, but Rinpoche was nowhere to be seen. There is only one entrance and I clearly saw him enter it. I asked the monks cooking there where Shamarpa was, and they said he hadn't been seen anywhere in the area. I argued and insisted that I'd just seen him enter this room, but the monks, holding knives and ladles, just stared at me in silence. I left the kitchen befuddled. Shamarpa has a distinctive appearance; I wasn't mistaken. I talked to a few other monks around the monastery, and they all concurred that Shamarpa hadn't yet returned to Nagi, but some ventured to guess that he might already be in Nepal. *Perhaps he was at Swayambhunath again?* I packed a daypack and set off back down the mountain, only to meet Rinpoche's retinue coming up the narrow path from his car on the mountain road minutes later. Shamarpa greeted me with the same silly smile I'd seen at the top, "Why are you going down? I'm going up!"

If I had turned back to Kathmandu when I first heard the news he wasn't there I would have missed him on the trail above the road. His doppelgänger from the steps-into-the-kitchen act delayed me just enough to meet him on the path. Shaman-yogi-lama doppelgängers have been legend through the ages, but this was only my second full experience of it. I later came to understand doppelgängers as manifestations of the All-Pervading Awareness, or Cosmic Mind, even when the lama, yogi, or shaman may or may not have even been consciously aware of it. I met also doppelgängers again in my shamanic training, and now my students sometimes report seeing mine, often smiling, waving, or trying to indicate a message to them.

One early morning after meditation I was eating a breakfast of tsampa and warm, salty butter tea, when through the wall came the deepest bellowing mantra I'd ever heard in my life. The entire stone wall vibrated! I had heard of such power mantras, but this sound was far beyond any normal human capacity. I could only compare it to the sound a gigantic bull elephant might make when belching after drinking hundreds of liters of soda water. The theories that such mantras could move physical objects such as heavy stones suddenly came home to me. I never learned such things; such powers are tightly held within the tradition, as the misuse could be devastating.

*The day science begins to study nonphysical phenomena,*
*it will make more progress in one decade than in all the*
*previous centuries of its existence.*

ATTRIBUTED TO NIKOLA TESLA

One afternoon a group of Western monks, scholars, and students came up to Nagi Gompa for a teaching given in the main monastery. Afterward I joined them for Tibetan butter tea in a tent and listened in to their conversation. The Argentinian nun I met in Kathmandu had been humbled by her experiences, but these students were hypnotized by the merry-go-round of Vajrayana studies. I was stunned at the competition and the one-upmanship rampant among them. "I've been initiated by so-and-so high lama," said one with her nose rising to the peak of the tent. Another exulted, "Well, I've received the secret initiation of the higher tantras from an even higher Rinpoche." Yet another crowed, "Well, I got the most secret, advanced teachings from Lama Too-High just last week!" Others brandished their Tibetan accoutrements and soon psychic envy darts were flying around the table. I could only watch and listen in amazement. To me, further teachings only meant annihilation of the false self, and while I suppose one could get ego gratification even from being crucified, it's not something for which the illusory self usually wishes. *Of their own funerals they boast!*

"Are you staying up here?" They turned to me, the silent stranger among them. I nodded and mumbled, "I've been here for some months." One asked, "Oh, I've heard of no guesthouses here. You're camping in the main hall then?" I shook my head. "No, I have a room up there." I gestured toward to the upper monastery. They looked puzzled. "But that is reserved for only high-ranking lamas?" *To stay there is only to die all the sooner,* I thought to myself. The guns of envy swiveled their sights toward me, and the interrogation began: "Who is your primary teacher then?" I replied evasively, "I've taken initiations from different lamas." From another, "Yes, we all do, but who is your root lama?" A barrage of envy-darts hit my back as I made a hasty departure. I've not spoken of my experiences and training until now, more than thirty years later.

Rinpoche had attended ten months of English classes at the University of California at Berkeley in 1982, a period he often harkened back to as "a time of freedom" from his many responsibilities (synchronistically also the start of my dream initiations in America). Even though Shamarpa's spoken English is quite good, I was asked to assist with writing English letters and so my linguistic studies again proved useful. Over my stay there I learned enough of the politics in Tibetan Buddhism to wish I had known less. As within perhaps all religions, disagreements exist among the four primary Tibetan sects, and the Indigenous shamanic tradition (Bön) as well. Considering the tragic situation in Tibet, all support the Dalai Lama out of political expediency, but within inner circles there are disharmonies. Still, this did not dissuade me from the power of the teachings.

After further breakthroughs in meditation, Rinpoche was pleased. "Very fine, yes! You'll attend the Tibetan university in Delhi for three years, and become a full lama and teacher in our tradition." Now, the true death knell of Kevin tolled. When I explained that I hadn't the money to do so, he said that he would personally pay my way through Tibetan university. I was deeply honored, but rather than pleased, a fear of complete annihilation again overtook my shivering, pathetic sense of separateness, my masquerade. Inner resistances reasserted themselves violently, and I trembled with fears of poverty, never being able to leave India or Nepal, and never having a family. Rapacious wishes for luxuries and pleasures of all kinds fell upon me night and day. Nevertheless, I stayed and carried on.

My spoken Tibetan was improving only very little, but Shamarpa's attending monks encouraged me to use it more often with the lamas. One morning, I was invited to eat breakfast with a group of high-ranking lamas, including the intimidating Tulku Urgyen Rinpoche, whom I'd never seen smile even once. The monks served us egg-fried rice, and silently waved me on to try out my newly learned Tibetan phrases. I had a limited vocabulary, but at least I had good pronunciation, probably from imitating animal sounds as a child and studying phonetics in graduate school. The ranking lamas conversed heartily in Tibetan, while shoveling in mountains of food (Rinpoches aren't shy about eating). There was a pause in the conversation, so I finally spoke up, and instead of, "I like to eat *ji*-eggs," I clearly but mistakenly said in near-perfect Tibetan, "I like to lick *ki*-eggs." The table exploded with uproarious laughter. Urgyen Rinpoche laughed so hard he shot a grain of rice out his nose. Shocked, I looked back at the servant monks nearby who were laughing so painfully they could scarcely stand. I knew that *ji* means chicken, and now learned that *ki* means dog. *Dog eggs* has a testicular connotation in Tibetan. Despite my best struggling attempts, the Kriya master had been right all along—I was still just "getting D-O-G."

# 29

# Yab-Yum

New initiations were granted, and stacks of texts for study were placed in my room, thankfully in English. "You'll get to the Sanskrit and Tibetan versions after your studies in Delhi." Shamarpa continued to lift my self-regard with further instruction and initiations, while simultaneously making use of me to edit his foreign letters. I pondered the real need for the butter in the tea, and in his words. Soon I learned more. He was building a contingent of foreign lamas and teachers and had plans of his own that might diverge from that of our larger lineage. I admit I was captured by the ideas of knowledge and power, and I now knew that many Tibetan lamas weren't celibate. Vague fantasies rose within of being a respected lama, loved by an adoring crowd, a spiritual teacher who needn't give up meat, drink, and fleshy pleasures. I started to ask more questions.

When I asked about the *Yab-Yum* (Tibetan: *father-mother*) symbol of union we often see in Tibetan sacred art, Shamarpa replied, "Yab-yum is the union of wisdom and compassion, but the real Yab-Yum is here." Shamarpa pointed to his head. "The hidden fire rises to the head, and later bliss descends into the body. You know *chakrabindu*? That is the union of sun and the moon (Tibetan: *nyi zla kha sbyor*) here at the center of the skull. The bindu (drop or point) chakra represents a deeply subtle level of consciousness. The pranic energy that flows through this chakra is concentrated into drops (elixir) and winds (*lung*) to help carry this elixir through the channels (*nadi*)." I felt compelled to ask him about the chakrabindu, this sun-moon union. He pointed to his head and said, "There are two glands here—when they are married, you can be enlightened. One must be empowered for this; see the Karmapa's crown." He would say no more, but I felt I was coming close the heart of the matter. The bindu chakra is the primal point, the consciousness that exists beyond time, space, energy, matter, or form.

In Tibetan *Tummo* (heat yoga), the alchemical marriage (Yab-Yum,

Fig. 29.1.
Chakrabindu
symbol.

Fig. 29.2. The ninth Karmapa, Wangchuk Dorje.
Note the sun and moon in union (chakrabindu) at the
upper cranium in Karmapa's crown.

or Yin-Yang) occurs with a slight twist to the metaphors: the father-mother (Yab-Yum) may be the pineal and pituitary glands. When the secret fire of kundalini is brought into the central cavity of the skull, it is said that the pineal impregnates the pituitary with light, creating youth-producing hormones, an alchemical elixir. The White Drop then falls to meet the Red Drop, which is ascending from the heart, thus producing a body capable of containing the voltage of enlightened consciousness. Intense preparation and purification for this is required.

I was sent elsewhere in the valley for initiations into Dream Yoga (*svapnadarśanayoga* in Sanskrit, *milam* in Tibetan) and Tummo, among other practices. Tummo came at the right time, as temperatures were dropping steadily. The male vital essence must be preserved in Tummo; semen retention is critical to keeping the heat (for men). This is an Indian tantric practice much older than the Tibetan preparation practices and also remarkably similar to the practice of the higher Kriyas of Sri Yukteswar (I would later learn). Tibetan *tögal* (*thod rgal*), or sky staring meditation may also be related to the older kundalini practice of *shambhavi mudra*. This can lead to spontaneous realization (*trekchö*, Tibetan: *khregs chod*), or the dissolution of solidity. Tummo is performed to accelerate one's evolution toward Enlightenment, to increase one's capacity to contain cosmic consciousness. Though the sequence is altered in Tummo to produce more heat, it is very similar to the initial stages of the Kriya Yoga of Karar Ashram. So similar, in fact, Evans-Wentz chose to place a photo of Sri Yukteswar at the front of his 1935 book, *The Tibetan Book of the Great Liberation*. Fortunately, Kriya has a different sequence of movements through the nadis (spiritual energy channels) for kundalini activation so less heat is produced—much more suitable for the hot plains of India. Tummo seemed more and more like Kriya Yoga each day.

Though I heard about the Bardo Retreat, I did not have the opportunity to practice it. This is a long and intense series of meditations in complete darkness, whereby one learns to navigate the Bardo, the in-between states as described in The Tibetan Book of the Dead (Bardo Thodol). The darkness is said to enliven and awaken the pineal gland. Navigating the Bardo states after death is said to occur over a maximum of forty-nine days, and if unsuccessful in "holding the Luminosity" one is drawn to take birth again. When I reviewed my journey back through the Bardo with Shamarpa again, he only said that a Bardo Retreat was unnecessary for me at this time, as I had already been initiated into it through the *backward* Bardo journey of my college days. I inwardly recalled that Swami Hariharananda Giri, the Kriya master, had gone into isolation for nearly a year before his enlightenment.

Only in 1986 was the first outsider allowed to formally photograph the Lukhang Secret Palace of the fifth Dalai Lama, where Indian yogic secrets, much older than most Tibetan practices, are contained in fantastic wall murals, never seen publicly. These were considered so secret and so advanced that only the Dalai Lamas alone were allowed to enter the inner room. Many of the positions are remarkably similar to those in Kriya Yoga.

*Phowa* is the ability of a lama or even a layman to fully consciously exit the top of the head at or near the time of death. I learned about this but did not take initiation into it at this time. Kriya Yoga has a similar practice, that is, to merge with the *All That Is*, but this is done only gently, as preparation for a final departure. Phowa on the other hand is rather proactive, resulting even in physical (pin) holes at the top of the head. If not practiced carefully, it could result in a premature departure from one's "precious human birth." Kriya Yoga seems safer. Yogananda called this process *mahasamadhi*, or conscious excarnation, that is, choosing to leave this world while fully in the samadhi of God-consciousness. This may be similar to concepts of ascension, or perhaps how the prophets Enoch and Elijah were "taken by God."

Tibetan guru yoga is essentially merging one's consciousness with a spiritual lineage, and the same as merging with the Kriya lineage, or in another case, a transcendent spirit lineage in the shamanism I would learn and study a decade later. The ancient practice of *Chöd* was ahead of me, and yet after a bit of reading I realized this also is a classic shamanic initiation from central Asia (though performed differently) and had rather little to do with the original Buddhism of Siddartha Gautama. Clearly, the roots of Vajrayana, *the lightning or diamond*

Figs. 29.3 and 29.4. Yogic postures on the North Wall of the Lukhang Palace.
Personal photos courtesy of Ian Baker, co-author of *The Dalai Lama's
Secret Temple*, with photographs by Thomas Laird (2000)

*vehicle*, may be the marriage of an ancient shamanism and Hindu yogic
Tantrism, with Buddhist philosophy only painted over the top—an
extraordinary combination for spiritual liberation.

I make no claims to be a scholar of, nor an expert practitioner of Tibetan Buddhism. I was a novice, though moving quickly. In a casual meeting over butter tea with Shamarpa and some other lamas I asked about the similarity between Tibetan Tummo and Kriya Yoga. They briefly acknowledged that the esoteric Buddhism now in Tibet had originated from Indian tantric mahasiddhas (yogis with great spiritual powers) and Sanskrit texts, so that there must be some overlap. But the conversation soon shifted to how degraded Hinduism is, and how "greedy, filthy, and useless Indians are." I was stunned at the lack of respect and compassion, especially for the spiritual forefathers of Indo-Tibetan Buddhism.

On another butter-tea afternoon with a group of lamas, looking out over the valley from the rooftop of the upper monastery, I mentioned that I had met a Hindu kundalini master of the highest order, and that he was outstanding in character and had reached the most profound levels of yogic cosmic consciousness, nirvikalpa samadhi. Shamarpa translated to Tibetan for the other lamas and my words were met with scoffs, shaking heads, and downturned waves of the hand. Laughter and derogatory comments about Hindus again continued round the circle in Tibetan and I fell silent. Shamarpa turned to me, and with some perturbance as I recall, said in English, "Those Hindu babas may have a few spiritual powers, but we Tibetans have the wisdom now. Don't be distracted by Hindu fakirs and cheats." Other lamas then mumbled rough grunts about their meat, *rakshi* (Nepalese vodka), *chhang* (Himalayan beer), their political intrigues, and mistresses, while ordering about the servant monks as though they were slaves. I suddenly felt distinctly uncomfortable with Lamaism. Its narrow ethnocentricity and priestly hierarchies increasingly reminded me of the Vatican and its *inconsistencies.*

# 30

# Inward Spiral

*The attainment of enlightenment from the ego's point of
view . . . is the ultimate and final disappointment.*

CHOGYAM TRUNGPA RINPOCHE,
*THE MYTH OF FREEDOM*

As further texts were stacked in my increasingly crowded room,
the immense complexity of the Tibetan mystery school struck
home. I was flattered, rather *buttered*, so to speak, by promotions and
praise, but something felt increasingly off-kilter. I knew the tradition
to be real and grand in every way, but wondered now if it wasn't my
spiritual materialism that had hold of me, more than the lineage itself.
Hariharandanda, like a Zeus with thunderbolts, had been relentlessly
honest with me, pointing out my faults and egoic wishes with ruthless
efficiency. *Have I been seduced by the powers in the Tibetan magical system?* Suddenly my hidden intentions became apparent, and I felt sickened
by my own hypocrisy—the very term Baba had used. Now that I knew
many of the advanced initiations in the Tibetan tradition were identical
or at least similar to not only Kriya Yoga but shamanic traditions as well,
I pondered my stay. I discovered more about the Shamarpa lineage as well.
The previous Shamarpa incarnations had a reputation for being

rebels. About 200 years ago a conflict occurred between the Gelugpa-controlled Tibetan government and the Karma Kagyu School resulting in the tenth Shamarpa being exiled from Tibet and all future official recognitions of the Shamarpa incarnations banned. Subsequent Shamarpas were recognized in secret and protected by the ensuing Karmapas. The official ban of the Shamarpas was lifted when the fourteenth Shamar Rinpoche was formally recognized and enthroned in 1963 by the sixteenth Karmapa at Rumtek Monastery in Sikkim. The sixteenth Gyalwa Karmapa then invited all the dignitaries of Sikkim to the enthronement and publicly proclaimed Shamarpa as a spiritual head of the Kagyu lineage, second only to himself.

Awakening one cool morning at 3 a.m. highly agitated, I decided to sit in meditation until my inner conflict could be resolved. Hours of spiraling inward led to the sunrise of a new day with the realization that I can overlook the imperfections in human teachers, to become the *Dharmakaya* and know the *Dharmadhatu*, the universal, spacious, enlightened intelligence that speaks and acts as a force of its own through adepts of all esoteric traditions. The impersonal All-Pervading Awareness that I had touched so briefly in childhood now came to rest in my heart.

Oddly enough, this felt completely natural, not something special. There was no longer a desire nor an aversion to living life as a lama—I only knew that it wasn't necessary for me. The arrival of a dream gave confirmation: Hariharananda and a young blue Krishna appeared, both with huge, luminescent eyes. Smiling, they ask me in vocal unison, "Why are you still bothering with an ego? We don't need one." I awoke from this with a deep feeling of completion and gratitude. I would return to the practice of Kriya Yoga, a direct alchemical path to nirvikalpa samadhi, as a householder, a participant in the world.

With a deep bow, I informed Shamarpa that morning that I wasn't ready to become a lama, and that I would return to work in Taiwan. Perturbed, he fiddled with a *dorje* with notable disappointment. Then he looked out toward the rising white clouds and blue sky, smiled, and turned back to me with a gentle compassion. "Perhaps then, we'll meet at my home monastery *in a different kind of time.*" I wasn't sure what he meant, but I assumed he was referring to Rumtek Monastery in Sikkim. His last words later proved to be prophetic in an unexpected way.

A few years later Shamarpa became embroiled in an open clash with other Tibetan leaders over the discovery and confirmation of the reborn Karmapa tulku. Pitched battles between monks of different factions, including some non-Tibetan monks, were reported. I read the newspapers detailing it all and leaned back with a sigh. My precognitive dream of the "punk monk" battles came to memory. *Seems I left at the right time. I might have been one of those fighting monks.* Divisions in the Kagyu sect remain up to this day, and there are now two Karmapas—possibly both *emanations* of the original. This is a most curious phenomenon recognized in Tibet and little understood, though the older Hindu concept of *vasanic* emanation is undoubtedly the origin.

A decade after I last saw Shamarpa, he appeared in a dream of brilliant, rainbow lucidity, though older, heavier, and with graying hair. He warmly greets me with a smile and open arms and I prostrate my respect. I have never been to Sikkim, but there in the dream is the Rumtek Monastery in full detail, immense and powerful, just like a painted mandala or *thanka*, only with no brushstrokes—an *ideal realm.* We beam happy recollections back and forth to each other without the movement of lips. "You see, this is my home monastery, in this world." When I awoke, I recalled his last words to me in physical form, that perhaps we would meet *in a different kind of time.* As the Tibetans like to say, spiritual connections (*tendrel*) made in good faith are never forsaken or broken.

In year 2000 I returned to Nepal to be initiated into Tamang shamanism, but Shamarpa was in retreat at the time. When I returned again for further shamanic research, initiations, and training in 2014, I learned that Shamarpa's *Parinirvana* (conscious entry into Nirvana after death) had just occurred in Germany, a few miles from Strasbourg in France, shortly before my arrival in Nepal. Having died in Europe I wondered if he might be reborn there, as Karmapas and Shamarpas also often take rebirth within each other's families. I ponder still now

Fig. 30.1. Shamarpa photos and the author
at Swayambhu Monastery, Nepal, 2014.
Photo taken by a bystander

whether I might meet his next incarnation—*he in the new body of a child, and I the elder with a white beard?** I never carried a camera in my early Nepalese journeys, as I felt it an unnecessary distraction from the spiritual quest, but in late 2014 this photo above was taken in the altar room of Shamar Rinpoche's monastery at Swayambhunath.

---

*In February 2020, the two Karmapa tulkus, Ogyen Trinley Dorje and Trinley Thaye Dorje, issued a joint statemen that they will work together to recognize the reincarnation of the Shamar Rinpoche.

A few months after I left Kathmandu, the Great Earthquake of Nepal violently shook the valley in April of 2015. Shamarpa's monastery atop Swayambhunath was badly damaged. I returned yet again in 2019 to further my shamanic research and found only ruins of the building. A mandala of synlocality, spiraling inward to the self-arisen *Swayambhu* center, was now complete.

# 31

# Taoist Alchemy

*The immortal breath is hidden in the original cavity
of spirit.
Worldly men who discover this are very rare indeed.*

MASTER CHAO PI CH'EN, FROM *TAOIST YOGA:*
*ALCHEMY AND IMMORTALITY*
BY LU K'UAN YU

At the sprawling Pilgrim's Bookstore in Kathmandu, I spent my last Nepalese rupees procuring two books, Gopi Krishna's *Kundalini: The Evolutionary Energy in Man*, and Goel's *Third Eye and Kundalini*. Here the authors Krishna and Goel lay out the fascinating kundalini process. I devoured portions of the two texts in nonstop reading sessions on my way from Kathmandu to Taiwan. A deep, psychophysiological and alchemical kundalini process had occurred in these two men to an extreme degree. In alchemy, this is known as the *dry* way. This had activated for me three times and each time the process had shut down due to its severity, until I was initiated into the Kriya Yoga of Sri Yukteswar. What little I knew of Taoist alchemy so far indicated an East Asian *wet* way, also a universal alchemical tradition. I would find further clues in Taiwan, a home of living Taoism.

Arriving in Taipei nearly penniless again, I vowed to engage Chinese language and culture in a way I had not before. I immediately spoke my limited Mandarin at every turn, and within a week I had reconnected with old friends, had work, a flat, a telephone, and a motorcycle. More importantly, I met Master Lee, teacher of *TaiJiChuan* (Tai Chi) and *Chi Gong*. Master Lee had been a national Tai Chi Pushing Hands (*tuī shŏu*) champion in his younger days. He was now retired and had a home outside the city, but enjoyed coming downtown to an alley where he owned an old storage shanty in which he taught small groups of students, including some foreigners. He spoke Mandarin, Taiwanese, and perhaps other dialects, but no English. He had been schooled in Japanese due the annexation of Taiwan before the war, so we started our friendship in that language, later switching to Mandarin.

For weeks Master Lee had me do deep diaphragmatic breathing and forward bending exercises, so similar to Kriya Yoga, which considers both breath control and bowing to stretch the spine of paramount importance. Through him, I often felt as though Hariharananda was working again to stretch and open my shushumna. I asked for the first Tai Chi movements, but Lee insisted I wasn't yet ready. I continued on with the tedious preliminary exercises for a full two months, until one day a great rush of power came up my spine, flushing my face red and producing a great heat. A wide smile broke across Lee's face. "*Sore da! Kore de yatto hajimerareru*" (Yes, that's it! From here we can start). The inner power and grace had been activated, and with his guidance my body was now effortlessly drawn into the new Tai Chi movements.

Weeks later, while enjoying a tea break with Master Lee, I brought up my practice of Kriya Yoga with him. He listened, nodded, and had only one word to say: *Neidan*. With my dictionary, I found this meant "inner alchemy." A week later I procured a copy of *The Secret of the Golden Flower* in English and showed it to him. He raised a finger, stood, and rummaged through his many piles of indiscernible items strewn about his storage hovel. "Your book's good, but this one is better," he said, handing me a tattered 1970 edition of *Taoist Yoga: Alchemy and Immortality* by Lu K'uan Yu in English. This was 1989, well before the many Taoist alchemy translations now available. I hungrily pored over the text and discovered time and again, very similar practices to that of the Kriya Yoga I learned in Sri Yukteswar's ashram in Orissa, as well as similarities with Tummo, the heat kundalini yoga of Tibet. The Taoist microcosmic orbit is identical to the initial stages of Kriya Yoga, circulating the *chi* (*prana*) up the chakras along the spine and down the chakras at the front of the body. Master Lee also confirmed that the practice of Taoist alchemy leads to the breathless, pulseless state (immortality), as does the advanced stages of Kriya Yoga of Yogananda and Hariharananda. Lu translates Taoist master Chao Pi Ch'en thus:

> Lao Tsu called [the spot at the center of the brain, the *tsu ch'iao* cavity] "the gateway to heaven and earth"; hence he urged people to concentrate on the centre in order to realise the oneness (of all things). In this centre is a pearl of the size of a grain of rice, which is the centre between heaven and earth in the human body (i.e., the microcosm); it is the cavity of prenatal vitality. . . . He who knows this cavity can prepare the elixir of immortality. Hence it is said: "When the One is attained, all problems are solved."[1]

This "pearl the size of a grain of rice" was surely the pineal gland, so important in the practice of all advanced yogas. The pineal rests at the center of the brain in the hermetically sealed third ventricle, or Cave of Brahma, also known to Lu as the tsu ch'iao cavity, the Heavenly Heart (higher heart in the head), or the Crystal Cave in other Taoist texts. Lu also writes of the Immortal Breath, or breathless, pulseless state, which is only found when one fixes the attention at the center of the original cavity (tsu ch'iao, or center of the brain):

> Worldly men who discover the original cavity of spirit are very rare indeed . . . during the training both eyes should turn inward to the center (between and behind them) in order to hold on to this One which should be held in the original cavity of spirit (tsu ch'iao) with neither strain nor relaxation; this is called fixing spirit in the

original cavity which should be where (essential) nature is cultivated
and the root from which (eternal) life emerges.[2]

"Fixing spirit in the original cavity" clearly stood out for me. *This
was surely key, but how?* I learned more about Chinese alchemy: *Shen*
is the original spirit, and Taoists become conscious of shen through
meditation. *Jing* or "essence" refers to the (sexual) energies of the physical body. Based upon the idea that death was caused by depleting one's
jing, Daoist internal alchemy claims that preserving jing allows one to
achieve longevity, if not immortality. The world of Chinese alchemy
and mysticism is a large one indeed, a complete path unto itself, and its
secrets are closely guarded.

Balance in all things is a key concept in Chinese thought, exem-
plifying the Yin-Yang duality in life. While thoroughly monkish in
India, I found Taiwan to be an energizing flow of feminine-masculine
energies. Ying Yue and I met when I had previously lived in Taipei.
My letters from India and Nepal had kept our connection, and upon
my return we became steadies. Her natural brilliance had graduated
her with honors from one of Taiwan's top universities. Sadly, she was
rigidly opposed to spirituality. Science held all the answers she sought,
and her intellectually flawless arguments in fluent English ground my
spiritual conceptions to dust. However, for her no rationale of any kind
applied to sensuality, and this left me enjoyably exhausted to the bone
each morning. I took on more work for more income, slept more, ate
more, meditated less, and skipped Tai Chi training often.

I returned to Master Lee in a state of exhaustion, and he asked me
about my love life. I cheerfully admitted that my girlfriend was *exceptionally dynamic.* He only shook his head, and mumbled something I couldn't
understand. He then told me to reread the parts of Luk's book about con-
serving the *jing li.* A young male brimming with testosterone believes this
to be inexhaustible, but this soon gives way to spiritual exhaustion. The
female on the other hand, only loses her vital essence during menstruation
and childbirth, not during sexual activity. It is a fundamental difference in
the genders. Master Lee could already detect the signs of jing li depletion

in my eyes at just twenty-eight years old. I set to studying how to sublimate this power inward and upward. I was sure Kriya master Hariharananda was doing something similar, though in conservative India they rarely spoke openly about such matters. Lu writes in *Taoist Alchemy*:

> Preparing the Elixir of Immortality: The deficiency of the immortal seed can be remedied by the use of slow and quick fires (from regulating the breathing) so that the genital organ will draw in, the inner light will manifest before the eyes, the dragon's hum and tiger's roar will be heard in the ears, and the heart (the house of nature) will be luminous. When the practiser is aware of the maturity of the immortal seed, he should stop the fire (by no longer regulating the breathing) to gather the macrocosmic alchemical agent for the final breakthrough (i.e., forcing open the original cavity of spirit between and behind the eyes, which will emit the precious light). . . . The above are the four stages of serenity, the sequence of which is: (a) thoughtlessness (*nien chu*), (b) breathlessness (*hsi chu*), (c) pulselessness (*mo chu*) and (d) extinction (unmindfulness) of worldly existence (*mich chin*).[3]

Though I was eventually able to sublimate and transform this power, moving it up my spine (instead of out of my loins), the vibratory disharmony between Ying Yue and myself was rendered more clearly over time. Her busy, hungry mind drew her to scientific studies in chemistry. The divide between my inner alchemy and her outer chemistry widened. She and I were both actively seeking the *Stone*, yet in very different ways—she in the psychopharmaceutical aspect, and I in a psychophysiological alchemy. We sadly parted and Ying Yue left Taiwan to complete a doctorate in biochemistry in a German province historically known for seeking alchemical transformation centuries ago. I recalled the Dancing Incarnationers and marveled at the ties back to Central Europe: *It is all a Great Game whose completion and secret exit lies hidden behind our eyes.* "The Stone of the Philosophers is everywhere and yet hidden from the uninitiated."

Lonely and adrift without Ying Yue to ground me, I was nevertheless free to soul direct my life again. I returned to Chinese language
studies and my practice of Tai Chi, Chi Gong, and Kriya Yoga. Though
far from fluent I started to dream in Mandarin, my first foreign dream
language. I took up the study of the I Ching, the famous Chinese book
of divination, and learned how to toss the coins to discover what I
needed to know about life situations. Though I sometimes misinter-
pret, in retrospect I've never known a poor response, and I still make
use of it now.

Every culture, it is said, has a particular astral vibratory realm that
lives as a reflection of earthly life (and vice versa), but I did not understand this until I met a living connection. I lived in Gongguan, an old
neighborhood near Taiwan University. One afternoon, I came down-
stairs to collect my mail from the row of boxes on the ground floor of
my old apartment building and noticed a very elderly man of inestima-
ble age in traditional Chinese clothes, also there to gather his mail. His
spine was ramrod straight; he turned toward me, and as we met eyes I
became unable to move or breathe. I disappeared into his eyes, falling
into a merging of minds and memories. In those seconds I seemed to
enter a China of centuries ago. That evening I soared through Chinese
astral planes, and I understood that each culture and epoch has such
twin astral spheres, accessible to sensitives. In the astral realm, like
attracts like, and I felt I had been vibrationally invited.

After extended practice of Tai Chi, the inner fire of kundalini was
again activated. Unlike Gopi Krishna who feared madness throughout
his ordeal, I knew in my heart of hearts what was happening. Though
ignorant of the precise twists and turns of the path, liberation seemed
at hand. However, I could not have predicted the intense feelings of
psychic isolation and imminent death of the small self, stepping aside to
allow spirit full expression and embodiment in the Earth plane. Gopi
Krishna writes:

The awakening of Kundalini is the greatest enterprise and the most
wonderful achievement in front of man. . . . It provides the only

method available to science to establish empirically the existence of life as an immortal, all-intelligent power behind the organic phenomena on earth, and brings within its scope the possibility of planned cultivation of genius in individuals not gifted with it from birth, thereby unfolding before the mental eye of man avenues and channels for the acceleration of progress and enhancement of prosperity which it is impossible to visualize at present.[4]

I returned to Kriya practice and the hidden fire was cooled, channeled into a calmer evolutionary drive. Simultaneously an increasing workload began to take a toll on my practice of both Kriya and Tai Chi. I had university loans still to pay, and this fact slowed and stabilized the process. Burdened by debt yet also wishing to return to India, my soul cried out for guidance. That night I dreamt:

*Walking through a small Indian village, I'm seeking Hariharananda. Slowly the village transforms into a Dutch suburb where I spot a small, white house. I knock on the door and Baba answers. I can only gasp in astonishment, "Hariharanandaji!" He smiles, greets me, and invites me in and I sit with a gathering of other disciples all in white. I ask him what I should do next, and he says, "Get some milk—a large amount of milk." Puzzled, I depart to search and soon find myself in a Taiwanese market where I spot a great metal canister of milk. I smile and awaken.*

I understood, *the abundance of work in Taiwan is the perfect cash cow I need to be free of debt!* Oddly enough, a week or two later I received a postcard from a friend in Europe, informing me that Baba had visited Holland recently. This confirmed the potency of the dream for me. As Sri Yukteswar often advised that one should never go into debt, I soon procured a full-time job working for a large agency representing several offline airlines. Even this wasn't enough to pay off my university loans, so I also took on a half-time position teaching at a local college. For a full year I worked ten hours a day, six days a week, slept on Sundays, and at the end of it wrote a single check to pay off the entirety of my university debt. I was now free, and have never entered debt again.

Shortly before I left Taiwan I came upon a local shaman in Tainan, an older city in southern Taiwan. He was shaking and vibrating, thrashing about while merged with his spirits, performing healing and divination. He climbed a ladder of knives, and then hung upside down. He descended and appeared to be removing invisible intrusions from his clients. I was spellbound and knew that I was witnessing something profound. Steeped in the silent inner meditations of Hindu and Buddhist traditions I was blind to shamanism at this time, but inwardly I noted: *There is far more here than meets the eye.*

I hadn't achieved high proficiency in Tai Chi practice, nor was I adept in Taoist alchemy, but I had found more pieces of a universal alchemical puzzle spanning centuries, cultures, and continents. A mysterious restlessness drove me to sell off everything I owned in Taiwan. I packed up for adventure in Southeast Asia. I would return to the Kriya master in India, but first I would seek out a new working base in Indonesia. Before departure, I read and put to memory an alchemical spell from *The Secret of the Golden Flower*:

> *In the water blows the wind of the Gentle.*
> *Wandering in heaven, one eats the spirit-energy of the*
>    *Receptive.*
> *And the still deeper secret of the secret:*
> *The land that is nowhere, that is the true home . . .*[5]

# 32

# Bali to Java

B ali, *the Island of the Gods*. No dancing goddesses met me at the airport, nor at Kuta Beach where I quickly left the drunken tourists to themselves. A month-long solo journey by scooter around the island would be my introduction to Bali. Milton wrote, "Solitude sometimes is best society." As idyllic as Bali still was in 1990, Milton was right about another thing—paradise had been lost. The island sanctuary has been a tourist destination for over a century, and it shows. However, a unique shamanic Hindu mysticism still invisibly permeates the culture, the people, indeed the very land. All of Indonesia had once been shamanistic, then Hindu-Buddhist, but the rise of Islam among the merchant class pushed what we call Hindu-Balinese culture from Java to the smaller island resting to the east about 400 years ago. Bali is now the *Island of the Spirits*, and indeed the atmosphere here is the most spiritually dense I know outside the Indian subcontinent.

Riding my scooter from village to mountain village, I stayed in small lodges (*losmen*), and in family homes when there were no losmen to be found. In the evenings I often followed gamelan music wafting over the rice terraces, through the jungle to find spirit-embodiment dances in forests where I was the only foreigner. I knew then I was in the presence of genuine spiritual power, called *Taksu* in Balinese, an authentic form of shamanism wrapped in Balinese Hinduism. Twenty-five years later

I would base myself here and teach a universal shamanism to sincere seekers.

One evening I returned from such a séance-dance of spirits to my bamboo hut, and slept early, only to be roused by the inner siren. I again plummet into the center of my head with a collapse like the sound of that heavy rain, then a rumbling train. Once I'm away from my body it is nearly pure silence. I hover over the Balinese treetops, gazing over distant lights and tiny fires. Then, just as they see me, I see them. Mischievous spirits of varying sizes and types, hiding in the palm tree tops, glaring at me with wild eyes! They are as curious about me as I am stunned by them. Some have the classic Balinese *leyak* appearance, and in retrospect, these are the shamanic definition of Middle-World spirits, neither good nor evil; only they have their own agenda and it isn't all-compassionate. As they look me over, perhaps pondering how I could be made use of for their own ends, I soar upward over Bali Island and away over distant waters.

A month is hardly even a start on coming to know or understand Bali, but one thing I knew for sure—Indonesia would become my new home. A short flight landed me in the wondrous old city of Jogyakarta, the ancient capital of Java. After seeing a few major sites in central Java, I planted myself in *Jogya* and threw myself fully into the study of Indonesian language, with four hours of private lessons every day and another four hours of homework each night. I raced through two thick textbooks at lightning speed and spoke only Indonesian at every opportunity.

Money is an energy that belongs to no one, and as with everything, follows the path of impermanence. After a month of study, I needed more cash flow in my direction and, like so many Indonesians, I made my way to the capital to seek my fortune. Jakarta is one of the great cities of Southeast Asia, and the sheer size and breadth of it stunned me. After a number of inquiries at Indonesian universities it became apparent that I simply would not be able to survive on an Indonesian salary, which averaged about $32 per month at this time.

"Go to the Universitas Pendidikan Ekonomi–they are funded by the government, an Indonesian bank, and a foreign university," advised a professor at the Universitas Indonesia. As luck would have it a foreign professor had just departed for an emergency return to his country in the middle of a large project that prepared government ministers for graduate university work in New York. They couldn't believe my sudden fortuitous drop out of thin air. With a master's degree in linguistics and university teaching experience in Taiwan, I was immediately hired. The salary was average by Western standards, but it was a small fortune in Indonesian currency at the time. I breathed a sigh of monetary relief. *Now I have only to find a home. Something humble, perhaps in the Javanese neighborhoods, so that I can save money and mix in with the locals.* I was then informed, "Oh, your house is being prepared. We'll take you there in a few days." *My house?*

My mouth hung open as we drove through the gate, opened courtesy of *my* guard. I was introduced to *my* maids, *my* pool cleaning man, *my* gardener, and *my* car and its driver—his broad smile displayed missing teeth. One of the largest banks in Indonesia supported the special research program, in cooperation with the Indonesian government and an American university. The bank had repossessed the house from a fallen millionaire but was prevented from selling it due to a court case that looked never to be resolved. So it was, for the duration of my work, my new home. I had nothing but a backpack, some raggedy clothes, and a pair of sandals. The first thing I had to do was look the part. Tailors soon supplied all the accoutrements of success, and my house staff breathed a sigh of relief that I already spoke conversational Indonesian. My living room, devoid of any furniture, was so large that I played tennis against the wall with room to spare. My private swimming pool, surrounded by a high wall, was a deep blue. A single coconut palm leaning over the water often left me a floating morning delicacy. The carpeted master bedroom was the only furnished room, and included a huge desk set back against rear windows and an enormous bed set before six sliding glass doors facing the pool. *A king's palace, indeed.*

In time I was introduced to the expatriate community, most of whom also had ex-pat packages with large houses, servants, and private swimming pools. Stepping into the first of their many parties I thought, *Surely this must be as close to the paradise of the gods as can be reached here on earth.* Lavish food, cocktails, and Javanese beauties blanketed the grounds. I was now in the club of neo-colonialists. As I had the money and palace of a god, *perhaps I might just be one too?* Equatorial sunshine blesses Java each day, and the temperature rarely wavers. After morning swims, my maid served me breakfast. I'd find the shirts that I'd carelessly tossed on the floor the night before, starched and pressed in my closet. With a wave of my hand, my waiting driver would appear with the car. My colonial inflation and feigned godhood worked so well I almost came to believe it myself.

Until an encounter with the invisible sorcery rife in Indonesia. Along with the boons of shamanic healing and divination, sorcery remains a part of Javanese life and the *dukun* make money on producing real results, for healing or for harm. I befriended the daughter of a wealthy Chinese Indonesian industrialist, and when I brought up the topic of Indian spirituality she asked for advice. Her father was ill. No doctors could diagnose his affliction, no treatment alleviated his pain. After his health deteriorated further, cursed items had been found, carefully placed and hidden in the house; he appeared to be a victim of sorcery. While in India I had heard that a Sathya Sai Baba was the most powerful healer on the planet at this time, and so I suggested she might go see him. She flew to India immediately and told me her story when she returned to Jakarta. "When I arrived, Sai Baba already knew my father's situation; he simply said to me, 'Your father is now healed.' Shortly later, I telephoned my father in Jakarta and discovered most of his symptoms had disappeared. By the time I returned to Jakarta he was completely healed!" Stunned that a spiritual master could perform a healing of such astonishing power across time and space by the mere flick of a thought, my palace, money, and lavish lifestyle suddenly felt empty compared to such a compassionate feat.

Nevertheless, at my greatly advanced age of twenty-nine, Java had me charmed. Only five months after my arrival in Jakarta, I delivered a tall stack of postcards to the postman, embossed with my home address, proudly announcing to everyone I knew worldwide that I would be spending the rest of my life on Java. I was even considering a white linen suit with a Sumatran king parrot atop my shoulder. But it was not to last. My palatial cage, no matter how gilded, grew increasingly oppressive. I had every interest in learning to speak fluent Indonesian but little in preparing government ministers for their doctoral dissertations. I was meditating less and partying more. As life would have it, Providence stepped in.

Weeks later, one early morning, like a kindly king I grandly waved off an offer by my maid to fetch the morning newspaper. I leisurely strolled out in my silk robe under the brilliant sunlight, past my pool to my fortified gate to retrieve my Jakarta Post newspaper. My driver sat up at attention, and my guard saluted. Unfurling the newsprint, I confronted a headline consisting of only three gigantic words in bold: BANK DUTA SCANDAL! Half a billion dollars had gone missing. Within a month of reading that headline, my Javanese palace was gone, and with it my job, the money, and my fair-weather, neo-colonialist friends. I was again on the road with a backpack, a pair of sandals, and money to last only half a year at best. Gold and pleasure palaces—*easy come, easy go.*

As much as I loved Indonesia, I took the opportunity to explore. I made my way up from Singapore through the Malaysian peninsula to Kuala Lumpur where I played mah-jong in the streets of the old Chinatown, enjoying claypot chicken and other delicacies. Then I boarded a flight for Ho Chi Minh City, and soon found myself with a job offer at the Open University in Saigon, but no work permit. "You can't process a work visa here; you must apply from outside Vietnam." This disappointing news at the Immigration Office led me back to slump at the hotel lobby bar with a cold Saigon 333 beer. Ceiling fans kept the flies and the heat at bay, but not my depressive mood. A friendly Aussie sat down at the bar to join me. "Why the long face, mate?" I explained my visa situation to him. "The Vietnamese embassy in Phnom Penh is easily bribed," the Aussie expat assured me, also sipping a cold 333. "Don't mind the civil war in Cambodia—you'll be back here in no time, having another beer with me right here, your work visa in hand." The next day at the Cambodian Consulate, in the midst of a shouting, chaotic scrum, I slipped two U.S. twenty-dollar bills hidden in my palm to the staff and my passport received a large stamp with scribbling in Khmer—I had no idea what it read.

# 33

# Cambodian Ghost Battle

*To end the greatest work designed,*
*A thousand hands need but one mind.*

GOETHE, FAUST, PART 2

From the plane window I gaze in shock—Cambodia is fully in civil war and the airport is a military garrison. Armed soldiers and military vehicles cover the area to secure arrivals. After sitting already too long inside the steamy plane, armed men entered and instructed us to deplane one at a time. We stood on the hot tarmac surrounded by guns until everyone was off. An officer looked us up and down, mumbling while a soldier next to him made notes of his comments. Perhaps the only Westerner onboard the flight, I'm the first to be waved to a battered, wooden desk in a hangar just off the mortar-shelled tarmac.

The lone immigration officer looked over my passport with a frown. "Your visa shows no sponsor—you cannot enter Cambodia. You must leave on the next flight!" Just as I took a breath to speak, a boisterous group of heavily armed men burst into the hangar and began to shout at us all, including the desk officer who looked in their direction with notable anxiety. While he shouted back at them in Khmer, without thinking I slid my passport off the desk, turned, and slipped through the gate, smiling and nodding casually to guards outside. I found my bag on an open cart, flung it over my shoulder, and strode out of the airport with absolute confidence, never looking back. Outside I hailed a ramshackle cab held together by wire and duct tape and flopped in the back in disbelief at what I'd just done. Half the back-seat floor was missing from either rust or roadside bombs, so I had to spread my legs apart to brace myself against falling through to the road. In this way we rattled and hobbled our way into Phnom Penh to one of only two hotels still operating. I was in.

A country at war can never be adequately described, only experienced. An all-pervading stress is embedded into the fabric of Cambodian time itself. I'm not a soldier, and have never experienced combat in this life, but I would come to know the surreal atmosphere firsthand. And here, I would learn an unexpected portion of afterlife knowledge as well. The nightmare of the Khmer Rouge years had resulted in the death of one-quarter of the entire population, and the continuing civil war between four different factions threatened the rest. I had read about the Pol Pot years, but nothing prepared me for the legacy of that nightmare. The situation at times seemed hopeless and all feared that the *Terreur Rouge* (Red Terror) might return from the forests in the west. Pol Pot still hid there, and he wanted Cambodia back.

At the Vietnamese Embassy the following day, officials refused any discussion of a business visa, and even refused me a transit visa back to Vietnam. Now I could neither stay, nor return to Vietnam. Dripping with sweat, nursing yet another warm beer in one of the few operating restaurants in the city, I dropped my head to the table in resignation, recalling the Kriya master's words, "Don't make too many plans."

"What's the problem?" in natural Mandarin came my way. My head lifted from its bow of surrender to too many beers and one visa too few. I hadn't heard such refined Chinese since I left Taiwan. I replied only that I couldn't get a proper visa. The *laoban* (proprietor) was from Beijing. He suggested, "Why don't you try the Norwegians? I hear they pay well." The next day I searched for the office of *Redd Barna* (Norwegian Save the Children), and they could scarcely believe the arrival of this gypsy linguist out of nowhere. I was immediately hired to oversee a UN advance translation project, and my work permit arrived a week later. I was in—and this time legally.

Cambodia, so cut off from the world, became my new home. Time here had come to a near standstill and those six months felt like six years. For both work and local menus, I quickly gained some basic French, which I learned only from Cambodians—this would later prove to be humorous in Europe. Russian and Cuban "diplomats" were everywhere in Phnom Penh, and they were most interested in the few Western aid workers. I was all too often met by the *overly friendly*, anxious to learn why I was there. In any case, all foreigners had to take armored personal carriers outside the city for safety from gunfire and mines. We were regularly frisked for arms at the two operating nightclubs; otherwise, the capital was usually calm.

After three months of work, I had a break and flew on a near-empty plane to western Cambodia to see the glory of Angkor Wat. The grand ruins of the capital of the Cambodian Kingdom, which ruled much of Southeast Asia for a century or two, is the largest religious structure in the world by land area. Two other Western aid workers and I walked the vast temple complex alone, except for our guide who informed us he was obligated by law to escort us due to the dangers. He advised us against stepping off the main trail. "Mines are everywhere, but the main paths are swept regularly."

We three were the only guests in the grand old French colonial hotel, now a faded glory and unpainted since better days. At night the sprawling hotel sat in near-total darkness, as power was so precious lights were kept on only in a small portion of one wing. At dinner late that evening under candlelight (only) we heard gunfire and mortar shells close by. With a subtle tremble and eyes that had seen too much, a young waiter leaned toward us, poured more tea, and whispered, "*Le Rouge.*"

Back in Phnom Penh, a French doctor invited me out to the provinces to visit his clinic. Dark circles under his eyes told me he needed help. He amputated at least three legs every day with or without anesthesia, due to the thousands of land mines planted all over the country by all sides of the conflict. I won't burden the reader with what one can imagine. Prosthetic devices were in short supply, lives were devastated, children were orphaned every day—and these were the easy days, compared to when Pol Pot and the Khmer Rouge had total control of the country, when torture and death were daily fare. I declined further trips outside Phnom Penh after a laughing soldier fired shots over my head just for fun. The capital was safer, but never truly safe. Fortunately, the largest UN election project in history would be getting under way before summer and everyone was hopeful for a positive outcome.

> *Now I understand what wise men see:*
> *The world of spirits is not closed.*
>
> GOETHE, *FAUST*, PART 1

Fig. 33.1. *Faust's Dream* (Walpurgis night's dream). Charcoal drawing by C. G. Carus, 1852.

The Realm of the Hungry Ghosts is part of Buddhist cosmology, but I was unsure of quite what this entailed. My spiritual education would continue. This night in the once-grand old French hotel where diplomats were held during the Khmer Rouge's initial takeover of the city, my eyes would open to these sad, tortured realms:

*Just after midnight, the pineal siren splitting my brain became the deep rumble of a freight train completing a coalescence into the center of my head, and out I popped, astrally standing in the middle of the old hotel room with its high ceiling and faded glory. Ahhh, free again! Hardly a moment had passed when blood-curdling screeches from above broke across my astral-aural perception! I gazed upward to find over a dozen half-desiccated astral corpses wearing shreds of rags that had once been military uniforms. They grinned at me with hellish malice. Screeching demonically, they rushed at me, contorting their faces into the most fearsome shapes and forms. I nearly shat my astral pants, so to speak.*

*Nothing brings one into the present moment like battle. Tai Chi forms learned in Taiwan began to move through me, as I motioned around the room. I looked slightly down so as not to face the hideous forms directly. Nothing can harm me—no fear, no fear, I told myself. I continued the Tai Chi forms around the room in my astral body, inwardly amused at the absurdity of it. My sublimation of fear did not send these lost souls away; rather it made them even angrier. They wanted to feed on the energy of terror, and I wasn't offering any snacks! Their hideous faces contorted into extremes of depravity and malice, and I nearly lost my cool. They rushed at me from every direction with shrill cries so terrifying I thought I might die of fright.*

*I then switched from forms to pushing hands, the way of Tai Chi competition. I send powerful beams of thought-intention energy out from my palms and push several of the hellish apparitions back and out of the room. I knew then that it was a battle of wills— of thought itself. My only enemy is fear. I shouted at them, "Be gone!" Now it's fun, as I shoot imaginal lasers out of my hands, they scamper away through the walls and windows, screeching and wailing.*

I returned to my cataleptic body, slowly reidentified with it, and got up to relieve my bladder. Just to further prove my fearlessness, I didn't even turn on the light, navigating my way to the toilet in near-total darkness, growling like a powerful animal. I returned to my bed and laid back down. Soon the siren came and I again sat up and out of my body. This night I would learn that positive intention set, invites positive experience:

*This time I'm not going to waste time with troublemakers—I will meditate! I sit at the end of my bed, and chuckle to myself at my novel idea and how easy it was to sit in full lotus outside my physical body. I picture one of my spiritual teachers above my head, and attempt to merge my consciousness with him. Then without warning I float up and over into the middle of the room and settle on the floor. Streams of light swirl into the room, coalescing into the form of an Indian yogi. His long white hair and face are known to me, but I was not a follower of Sri Aurobindo. I had seen his books but after a perusal they had seemed dry and I took no further interest. But his presence here now is powerful and full of light. He beams to me scenes of what looked like outer planets, possibly other dimensions. "Look! This world has been protected for long, but things are taking a turn. Do not lose a moment!" What does he mean? I didn't know, but the desperation in his voice led me to believe that spiritual progress may become more difficult in the years ahead, and that I should not waste time.*

Sri Aurobindo had not only been nominated for a Nobel Prize twice, he was also a yogi. A year after my time in Cambodia, I passed through Pondicherry, India, and visited his grave site. As discussed in previous chapters, master yogis are not burned in India, rather buried intact to preserve their enlightened vibration.* I meditated at the edge of his tomb and clearly communed with the same vibration that had entered in my room in Cambodia. Aurobindo's presence permeated the grounds. Masters do not die; their consciousness lives on.

> *Yesterday I wanted to know about the life of Sri Ramakrishna. I was meditating on my bed, and he materialized right beside me. We sat side by side, holding hands, for a long time . . . [and] in the interchange of vibration I got the whole picture.*
>
> PARAMAHANSA YOGANANDA,
> FROM *THE NEW PATH*, BY KRIYANANDA

As for Cambodian ghosts, I had learned of the hellish plane of suffering here in samsara, but I knew not yet how to help them move to transcendent worlds. Shamanic training in the country of my birth some years in the future would open further doors on the secrets of life and death. I also learned that astral journeys here in the confused realm (the shamanic Middle World) without intention can invite the presence of disembodied derelicts. Before sleep, we may be wise to set positive intentions.

The United Nations finally arrived in Cambodia to hold the first democratic elections in years, the largest such undertaking in UN history. Redd Barna offered me a new project position that would start in a month. I tentatively accepted, but needed a break and so made the long trip to America to attend a family wedding with the vague notion of returning to Cambodia after the month's holiday. After the relative deprivations in Cambodia, I wasn't prepared for the American gorgefest at the wedding, as well as the complete ignorance of geopolitical situations in the rest of the world. Though a joyous occasion, the contrast between such opulence in the United States and the poverty/terror

---

*An account of Sri Aurobindo's burial, "Sri Aurobindo's Last Darshan," by Rhoda P. LeCocq, can be found at the website Collaboration.org.

in Cambodia left me numb and speechless. The rise of Pol Pot was the direct result of Nixon-Kissinger's illegal bombing of Cambodia, bombing on a scale only rarely seen after WWII. The U.S. military had simply hoped the Viet Cong would be standing under Cambodian trees. At the nuptial fest no one seemed aware of how America so greatly affects the world, for better or worse. I turned thirty years old there, and feeling severely disoriented, I soon prepared to return to Asia.

A vague sense of obligation drew me to return to Cambodia, but I refrained from giving the Norwegians my return date. As my return flight had a stop in Japan, I would first visit a lovely couple I had known years before in Osaka, who had married and moved to Kyoto. On arrival in the ancient capital of Japan, I was charmed by the serene temples and gardens, especially after the heartbreaking catastrophe of Cambodia. My old friends and I laughed, ate lots of wonderful Japanese food, and I found myself once again taking an interest in Zen and the esoteric Buddhist sect *Shingon*. They lent me their scooter and I soon met an alternative artistic community in a Japan I had never known existed.

Pol Pot was still in the jungle vowing to return to Phnom Penh, but the UN elections were successful and Cambodia didn't need me. Offers to lecture at two universities in Kyoto settled the matter. I regularly sat for meditation at a temple in eastern Kyoto, and there made connections to rent a 150-year-old mud-and-straw house on Mt. Yoshida, a hill in the midst of the city upon which rested an ancient shrine and forest. My teetering birdcage of a house contained a white stone garden complete with bamboo and flowering tsubaki trees and a heated Japanese bath outdoors in the garden. The idyllic peace felt like another planet.

Weeks later a vision of a gossamer woman with long flowing hair in an ancient Heian-era kimono hovered over me one night, sadly trying to tell me something. As indicated in Cambodia and now in Kyoto, ghosts need help, not condemnation. I didn't yet know how to guide souls into transcendent realms. The call for shamanic training was now released into the ethers, sure to manifest in a few years' time.

# 34

# Kyoto

*Naturally a single truth surpasses ten thousand vanities.*

Eihei Dogen, Soto Zen master in Kyoto,
from Thomas Cleary's *Dogen Zenji Goroku:*
*Record of Sayings of Zen Master Dogen*

The damp Kyoto winter warmed into a flowering spring, and the Philosophers' Path (Japanese: *tetsugakunomichi*) and its accompanying canal is blanketed with tiny pink *sakura* (cherry blossom) leaves. My crumbling mud-and-straw-walled Japanese house backed into the forest of Mt. Yoshida, and closely behind this hill to the east lay the famed path, a two-mile meandering canal-side walk that passes a score of mountain temples. The path is named after the Kyoto philosopher Kitaro Nishida, who walked along this canal each day on his way to Kyoto University. Nishida's creative philosophy, merging both Zen and Western philosophies, aimed at bridging the East and West. Nishida founded the Kyoto School of Philosophy, and his daily walk was a key point in his meditations. I walked the path often, pondering the intentions that draw us all along our winding, individual paths.

April also brought new lecturing invitations from other universities, and I quickly fell in with the social life of the young and single intelligentsia. Dinners led to after-dinner parties, which led to even later parties into the wee hours. Now with money and a bit of academic prestige, one of Kyoto's most eligible bachelors moved into a larger home on the fashionable Kitayama Boulevard in the northern part of the city. Though also an older wooden house, it had a large living room, four bedrooms, and rested only a stone's throw from the Kamogawa River, lined with cherry trees on both banks. A car and a motorcycle joined my new home, and soon Saturday night dance parties rocked my home until Sunday sunrises. Kyoto became my playground, and like a child grasping at tinsel I fell into the trance of sensuality. If I meditated regularly, soul awareness kept afloat through the worldly maelstroms, but if not, I was pulled under and half-drowned in samsara, the illusory world. I was soon meditating less and socializing more. The spirits would shake me from my stupor with a powerful and humorous dream:

*Gazing over the Earth from a great blue light on the edge of space, I calmly watch holographic Earth eras spin and slide over and through each other in time. I am somehow an agent "Double-0-Something" and have been summoned by boss agent "M." A woman clearly bearing the likeness of actress Judi Dench appears and shrieks at me, "Stop fooling around down there on Earth, and get on with the mission!"*

*I could only nod my obeyance like a naughty and confused schoolboy. M then points to two television screens well above me that contained images of what was happening on Earth, flashing at high speed. "You've got to wake up and help us fight our enemies, or we'll have to send someone else to do it!" The velocity of the images is such that I can make no sense of them, so I simply think, "Slower" and the disturbing images decelerate. Then I inwardly ask for the meaning: one word appears over each screen, GREED on the first, and FEAR over the other. Jolted now into remembrance, duty calls! I brace up, and the dream fades.*

I awaken and know it's time to ease off the playtime parties. I must continue *the Project*, and my training. Naturally, I understood the dream to be metaphorical, not a literal command from the stars. I laughed, *A female M for the Bond films? No, that'll be the day.* Oddly enough, three years later, Dame Judi Dench did verily play the role of M in her first Bond film. I marvel still at the precognitive nature of the dream.

I set aside the smallest room in my new larger home solely for meditation and returned to regular sits. Time now became slippery, like oil atop the water, and precognitive perceptions became a daily life experience. Sadly, much of humanity felt so asleep that I descended into a lonely melancholy. *Why awaken when nearly everyone else is asleep?* The Kriya master's compassion, and his loneliness, struck my heart. While most of his students sleepwalk through their lives, he among the few stays awake. Such a Herculean heart is rare, and I felt small indeed.

When I learned Hariharananda would be visiting the Netherlands this coming summer for the opening of a new ashram by one his advanced disciples, I made my summer plans. After a fourteen-year absence, a return to Europe was overdue, and I looked forward to leaving Asia for my annual two-month summer holiday from the universities. I gave my exams, packed up, and the night before my flight I received a mysterious dream:

*A blue-skinned Krishna appears before me, but this time there are geometric coffers covering his entire bald, blue head, reminding me of angular golf ball dimples. I ask why his head looks this way, and he only smiles. He again pushes a mirror before me, and I perceive familiar images of old Europe flashing at high speed. . . .*

# 35

# Mirror of Souls II

*Mercury, the universal solvent . . . perfects the*
*[Philosophers'] Stone. Mercury is the alchemical*
*symbol for consciousness because the metal mercury,*
*quicksilver, is used to coat glass to make mirrors. The*
*mirror, in both Eastern and Western traditions, is*
*often used as a metaphor for the inherently pure and*
*transparent nature of mind, pure awareness, the light of*
*Primordial Consciousness. It is in the "mirror" of human*
*consciousness that God beholds God.*

THE TOWER OF ALCHEMY

Upon my arrival in Paris, I was immediately greeted with smirks and laughter. I thought it was only my poor French that drew the scorn and scoffs, until a young fellow working in a delicatessen laughed out loud and informed me that I had a severe *accent d'Indonchine.* For most French to hear a strong Khmer accent on their language from a tall, fair Caucasian is both absurd and possibly considered mocking, but of this I was completely unaware. Thoroughly embarrassed, I stopped speaking altogether for a while, and listened to Parisian French carefully.

Fig. 35.1. *Alchemists Revealing Secrets* from the *Book of Seven Seals.*
Detail from The Ripley Scroll, 1690.

*Follow the Footprints of Venus and Apollo*
*And you shall find the Rosicrucians.*

SAMUEL ROBINSON, "SECRET TEMPLES OF THE
ROSICRUCIANS," ROSICRUCIAN TRADITION WEBSITE

At the astounding Palace of Versailles outside Paris, I was greeted
at the gate by Venus holding a caduceus (fig. 35.2). The sphere at the
top of her winged staff or wand bears *the hidden alchemical gemstone*
*that everyone has but does not normally perceive.* The Hall of Mirrors
is especially striking, as these mirrors have reflected an especially large
number of historic events. I recalled my initiatory dream of the elderly
teacher with the head of light, and his alternative history of the world.
He would likely agree with Napoleon who stated on more than one
occasion that "History is a set of lies agreed upon."

Events held in such chambers often have a peculiar gravity about

Fig. 35.2. *Peace*, detail of Venus/Sophia with a caduceus at the gate of Versailles. Statue by Jean-Baptiste Tuby (1635–1700), after a drawing by Charles Le Brun (1619–1690).

them, as though *the eyes of the world are upon us here.* Events debated, decided, and announced in the Hall of Mirrors greatly affected Europe and the world at large—another example of the locational, psycho-gravitational force of which I have earlier written. Though this hall is no longer a seat of negotiations, decisions, and proclamations, it remains an important centerpoint of synlocality.

In the Hall of Mirrors, my mystagogue with the face of light reappeared only momentarily to my inner eye, silently pointing out to the gardens. The gardens, it is said by those few in the know, are of Rosicrucian design, accommodating a revival of an earlier Apollonian (sun deity) and Pythagorean mysticism. Louis the XIV was known as the Sun King (*le Roi Soleil*). This focus on the Apollonian solar logos

Fig. 35.3. *Christus-Apollo im Zentrum des Zodiakus,* Christ-Apollo at the center of the zodiac. Illuminated manuscript page by unknown artist. Italy, eleventh century.

Fig. 35.4. Illustration of Venus/Sophia leading an initiate over delusion to the truth, in *Freymäurerische Versammlungsreden der Gold- und Rosenkreutzer des alten Systems,* from the Amsterdam branch of the Golden Rosenkreuzer, 1779. Note the Rosicrucian eyebrows and flame in the triangle is nearly identical to Sri Yukteswar's symbol of the Kriya Yoga at Karar Ashram, seen at top of the Karar Ashram gate and at their website.

reminded me of the Surya Sun Temple at Konark, near Puri, Orissa, and I pondered again the solar path.

The Rosicrucians are reputedly a hidden order of Hermetic Christian mystics offering a *universal wisdom* (pansophy). In the gardens of Versailles, it is thought that the Rosicrucian designer intended to build a Hermetic initiatory experience, thus bringing the ancient wisdom to life. The pansophy of the Rosicrucians would appear to be a much later manifestation of ancient knowledge regarding internal spiritual processes.

I later learned that the mystics Emmanuel Swedenborg and the Count of St. Germain had frequented the halls of Versailles, exerting their invisible influences. Here, intense diplomatic/spiritual efforts were made to sway self-serving policies and faulty treaties to a better evolutionary path, though they obviously weren't always successful. I left France with only one thought: *There is a universal esoteric tradition.* Rome would soon point me to far earlier lineages.

# 36

# Pantheon Pigna

*In some of the [Egyptian] papyri illustrating the entrance
of the souls of the dead into the judgment hall of Osiris the
deceased person has a pine cone attached to the crown of
his head. . . . As its name signifies, the pineal gland is the
sacred pine cone in man—the eye single.*

MANLY P. HALL,
SECRET TEACHINGS OF ALL AGES

ntering the Roman Pantheon, the "temple of all gods," one feels
swept upward within an immense cranial bowl to the perfectly
circular *Oculus* ("Eye"), an opening in the ceiling to the sky. I immediately note this to be the same goal of all kundalini practitioners, and
the final exit point for all Tibetan Phowa practitioners, the flowering
thousand-petal chakra, the exit portal of all yogis at the time of death.
The inner spherical aspect of the building is like a skull (*golgotha*) with
an exit point at the fontanelle, that is, liberation from earth into the
heavens, supported by the great deities that once lined the circular hall.
The Oculus is also just how I perceived the spirit of my aunt on that
Thai beach eight years ago, looking skyward from the eye at the center
of my head through an openning at the top.

*. . . a Pineal Door projection. This is the most difficult to achieve.*

OLIVER FOX, *ASTRAL PROJECTION*

The coffered, hemispheric ceiling immediately reminds me of the geometric dimples in Krishna's head from my dream before departure, and I know that no accident has brought me here. *Mirabilia Urbis Romae* (*The Marvels of Rome*), a twelfth-century guide, tells us the largest bronze pine cone in the world had once rested atop the Pantheon in Rome. Indeed, the spirits and adepts of ancient Greece and Rome had this knowledge of the pineal gland, so well displayed in this two-thousand-year-old architectural masterpiece. Likewise, the goal of all yogis and Tibetan lamas is to depart this aperture at the time of death, and one could say all the spiritual work of their lives is geared to this one goal.

The Pantheon may be a monumental three-dimensional mandala of the human seventh chakra, the sahasrara, complete with a giant pine cone atop, symbolizing the activated pineal gland. That this is hidden in

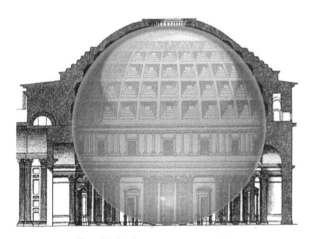

Fig. 36.1. Cross-section of the
Pantheon in Rome showing
a perfect sphere.
Derived by Cmglee, from an illustration
in *Meyers Konversationlexikon*,
unknown author, 1885.

Fig. 36.2. Awakened
sahasrara, the seventh chakra.
Illustration by Sandeep Johari
from *Breath, Mind,
and Consciousness* by Harish
Johari, 1989.
Reprinted with permission of
the publisher

Fig. 36.4. Crown chakra,
the sahasrara.

Fig. 36.3. Cortile della Pigna (courtyard
of the pine cone), Vatican.
Photo by pWknight94

plain sight for all to see is simply astonishing. The *Self* is clearly the central deity of all the deities that once encircled the giant mandala of the metaphorical cranium. This *Temple of the True Self* points to the interiorization of consciousness, squaring the circle, entering the pine cone of gold, the enlivened pineal gland, atop the single eye staring skyward, the seventh chakra. Along the ring of deities were once the symbols of the pineal-pituitary marriage, male-female, sun-moon, Apollo and Venus.

The *Marvels of Rome* states: "In the top of the Pantheon . . . stood the golden pine-cone that is now before the door of Saint Peter." It may be significant here that this writer (and/or translator) wrote not *at* but *in* the top stood the golden pine cone (gold indicates success in alchemy). This may imply "in the Oculus" (the Eye), which would be the crown chakra, where the thousand-petaled lotus blooms from the alchemically prepared pineal gland.

Nearly two-thousand years ago, the Roman Pantheon was rebuilt by Emperor Hadrian, a student of the Pythagorean Mystery School. Hadrian took prophecies and omens seriously. He was twice initiated into the Eleusinian mysteries, first into the lower grade then into the higher mysteries. He consulted oracles and was proficient in astrology, to the point that he kept journals even to the hour of his death. Among his friends were musicians, geometricians, and astrologers, and he himself was expert in arithmetic and geometry as well as painting and letters.

Under the mystagogue Pythagoras, initiates in Greece learned that all heavenly bodies are spherical in shape and move around a central fire, the sun, or perhaps a central sun, the center of our galaxy. For most Pythagoreans, Apollo occupied this position at the center. This Greek sun deity is also the prophetic deity of the Delphic Oracle. Abaris Skywalker, arriving from central Asia at the school of Pythagoras, claimed to have received his divine arrow (possibly a *phurba*, still in use in Tibet and Nepal) from Apollo himself. I later came to know Abaris "was described as a 'shamanistic missionary' and savior-figure."[1]

Centuries after reconstruction, the *Pigna* was taken down from the top of the Pantheon and reconstructed as a fountain that rested between the nearby Temple of Isis and the Temple of Serapis (Osiris). This location may suggest a direct connection to the Egyptians, who had knowledge of the sacred gland, the seat of the soul. The Roman Pantheon demonstrates to me that this knowledge did exist in the West, at least at one time. There may be any number of veiled, esoteric bridges from the Egyptian Mysteries to the Pythagoreans among the Arabian alchemists, and onward to the hidden mystery schools of Europe. The living knowledge once contained in the Western Mysteries has perhaps now been so well hidden that it might be lost or, at best, purposely withheld. A further pilgrimage across Rome to the Vatican brought me to the *Pigna*, the great pine cone, standing almost 4 meters high. In the twelfth century, the Vatican first placed the stolen *Pigna* in front of Saint Peter's, only later moving it to what is now called the Courtyard of the Pine Cone, where this Hermetic key continues to be symbolically held hostage.

*Enough of arcane remnants!* I packed up my things for the pilgrimage to a living Philosophers' Stone, who would be arriving in Holland soon. However, the train journey north from Rome to Holland would first pass through Switzerland, and I simply had to make a brief stop. The roof of Western Europe would offer new clues, and new views over unexpected landscapes.

# 37

# Swiss Synchronicities

*What is great in man is that he is a bridge and not a goal.*

FRIEDRICH NIETZSCHE,
*THUS SPOKE ZARATHUSTRA*

L egend has it that dragons once lived here atop Mt. Pilatus, perhaps due to the two peaks that give it a horned appearance. The
views overlooking the great *Vierwaldstättersee* (Lake of Luzern) and the
surrounding mountains are stupendous. Now, at the center of western
Europe, gazing over distant peaks and thin wispy clouds floating above
the five fingers of the lake, I'm silent within and without. Just as in the
Himalayas, at this towering height there are no mysteries, no questions;
it is enough just to be.

Descending the mountain peak to the town of Luzern I made my
way to the famous *Kapellebrücke* (Chapel Bridge), the oldest extant
wooden bridge in Europe, built in 1333. From this bridge I gazed out
over the lake and recalled how I had met the Swiss couple, Bruno and
Rosie, in Nepal five years ago. When they handed me their address
in Basel, they cheerfully admitted to being rather transient, moving
nearly every other year. The memory of Bruno and Rosie in the high
mountains bordering Tibet warmed my heart, and I wondered how I

might find them. Unfortunately, I hadn't carried their address with me, and could not even recall their family names. I pictured meeting them again in my mind, but quickly dismissed it. Yet this day I would learn in a most remarkable way that an intention held, even for a moment, has power.

Fig. 37.1. Kapellebrücke (Chapel Bridge) of Luzern.
Photo by author

Carl Gustav Jung may have been partially amiss in his psychologizing of Eastern mysticism, or *perhaps he might have known more than he publicly let on?* We may never know, but *anyone*, I thought, *who recommends studying the Bardo backward, and wrote commentaries on so many Asian esoteric texts must have at least been intuitively spiritual in his outlook.* I recalled Richard's remarks in Nepal about Jung's tower hermitage, and I had limited time to explore. The Tower called to me in a soft whisper—a new pilgrimage was in the offing. I boarded an express bound for Zurich and Küsnacht. After a brief visit to the Jung Institute and an *"absolut verboten"* from the office staff there, I learned that his Tower at Bollingen belongs solely to the Jung family, and has never been open to the public, ever. However, I had a deeply personal question and would not be dissuaded. I wanted to at least sit near his

Tower, and meditate on the shore of the *Obersee*, the upper portion of Lake Zurich.

The narrow-gauge local train wound around the lake passing rolling hills, idyllic farms, and villages. In 1993 this line still stopped at Bollingen village. There I found no gate, not a soul around—an unmanned station. I dropped my ticket in a small open box and stepped down into a pastoral scene—forest and meadows of grass dotted with country homes. Following a small path east along the lake, I came upon a family unpacking their cars, perhaps for a picnic. I hesitantly asked them in stuttering *Hochdeutsch* (standard German) if they might know the whereabouts of *der Turm von Herr Doktor Jung?*

The older man replied in friendly, yet incomprehensible *Schweizerdeutsch* (Swiss German). My silence was answer enough, and turning to introduce a woman now emerging from the other side of a car he said in English, "This is my wife, Professor Jung's granddaughter." Timeless blue eyes met mine, and with a gentle smile she offered the Swiss greeting, "Grüezi." They invited me to join them, and we carried their bags and baskets of food for their barbecue down a grassy meadow. Her husband continued in melodic Swiss English, "You're fortunate to meet us just here. We only suddenly decided on this picnic a few hours ago. No one has been to *der Turm* for a long while." Scarcely able to speak nor fathom my good fortune, I could only nod, smile, and thank the skies.

Passing through a small wood, fairy-tale turrets emerged into view, and we soon stood before the gate of a small castle set right on the lake. Inside the heavy wooden door to the courtyard, a dreamlike medieval atmosphere permeated every stone, like Merlin's forest keep, befitting a wizard who talks to wind, the lake, trees, and the spirits. I was courteously informed that Dr. Jung's hermitage has been left as it was at the time of his departure, with only a few modern additions and refinements. While they carried on with their barbecue lunch, they gave me free rein to wander the Tower's ground floors and courtyard. In a dining nook, curious items collected during Jung's travels covered high shelves. I read a local newspaper article, posted on the wall about the medieval-era bones discovered at this site in 1923. From a high shelf above, the wide-eyed statue of an ancient Hindu deity watched over me from the shadows of a timeless pilgrimage to the East (I would take better note of this mysterious deity when I returned to Bollingen twenty-five years later).

Outside the walled courtyard and near the shore of the lake, I sat next to a large cube of stone, also carved by Dr. Jung, as were all of the paintings and engravings that cover his little castle hermitage, his inner world in stone. I was so stunned to gain admittance to the forbidden keep that it had not occurred to me that this might itself be the response to the question I came here to ponder. Gazing over the lake I silently cast my inner question out over the waters and waited for a response. Not a sound. With great intention I again beamed it across the lake, and waited. I looked and listened for answers in any signs from the lake—the fall of a leaf, a bird cry, whatever may come. The lake was as dark and silent as any secret chasm, and not even a gentle breeze reached me.

> *It is impossible, that any Mortal understands this [alchemical] Art, unless he has been previously enlightened by the Divine Light.*
>
> DORNEUS, *THEATRUM CHEMICUM*, 1602

My question dismissed, I surrendered to the unknown, melting into the landscape, just as I had in the Nepalese Himalayas years before. An ageless peace fell over the lake, the greater valley, and eternity whispered an inner breathy stanza I could not discern. The sound of voices behind me snapped my attention back to shore. Now late afternoon, the family had packed up their lunch baskets, and were preparing to depart. They allowed me a few last photos of the courtyard of the Tower, including his enigmatic cube of stone resting by the water. Though Jung had spearheaded a revival of the study of alchemy, I remained unconvinced he had solved the arcane mystery of the Philosophers' Stone. The mute cube only stared back at me, its inscriptions and planetary symbols as much a riddle as the rest of his Tower.

Fig. 37.2. Jung's Tower at Bollingen, 1993.
Photo by author

Outside, the Jung family and I bid our farewells. I walked east toward Schmerike hoping I might reach the next station. After a short trek beyond the wood a meadow opened to the lakeshore. There I spotted a restaurant and stepped in for an early dinner. As I dined gazing over the lake, I felt an intuitive wave that something larger than myself has been at work, but I had no sense for what I should *do* about it. *Perhaps just* being *is enough?*

Finishing up my meal, I stood up feeling rushed to see more of Switzerland in my brief time here. Then I paused, held by a thought, *What's the hurry? Must I be slavishly tied to doing more and more?* I sat down again, ordered a tea, and enjoyed it leisurely while watching the sky gently dim to a gray blue over the Obersee. After a spell, the time felt right. I paid my bill and exited the restaurant. Outside, late afternoon rays of sunlight were still beaming upon the foothills. I decided to turn back west toward Bollingen Station, when I spotted two shadowy wisps coming over a high, green hillside upon bicycles. I stood entranced by these tiny beings, far away up the hill, watching them flow down the winding road. Soon it was clear they were coming this way—an inner command resounded, *Wait.* I could now see that it was a man and woman. The bicycles turned toward the restaurant and my heart beat faster—*could it be? Impossible!*

Bruno and Rosie with mouths gaped widely looked and said in unison, "Kevin!" We gleefully embraced at the entrance to the restaurant, and Bruno exclaimed, "*Mein Gott*, we were just sitting at home over the hill, and we suddenly decided we should come eat at this restaurant moments ago." Rosie chimed in, "*Welch eine Synchronizität!* So many years since we met in the Himalayas!" We sat down together, they to a meal and I to an *Apfelstrudel*. They had only moved from Basel to this location a year ago, so it was all the more remarkable that we should meet. They were even unaware that Dr. Jung's tower was nearby. If I hadn't paused for tea, and paused again at the door to watch the distant bicyclists, we wouldn't have met at all.

With a view of the lake and setting sun we reminisced over our Nepalese adventures and those since our last meeting. The odds of not one but two such impossible synchronicities occurring back-to-back in the tiny village of Bollingen on the same afternoon was not lost on me. Dr. Jung himself, the *Hexenmeister* of Bollingen, had coined the term *synchronicity*. I would no longer avoid Herr Doktor Professor Jung's work; he clearly had something to say to me. This power of intention to draw synchronicities reminded me of Swami Kriyananda's story of how Yogananda was led to the whereabouts of an anonymous letter writer:

> One day in Boston, Massachusetts, Yogananda received a letter criticizing him for "sponsoring" Jesus Christ in the West. "Don't you know that Jesus never lived?" the writer demanded. "He was a myth invented to deceive people." The letter was left unsigned. Yogananda prayed to be led to the writer. About a week later he was in the Boston Public Library. He saw a stranger there, seated on a bench by one of the windows, and went over, sitting next to him. "Why did you write me that letter?" he inquired. The man stared in amazement. "Wh-what do you mean? What letter?"
>
> "The one in which you claimed that Jesus Christ is only a myth."
>
> "But—how on earth did you know I wrote that?"
>
> "I have my ways," the Master replied quietly. "And I want you to know that the power which led me to you enables me also to know for certain that Jesus Christ did live in Palestine, and that he was everything that the Bible claims for him. He was a true Christ, a Son of God."[1]

Returning on the evening train along the dark lake I leaned my head against the glass, entranced by light reflections dancing inside and outside the train windows. The sky over the lake faded into a dark violet, as the little train chugged back toward Kusnacht and then Zurich. After a quick stroll by the cafés of Niederdorfstrasse in a lit-up Zurich, I returned to Luzern by high-speed express, and enjoyed a late *Wein und ein kleiner Imbiss* (wine and a light snack) with a view of the wooden footbridge and lake. Beyond this, the ominous silhouette of Mt. Pilatus stands sentinel. Legend says this mountain may be the burial place of

Pontius Pilate, who presided over the trial of Jesus. *Surely the Christ could have escaped this fate?* I thought. Elder Self inwardly replied, *A voluntary sacrifice.*

I paced back and forth on the bridge, both shaken and exhilarated by the impossible odds of the double synchronicity at Bollingen. From the old bridge I stared out over the dark waters of Lake Luzern, and wondered, *Is it time to leave Asia?* Bruno and Rosie had suggested I find work in Switzerland and stay. I left the question up to the night sky and the dark water: *Are the alchemical traditions still alive here, or have they been lost? Are the Rosicrucians still a force, or were they always a myth?* The waters were as quiet as the cool breeze. I returned to my guesthouse and dreamt of a boat on a lake before a castle. I awoke reminded of Parzival and his quest for the Grail. *Can a fool find what was lost and heal a kingdom?*

The following morning I tucked into breakfast with zest and sped out to discover more of Luzern, first with a walk to Denkmalstrasse to see the *Löwendenkmal*, the Lion Monument, hewn from the face of a rock wall to commemorate the Swiss Guards who were massacred in 1792, when the Tuileries Palace in Paris was stormed during the French Revolution. The sculptor expressed the lion's anguish like no other I've ever seen, and I couldn't help but mourn for the collective excesses of that revolution. Two centuries and a year had now passed since that time.

A thoughtful-looking Japanese woman then appeared and seemed as captured by the pain of that lion as I. Breaking the ice in Japanese, I learned she had just finished her graduate studies in England. She said she would soon be returning to Kyoto, and we laughed as we discovered we had mutual friends at the universities where I lectured. When she asked why I had come to Europe, I explained that I would be seeing my Indian kundalini teacher in Holland soon. She was curious and I mentioned that Yogananda's book had been translated into Japanese (*Aruyogi-no-jijoden*) and that she might find it interesting.

We looked back to the suffering lion in silence. The Kriya lineage and their sacrifice and fierce devotion to spiritual liberation came to mind: *Yes, they were like lions in this world.* As this thought turned, a powerful magnetic vibration coursed through me, and I began to tremble. I touched her shoulder, and she piped in English, "What a strange feeling—my entire body is vibrating!" I offered no explanation. We walked through Luzern sightseeing for the rest of the day. At dusk we reached the old wooden Kapellebrücke where we bid each other farewell.

Though I had a night train to Holland to catch, the ancient bridge held me like a magnet. I felt I now understood a bit about how Kriya initiation worked, how the Kriya vibratory state is passed from the lineage of masters through a practitioner, just like a bridge, to others. I asked the lake, *Might Kriya Yoga be the key to uniting Eastern and Western esoteric lineages?* The ancient bridge only creaked under the weight of passersby and the dark waters again whispered no reply. I retrieved my luggage, crossed the wooden footbridge one last time, and boarded the night train for Holland. As the train pulled out, I looked back at Luzern with an uncanny nostalgia in my heart. Weary from too many synchronicities and too few answers, I slept soundly over the rumbling rails, finding some comfort in the unknown. Rolling ahead into darkness, a new pilgrimage had begun. This time to *a living keeper of the Secret Fire.*

# 38

# Second Kriya

*The Self is a mirror that reflects the entire universe. The mirror reflects the many objects of the world, but doesn't retain any of them. Just like reflections, humankind remains absorbed in the pain of sense attachment, but the Self, the mirror itself, remains detached, luminous, and pure. Be the mirror, be the Self.*

PARAMAHANSA HARIHARANANDA

The new Kriya Yoga ashram in the small village of Sterksel in the Netherlands is an oasis in northern Europe, established by Peter van Breuklen, one of the most advanced among Hariharananda's Western students. Soon after my arrival on August 7, 1993, *Rajarsi Peter-ananda*, came to fetch me. Swamiji wanted to see me. I entered his room and pranam'd (bowed deeply, Indian style) to the Kriya master.

Before I could utter a word, Baba took me by the neck and pulled upward. "God, God, God. You're the living power of God. Your questions are being answered, are they not?" I could only nod, held in a vibrational suspension by the fiery voltage running through me. "Do you love Jesus?" he asked, as he released me and put his hand over the crown of my head. "This is Jesus . . ." An increasing power circulated through me. "Do you feel him vibrating within you?" he added, and I nodded. The master moved his hand and looked straight through me with his luminous, watery eyes: "Be the mirror, be the Self!" I was stunned. He let go of my neck and pulled my hair upward. "Always come to the top, here, stay at the fontanelle." He then pointed to his own fontanelle and then mine, and said, "The guru is a bridge. Cross this bridge and you'll be free." I nodded, and he smiled, "Good. Come to meditation this evening."

In a few short phrases he had encapsulated the whole of my experience with him, from our first meeting seven years ago in India to most recently here in Europe—the mirror man, the Pantheon, and even the Swiss bridge, as though he had observed me inwardly all along. The *spirit of illumination* is clearly embodied in him—the *Secret Fire* lived in him. I was speechless for the rest of the afternoon and only lay on my bunk until evening meditation. That evening during meditation practice, from my scrawled notes, he said:

"We are born for Self-realization—God-realization. Kriya Yoga is the simplest, most direct path to liberation. Theory makes us restless and selfish; practice gives us inner peace and liberation from ego. An ounce of practice is worth tons of theories! Feel that in every breath it is the Infinite who is drawing breath through you. Feel the Presence of God in every breath, sense, and thought. In the Katha Upanishad it is said that the indwelling Self is none other than Brahman, the Infinite, manifesting itself in the many forms."

The elderly master was as natural here in Europe as in any other environment—calm, compassionate, humble, yet also powerful beyond ordinary measure. A week passed basking in his enlivening aura, when I learned that many others in the ashram had taken second Kriya from Rajarshi Peter after only a year or two of practice, while I was still practicing first Kriya after seven years. I said nothing to anyone but tried to see Baba to ask him directly for the next level of initiation. He was busy with preparations for an upcoming public program, so was unavailable. That evening we silently waited for him to come to meditation. He arrived at the meditation hall, walking slowly in his brilliant

orange wool *ruana* (pancho) from Colombia, as the Dutch summer evenings were cool for elderly Baba, who was accustomed to the heat of
the Indian subcontinent. He gently sat down, looked over the crowd,
and with astonishing clairvoyant acumen immediately pointed at me,
shouting loudly in front of everyone, "You believe you're advanced, but
you're NOT advanced! When you are ready, you'll be promoted to second Kriya." I nearly melted into the floor. As usual, Baba was attuned
to even the least of his disciples.

Days later it was announced that there would be a special meditation session for all *Kriyavan* (practitioner of Kriya Yoga) with the second initiation. That evening I looked over the crowd entering the large
meditation hall in disbelief—many were less experienced, and from the
conversations at the dining tables, I judged them as less spiritual and
more worldly than myself. I felt robbed, incensed, and inwardly seethed
in burning anger for a day. *After seven years I'm excluded from this second
level meditation! Am I so unworthy, after all these years? Have I wasted
my time? Is he really a master?* With insolently clenched fists I fumed,
*Perhaps he's not the bridge for me!*

In a raging depression and egoistic resignation, I made plans to
depart the ashram the next day. I slept badly, tossing and turning in a
hot sweat. Skipping morning meditation, I went straight to breakfast
where I resentfully filled my muesli bowl, and sat at a long table, mis-
erably alone in a downcast, melancholy gloom. A few Dutch disciples
joined me, dropping a newspaper down on the table. Lifting my spoon
to my mouth, I glanced at the cover page. Upon seeing flames leaping
from a long wooden bridge I sucked a chuck of muesli down my throat,
sending me into a convulsion of gasping and coughing. The Dutch leapt
up to slap my back, and my breath returned.

Gathering oxygen, I seized the newspaper in disbelief: the headline read *Luzern verliest Kapellbrücke.* Just last night, Luzern lost the
famed Chapel Bridge to fire! We all moaned and lamented Luzern's loss
of the oldest wooden pedestrian bridge in all Europe, well known to
everyone at the table. More came to gawk at the cover page with much
shaking of heads and exclamations of sorrow in Dutch, English, and

German. One Dutchman read out the article and explained to me in English that the Swiss had vowed to rebuild the bridge, but that many of the original paintings in the upper panels had been lost forever. I sputtered that I'd come to Holland directly from that bridge just ten days ago. Deeply shaken, I ate the remainder of my breakfast in silence and understood. After nearly seven hundred years an ancient bridge had burned, but it would be rebuilt. A gracious surrender enveloped me, and I felt the ground under me like never before. *How can I cross the waters if the bridge is burned?* I must stay. That evening I slipped the newspaper away to my room and cut the article from the paper. I keep it still.

Sharp edges in my heart crumbled and burned away that day. The extraordinary bridge fire coincidence inspired me to plumb an inner silence. Spiritual experiences of all kinds filled my basket of ego, but

Fig. 38.1. Article, "Luzern Loses Chapel Bridge."
Dutch newspaper, August 18, 1993

I was missing a key point—transformation. It was high time to be focused, like a monk, at least while here. Touring more of Europe could wait for another time. I vowed to rebuild the bridge to my teacher; but there would be no easy promotion. I remained quiet and attended every meditation.

Rajarshi Peter had long planned the auspicious Founding Day and now the master had arrived. A low stage was built and scores of rental chairs brought in for the event. Despite the beautiful weather that day, Peter's wife confessed to me, "Yes, a glorious day, but the local people of Sterksel village are frightened this may be some kind of strange cult. Many of the village leaders will be attending today and it might just determine whether the ashram will be accepted in this rural community, or not." I understood as I noted a gathering of local villagers, many with pinched and scowling faces. They sat with arms folded in front of them, frowning as they awaited the appearance of the strange foreign master. On stage, Peter made several friendly announcements in Dutch and German, and then introduced Swami Hariharandanda Giri. In beautiful Indian English, Baba immediately turned on the charm and went straight to the point:

"In the Bible, it is said that God made man and woman by breathing into our nostrils. We say that this hasn't ended. It didn't happen just once, thousands or even millions of years ago. No, it is a continuous action. You are not breathing; God is breathing through you. Self is constantly inhaling. Without Self, Soul, God, there is no breath, no life. In the Holy Bible, does not Jesus say that the Kingdom of God dwells within you? And does he not also say that you are to seek first the Kingdom of God? How can you seek the Kingdom of God, within you, if you do not seek within? Kriya Yoga meditation means to look within yourself and seek God and his Kingdom. Therefore, if you follow the words of your master Jesus, and seek the Kingdom of God that is within you, it is then that you should feel that you are being faithful to Jesus and Christianity. Jesus is the living power of God.

"Kriya Yoga is the panacea for all the ills of humanity. It can transform nations and societies. Kriya Yoga is the most scientific technique to save humanity from misfortune and destruction. It is the essence of all the schools of yoga, though it is different from all of them. The ancient practices were extremely exclusive, requiring renunciation of all worldly affairs, and all one's time performing difficult postures and practices, but Kriya Yoga can be practiced by everyone. It is completely nonsectarian—you may be Christian, Hindu, Buddhist, or not have any religion at all. Kriya Yoga is the highway to realizing the Infinite!"

Baba continued speaking about Moses, Jesus, and John the Baptist with a powerful vibrational authority, answering questions about Christianity and Hinduism with a special magic only he could offer. Rather than intimidating, as he often could be, this was as though St. Nicholas himself had arrived on a summer sleigh and was explaining what the real Christmas meant. An ethereal light beamed from him like I hadn't seen before, bathing the crowd in an almost tactile love. Smiles broke out over the crowd and even the stodgiest of villagers opened up in the warming light of his words. He then stood beaming with an effulgent joy and said, "Now I will give my love to you . . ." Though frail at his great age, he stepped out into the crowd, hugging villagers right and left. Tears poured over the cheeks of many who were perhaps experiencing real divinity for the first time in their lives. The program was more than a success, it was a transmission.

The local community accepted the ashram and a communal sigh of relief was felt all around. I knew then that an opportunity like this may never come again, and I settled in to stay for as long as Baba was there. However, one afternoon only days later I pondered whether to tour some local sites. Baba caught me by the arm in the hall and pulling me closely said, "You have lived many lives for the world, now live one life for samadhi. You can get liberation just now." Power poured from his arm into mine, filling me with a subtle bliss. I remained and sat in silent meditation the rest of the day, experiencing no discomfort.

Days passed and I had long hours free in the ashram, so when I found a copy of Yogananda's book in English I reread it. I pondered the process of reincarnation, and how the knowledge of this had been obscured in modern versions of the Bible. In chapter 35, Yogananda clearly relates how the Old Testament prophet Elijah (Greek: Elias) was reborn as John the Baptist to announce the rebirth and return of Elisha-Eliseus as Jesus in the role of a messiah:

> The very end of the Old Testament is a prediction of the reincarnation of Elijah and Elisha: "Behold, I will send you Elijah the prophet before the coming of the great and dreadful day of the Lord." . . . Thus John (Elijah), sent "before the coming . . . of the Lord," was born slightly earlier to serve as a herald for Christ. An angel appeared to Zacharias, the father to testify that his coming son John would be no other than Elijah (Greek: Elias). "But the angel said unto him, Fear not, Zacharias: for thy prayer is heard; and thy wife Elisabeth shall bear thee a son, and thou shalt call his name John. . . . And he shall go before him in the spirit and power of Elias, to turn the hearts of the fathers to the children, and the disobedient to the wisdom of the just; to make ready a people prepared for the Lord." . . .
>
> Jesus twice unequivocally identified Elijah (Elias) as John: "Elias is come already, and they knew him not. . . . Then the disciples understood that he spake unto them of John the Baptist." . . . Again, Christ says: "For all the prophets and the law prophesied until John. And if ye will receive it, this is Elias, which was for to come. . . ." When Christ was transfigured on the mountain it was his guru Elias, with Moses, whom he saw. Again, in his hour of extremity on the cross, Jesus cried out the divine name: "Eli, Eli, lama sabachthani? . . . Some of them that stood there, when they heard that, said, "This man calleth for Elias. . . . Let us see whether Elias will come to save him."[1]

Both Yogananda and Hariharananda have referred to Kriya Yoga initiation as the true spiritual baptism of fire and light. As I wasn't raised in a church, nor even to be Christian, it struck me as odd that my sacred journey to India would lead to a reconciliation with a religion I had always considered militarized. I recalled Gandhi saying, "If you feel the need to change your religion, it's because you don't understand your own." I still have little interest in *churchianity*, but I now feel a deep connection to the original spirit of these early prophets who I now view as not only prophets but profound shamans, mystics, and yogis. Yogananda said a number of times that Jesus taught his disciples a technique similar to Kriya Yoga in which they were able to perform miracles and be in God-consciousness: "Kriya Yoga is a simple, psychophysiological method by which the human blood is decarbonized and recharged with oxygen. The atoms of this extra oxygen are transmuted into life current to rejuvenate the brain and spinal centers. Elijah, Jesus, Kabir and other prophets were past masters in the use of Kriya or a similar technique, by which they caused their bodies to dematerialize at will."[2]

Shortly before he was to leave Holland, Baba appeared in a dream and beamed, "You're still not ready, but I will give you second Kriya." I woke, dressed, and went to see Baba. Without a word I touched his feet, expressing my silent gratitude. He said only, "You'll take second Kriya now." Flowers were gathered from the garden, and he initiated me then and there. Hardened flakes of cast iron ego flaked away, and a new power rushed through my spine into my brain. Baba further describes second Kriya:

> By practicing second Kriya, you perceive the triple divine qualities of vibration, light, and sound at each chakra. Gradually the divine sound will fill the entire brain. Completing second Kriya is a great gain: immediately one can feel that any disposition in any chakra is coming from God, and when hindering propensities come, he can remove them. The samadhi of second Kriya is called *vicharani samadhi.*[3]

Chai was brought and I sat with him while he looked over letters and documents. He turned and added, "You should keep silence, always watching the soul. If you have a spouse, then you could not come here. You'll be bound in chains. Maintaining a family is like maintaining an elephant. You should not marry, if possible. You're a second Kriya yogi now. You must be highly moral—have one wife, or none." He then waved his hand over his groin and said, "Conservation of the male vital fluid is all-important in second Kriya." He leaned back and added, "After second Kriya you must be humble; you must not be guru now. You should practice second Kriya with love every day. Remain up here (pointing to his fontanelle). This is your freedom; all else is illusion. You remain with open eyes, looking up at the wall. See the divine light all over the world. You are this light." Before I left, he took my arm. "You should never boast to others you're practicing second Kriya. Once you complete second Kriya, the advanced initiations will come much more quickly."

Swami Atmananda filled in the lengthy details of the technique as I took notes (second Kriya has the most steps of all the six levels). After we finished, Atmanandaji, an M.D. neurologist, said to me privately, "As you may have noticed, you cannot think of anything when you look at Swamiji. You can travel the whole world and never find another one like him. I've been all through the Himalayas, and have met hundreds of yogis, swamis, and teachers, but there's no one like him. I've seen Baba in samadhi many times, even pulseless and without breath for over an hour. He's the real thing." He continued, "Kevin, you're more attuned to the mind of our master than most here. Make the most use of it and follow his inner guidance."

Baba was soon due to depart for Munich, where he would rest for a week before the program there. I made plans to visit friends in and near Munich for that week, but before I left he called me into his room. "You have questions?" I told him about the psychokinetic events with metals or electronics that sometimes occurred around me. He pulled his beard and said, "It's best not to make a display—this attracts the wrong kind of persons." He then paused as though hearing an inner cue. "You also have healing power. You will later do more with this, but only show it to a few."

# 39

# Munich to Dresden

In Munich I stayed with Rolf, the eldest son of my homestay family from fourteen years earlier. At this wonderful reunion we laughed and reminisced, and later visited his parents in the village near Neusäss where Rolf and I attended *gymnasium* (high school) the summer of 1979. Rolf's mother gasped in fright when she saw me, "You haven't aged a single day in fourteen years? How is that possible!" She backed away as if from a sorcerer and kept a cautious distance throughout the visit. I recalled Yogananda saying that Kriya Yoga slows the aging process, extending the yogi's lifespan. Kriya has been lauded as an elixir, a fountain of youth, but I hadn't yet fully understood it as an alchemical process. I spoke more German with his *Bayerisch* father this time, making up for my previous visit when I could scarcely understand his Bavarian dialect at all. I recalled the electromagnetic anomalies and telekinetic effects during my time there and concluded that the alchemists used the metals as metaphors for internal kundalini processes precisely because metals seem to be the most receptive to telekinetic effect. Of course, no one in the family spoke of the unusual events years before, and neither did I.

Hariharananda arrived in Munich and the meditation programs and initiations started shortly later. A special meditation was held for those with the second initiation in Munich, which I now gladly joined.

Baba launched the sit with, "You should love God with all your heart. The Kundalini Shakti in the lower chakras is the devil's kingdom. If you don't look ahead of you, then surely, you'll fall. God has given you eyes to see, is it not? Limited sex is important in the higher Kriyas; it is imperative! You must be pure in God, beyond thought. Each petal of the seven lotuses has a vibrational sound, the letters of the Sanskrit alphabet." Tremendous power poured from him this night, and I felt pressure at the top of my skull. Baba continued:

"Bow deeply, stretching the spine. The moment you get vibration, pulsation, and pendulum movement sensation, then you take a turn on the right, this massages the liver and internal organs giving you secretions for your health and vitality. You live a long and full life. Mary Magdelene, Peter, and others changed in a moment's time. You can also change your bad habits, your animal qualities in a moment's time. If not, you'll never be free. Even if very busy, take ten minutes to bow and get the vibration at the fontanelle, merge with the sound, eyebrows up, see light in the cranium. Open your eyes while merged in the God center, the seventh chakra, and know He is looking through your eyes from the seventh center at the fontanelle.

"You are the power of God; you are the energy of God, beyond thought, beyond mind, beyond concept. Many of you have failed. You must make the most sincere efforts. Feel the vibration of God's presence in the seventh center always. Take a breath from the pituitary up to the fontanelle, and remain there with feeble breath. You must feel it. You're accumulating spiritual wealth. The practice of Kriya dispels negative astrological forces, and frees you from the astral influence with which you were born. Be free!"*

He sipped from a glass of water, looked over the room with shining eyes of light, and continued:

"The Kingdom of Heaven is at hand. You must sit with deepest sincerest effort. Reach for samadhi stage now. Feel the movement sensation, the pendulum swinging, pressure, heaviness, you all like to think you are

---

*Transcribed from the author's personal notes.

advanced, but you are not. You're full of animal qualities—you all kiss your girlfriends and boyfriends, then kick them. This is kiss and kick! By the practice of Kriya Yoga, one will become a *jivanmukta* (one who is free from the cycles of birth and death). Kriya Yoga greatly reduces the time required for liberation, making it possible in just one birth."

Baba later pulled me aside and reiterated, "You'll hear more sounds, if you can feel the pendulum swinging inside you. Don't move the body; just feel the pendulum inside. See the illumination within the brain." Later, in his room Baba asked me to write an article in Japanese about Kriya Yoga, adding, "I will come to Japan when you are giving Kriya initiation." Thus, it was the first of his predictions about Kriya coming to East Asia (Kriya Yoga did indeed come twenty-seven years later to Japan, through his disciple Don Abrams). Seeing Baba's increasingly frail condition, Atmananda said to me, "Every opportunity to meditate in the presence of a realized master should be treasured. He is cleansing you. You may not feel it, but you are reaping boundless benefits from his presence."

Before my departure I spent an hour with Baba. At one point, he got down on his hands and knees, crawling about on the white-carpeted floor to search for a pen that had rolled off the desktop. I assured him that I would find it for him, but he only continued crawling under tables, giggling and carrying on. He then turned, glancing back at me from there on the floor, and through his eyes looked a divine, child-like deity permeated with cosmic consciousness. I cannot adequately describe this experience.

Baba returned to his chair with his pen, and said, "Once I broke my arm, and the doctor insisted on anesthesia before resetting the bone in place, but I refused. I went into samadhi—no breath, no pulse. The doctor thought I was dead, but Atmananda insisted he set the bone immediately. He did, and I returned from samadhi. The doctor was so shocked he followed me from that moment, even leaving his patients behind that day. I sent him back to his medical duties later." Like Peter dropping his fishing net, that doctor knew he encountered true divinity at that moment. Swami Atmananda later confirmed the event. My attunement, on the other hand, was still weak, and I needed constant reinforcement and confirmation.

After a blissful week in Munich, Baba bid me farewell. "You have received more than anyone here—make good use of it. Lift the hidden fire up, as Moses raised the serpent, and enter the Kingdom. Fight with your evils and become what you're destined to be!" He took my arm. "You can get samadhi. You've lived many times; leave all that behind, be free!" I turned to the door, but he spoke again, "You must practice every day with deepest concentration." He made a cross sign at his forehead, and added, "No *I*. Complete the inner sacrifice, the inner crucifixion!" Bowing low, I departed.

> *Transform yourselves into living philosophical stones!*
> GERHARD DORN, ALCHEMIST (1530–1584),
> *THEATRUM CHEMICUM*, 1602

At the *München Hauptbahnhof* I boarded a train, and soon passed through Vienna, bound for Budapest. After days in the beautiful Hungarian capital, I trained back north, again passing through Vienna Station to spend a week in equally beautiful and curiously familiar Prague, another early European center of alchemy. I sensed the capital of Bohemia still held a secret magic, though perhaps largely squelched during the Soviet era. My return flight to Asia was in a matter of days, so I boarded an early morning train bound for Berlin. The train sped north, passing the mountains of Sächsische Schweiz to the east. Shortly later, we stopped briefly in a large city and I felt an overwhelming desire to jump off the train. Holding a train pass that offered such flexibility, off I stepped. I placed my baggage in storage at the station and strolled about the old city. Dresden, the city where the Project began.

Here lived the spiritual alchemist, healer, and early Rosicrucian, Dr. Heinrich Khunrath (1560–1605), whose emblems grace the frontispiece and end illustration of this volume. The esotericist Eliphas Levi wrote that Khunrath was forty-two years old when he attained transcendent theosophical initiation: "He is a sovereign prince of the Rosy Cross, worthy in all respects of this scientific and mystical title." Forshaw quotes the German poet and mystic Quirinus Kuhlmann (1651–89), "'The remarkable man Heinrich Khunrath [is] inflamed by the Divine Fire with an ardent desire to search out the deepest matters,' and his *Amphitheatre* is a 'real Wonder-Book.'"[1]

Born in Leipzig, the shamanistic Khunrath studied medicine in Basel, Switzerland, wrote a Paracelsian dissertation, and then spent his late life in Dresden. Khunrath wrote that the spiritual alchemist is a "wonder-working discoverer of the treasures of Eternal Wisdom, [who] 'has the power of [performing] miracles,' and will consequently indeed be obliged to 'perform and accomplish marvelous and rare things.'"[2]

> *Hyperphysical or Supernatural Magic is "pious and useful conversation, as much when awake as when sleeping, mediately and immediately, with the good angels, God's fiery ministers."*
>
> HEINRICH KHUNRATH, *AMPHITHEATRE* II

Dresden was nearly destroyed in 1945 and had until recently been part of the GDR, East Germany. Though largely rebuilt since the war, portions of the ruined inner city still remained, perhaps as a memorial reminder. Just like Khunrath, the old doctor I once was had also been born in Leipzig and died in Dresden, though two centuries later. Khunrath's writings in Latin and German were a likely influence on him, as the Saxon court in Dresden had been one of the major centers of alchemy in the seventeenth and eighteenth centuries. I walked to Grosse Borngasse where this other self once lived, and later to the cemetery near the university where lay his remains, silently resting in the synlocality of this day. The whole of the summer journey had been a rebuilding of bridges, and a tying up of loose ends.

I sensed no further clues, only that the Project was progressing. The wide swing of a pendulum returned me eastward to Kyoto, naively convinced that now with second Kriya I would soon be liberated from the bondage of illusory identities. Significant trials lay ahead; I would soon confront a shadowy force, *a darkness that yet teaches . . .*

# 40

# Pendulum

*Your history is animal; your future is divinity.*
*Right now, you are like the pendulum, swinging between*
*the two.*

JAGGI VASUDEV

R efreshed from summer holiday, I enthusiastically delved into the
regular practice of second Kriya in my meditation room in Kyoto.
As the fascination with rediscovering a pan-Eurasian tradition also grew,
I made use of the university libraries in Kyoto to further search out the
Western counterparts of this universal alchemical process, documented
so well in the Indian Tantras, *Rasayana* (Indian alchemy), and Chinese
*Neidan* (inner alchemy) sources, but so unclearly in Western sources.
The European alchemists and the Rosicrucians had surely known techniques similar to Kriya Yoga, but these references remained obscured,
their writers purposefully evasive. Alchemy seemed to be a maze of symbols only understood by insiders long ago. There was no need for confirmation regarding Kriya Yoga, as I had a living source, but as part of
an archaic wish to reconnect Europe and Asia into a universal tradition
I collected any references I could find regarding Western esotericism in
hopes of bridging the historical chasm.

*Anyone who attempts a literal understanding of the writings of the hermetic philosophers will lose himself in the twists and turns of a labyrinth from which he will never find the way out.*

LIVRE DE ARTEPHIUS (TWELFTH CENTURY),
STANZA 29, BIBLIOTHEQUE DES PHILOSOPHES
CHIMIQUES, PARIS, 1741

While the puzzle of alchemy absorbed my intellectual interests, the next three years would bring a challenging period of oscillation between the extremes of material indulgence in Japan and spiritual refuge in India. This dizzying pendulum of duality swung with the university holidays; every half year contained an extroverted four months of stressful academic work and sensual pleasures in Japan, with two months of holiday completely free for spiritual interiorization. Shifting attention between descending energies into materiality and separateness (*apana*), and consciousness rising up the spine into a transcendent unity (*udana*) confounds most spiritual seekers. For the youth, descending energies are a necessity if a soul is to have a fully *in-the-body* experience; for the mature, it is best to reverse the downward flow, upward away from the material existence to the uppermost chakras in preparation to embody one's higher self and later for eventual departure. For a Kriyavan of any age, one seeking liberation must bring this motion under one's conscious control.

With the stress of lecturing at four different universities came the wish for a release of the pressure valves. Invitations for drinks after work led to a widening social life, thanks to a handful of close-knit friends, all gypsy scholars on the university lecturing circuit. Parties

---

*An alternative translation from *The Secret Book of Artephius* (Global Grey Books: 2018):

Stanza 29: "Truly, I tell thee, that as for myself, I am no ways self seeking, or envious as others are; but he that takes the words of the other philosophers according to their common signification, he even already, having lost Ariadne's clue of thread, wanders in the midst of the labyrinth. . . ."

at regular intervals again rocked my quiet neighborhood and I had more social interaction than I needed or wanted. Kyoto again became a playground of sensuality. I awoke one weary morning recalling my dream of the Dancing Incarnationers, and wondered if I wasn't heading for a fall.

> *In contradistinction to the historical depth of anima, eros is forever young, has no history and even wipes out history, or creates its own, its "love story." And where anima withdraws toward meditative isolation—the retreat of the soul—eros seeks unions.*
>
> JAMES HILLMAN, *ANIMA: AN ANATOMY OF A PERSONIFIED NOTION*

As my social extroversion reexpanded, my inner life became a hyperactive battleground for powers beyond my control. In dreams, struggles between seductive women and aggressive rivals tore at me savagely, interspersed by joyful appearances of spiritual teachers. Forces larger than myself were at work, call them archetypes or the gods, it didn't matter. Clearly something was both inspired and unresolved in me; I needed help. My distress became a beckoning call to investigate, to introspect, to seek, and to discover. I again returned to India for the two-month winter university break.

> *Ecstatically, you think, "sex is bliss."*
> *. . . Like a monkey's wrinkled skin. You grow old*
>   *soon . . .*
> *When the dark Lord of Death comes,*
> *Who will protect you, O sinful mind?*
>
> TAMIL SAIVA, POET, CIRCA 1725, FROM WHITE, *THE ALCHEMICAL BODY*

"The Lord is giving you so many beautiful dolls to play with and you're forgetting all about Hariharananda!" shouted Baba. Though I had said nothing to him of my life in Kyoto, my arrival at the ashram was greeted with ferocity. "You're not getting change—you're not getting G-O-D, only D-O-G!" Baba taught with love when he could but was fiercely truthful with those whom he felt he could teach no other way. "You're not remaining here in the cranium; you're not ready for higher Kriyas yet."

> *Behind all physical phenomena lies the Truth. Self-realization is not for the weak or cowardly; it is for the courageous who can face all the storms and sacrifice their ego on the altar of Truth.*
>
> PARAMAHANSA HARIHARANANDA

The cosmic intelligence Baba so remarkably embodied adjusted its teachings to each pupil, and in their own way everyone felt Baba was their own best friend. To those who stayed near him longer, he was like a bonfire burning away impurities. The false persona could not survive near him, as we were purified in *the fires of the Solar Logos* in our midst. Yet, he was also human and fallible, and perhaps not a professional manager. His was the traditional style of ashram management, and even though others might have wished to improve upon it, his methods in the end usually proved effective.

Days passed in Puri, but I remained distracted and wanted to run away from this blazing bonfire. "There must be no negativity in you. None! You must be purified. Only love, love, love!" Baba shook his finger. "You could be ready, but you're not. You must hear the sound always, plug one ear if you must, and hold until you hear the divine sound always. Merge into that." Higher Kriyas require an intense degree of focus, concentration, and mental purity. In profound esoteric work negativities may not only derail one's meditation but lend to the manifestation of unwanted and unhealthy results. Such is the power of this universal technique. One of Baba's monks, Swami Brahmananda, taught me an obstacle-dispelling technique that week, as a prelude to third Kriya, and this greatly helped.

*Do not roam about searching for God; but sit calmly at home, and God . . . will come to you.*

Zosimos of Panopolis, third-century alchemist of Alexandria, Egypt, *The Book of the Keys of the Work*

Reversing the spinal downward flow into upward flow here in India proved difficult after the months of material indulgence in Japan. Bored with silent, isolated meditation, I explored Puri on free days, chatting with townspeople. Returning to Baba at the ashram, he was again fierce. "Do or die! If you don't do, then do not come to Hariharananda anymore. Chatting only keeps you in ego." Baba howled, "Many people go to church or the temple mechanically, but they get no change. You have no depth in your meditation—you sit with me longer!" I plunged into the moment, and sat longer with him in his room in silence. Distractions tore at my mind, and I sensed him scan my brain and very soul. Baba intoned, "More obstacles, more realization!" After meditation he asked me, "Is the field prepared? Is the mango (cranium) ripe?" We both shook our heads, no.

Like a yo-yo, pushed and pulled, swinging back and forth between monastic India and sensual Japan, I felt chained to samsara. The sedating comforts and soul-numbing gratifications pulled at me with an irresistible gravitational force. At the end of two months, I returned to the far eastern island of exquisite food and no original sin, to Japan—kingdom of pristine materialism.

Mephistopheles' contentious, often ambiguous relationship to Faustus is a reference to tantra just as it is to alchemy. It resembles the shifting tactics of a guru who varies his approach to his pupil in order to dissolve his resistances and prepare him for wider states of consciousness. Both Faustus and the tantric aspirant stimulate and indulge their senses under the guidance of their teachers who encourage them to have sexual encounters with women in their dreams. Both work with magical diagrams or yantras, exhibit extraordinary will, "fly" on visionary journeys, acquire powers of teleportation, invisibility, prophecy, and healing, and have ritual intercourse with women whom they visualize as goddesses. The tantrist is said to become omniscient as a result of his sacred "marriage," and Faustus produces an omniscient child in his union with the visualized Helen, or Sophia.[1]

Spring semester in Kyoto brought both the gentle fall of pink cherry blossoms, and a busy recommencement of worldly life. My dream life rebelled, bursting with a surplus of archetypal imagery, and I became frightened that perhaps my inner world was spiraling out of control. I sensed a spiritual disintegration, a breaking apart. I recalled the proverb, *Fertile soil comes from the bloodiest of battlefields*, and held on for dear life.

"Kevin, your rich dream life is incredible material for inner work." My psychologist friend and I dined in a famed noodle shop near *Ginkakuji*, the Silver Pavilion. Robert continued, "You simply must look into Jung's psychology." I recalled the stodgy Swiss doctor and countered, "Isn't Jung passé now? His psychology seems like a rehashed shamanism to me." Robert continued, "*Analytical Psychology* is far more than meets the eye. Jungian dream analysis starts an archaic process deep inside you—the integration of the unconscious and the conscious, soul and personality." Now this spoke my language. My dual selves, the Elder and Younger selves, had moved far apart again, and seemingly more so each day in the frenzy of lecturing at several universities and parties every other weekend. Robert slurped the last of his noodles and closed his discourse, "You won't regret it. Just reading books won't do. Sit with a Jungian analyst and see."

While the double synchronicity at Bollingen Tower astounded me, I still found Dr. Jung's Eurocentric psychologizing of Eastern mysticism constrained and outdated. Nevertheless, I contacted the Jungian Association in Japan and was introduced to a kind analyst. She and I delved into dream analysis, and immediately Hermetic archetypes emerged in my dreams and I was tossed about in deep inner processes.

One afternoon she said with exasperation, "I'm just not sure what to do with this material. I'm going to recommend you work with Dr. Toshio Kawai, the son of the first and most influential of all Jungian analysts in Japan. He partly grew up in Zurich and is fluent in German, but he can also work with you in English. He lives in Kobe but comes to Kyoto each week—and he has already agreed to work with you." The timing was ideal, as the emergence of inner dream figures was rising to a crescendo along with an expanding social extroversion. The time was now; I could avoid the pain of this division of my soul no longer. I kept a dream journal and discussed the dreams with Dr. Kawai each week. Through analysis my inner life was transformed from a slipstream of rushing images into initiations of the arcane.

*I give birth to the light even though my nature is darkness.*

HERMÈS MERCURIUS TRISMEGISTUS,
*THE DIVINE PYMANDER*

"Another party!" the Kyoto party crew shouted and I was easily convinced, also seeking relief from the academic drive for tenure, the pressure to publish or perish. Though I had vowed to bring such effusive gatherings to an end, I relented to one more on a Saturday evening. I lost count after seventy guests, well over half in alarmingly short miniskirts, squeezed into every space in my large but rickety old Japanese house. I wondered if the thunderous music and dancing might not just bring the wood-and-paper birdcage down. As the night passes into morning, the mystic feminine again enchants and captivates—and I am again possessed.

*Everything the anima touches becomes numinous—unconditional, dangerous, taboo, magical.*

C. G. JUNG, *ARCHETYPES OF THE*
*COLLECTIVE UNCONSCIOUS*, PARA. 59

Autumn fell like a living canvas over Kyoto, leaves of resplendent gold and deep red cover the city, but I'm imprisoned in a hellish storm of my own passions, a dark abyss of such gravitational force that it seemed even light could not escape it. Dream analysis with Dr. Kawai put into motion a most interesting process: the Hindu Goddess Kali and Western Hermetic figures flitted through my dreamscapes, pointing to symbols I could not yet understand. The further I fell, the more Kali appeared in my dreams. Making further use of the university libraries in Kyoto, I discovered a painting of the Hindu deity Kali holding a severed head. *This process of transformation is known to history; I'm in good company.* Throughout my continuing dream analysis, Dr. Kawai mentioned Jung's concept of *Anima Projection*, but I had as yet no real understanding of the psychological importance.

Fig. 40.1. Kali with severed head, standing on Shiva. Lithograph, unknown artist, Calcutta, circa 1895.
British Museum

*The primitive mentality does not invent myths, it experiences them.*

C. G. JUNG, *ARCHETYPES OF THE COLLECTIVE UNCONSCIOUS*, PARA. 261

The Great Hanshin Earthquake struck on January 17, 1995, in nearby Kobe, sending dishes flying in my Kyoto home. I already had my flight to India arranged, and all roads to Kobe were blocked. So a week later I escaped the cold, trembling, and destructive insanity of life in Japan for the spiritual warmth of India.

Arriving at Karar Ashram in Puri, I was led to Baba's room and greeted with head bops and scoldings. "You're just a baby—you know nothing!" Baba's penetrating eyes scanned my brain, and I wanted to run away. "Can you have one wife on Monday, another on Tuesday, yet another on . . . Thursday? You should marry," he said with a wry, mocking grin. I could only hang my head. After a silence, he added, "You mustn't talk with others, and you must clean your shirt. No hypocrisy!" Within days I soared in the bliss of meditation, but on breaks I was racked with attachments that would not release their holds on me. *Solve et Coagula.* The fierce bonfire of meditations in his presence dissolved and coagulated my personality, over and again.

If the sexual impulse were taken away from you, you would realize you had lost your greatest friend. You would lose all interest in life. Sex was given to you to make you strong. The more you give in to it, the weaker you become. But when you master it, you'll find that you've become a lion of happiness.

PARAMAHANSA YOGANANDA[2]

Weeks passed in Orissa. One day the master called me to his room, "If you gain the whole world, but lose your soul, then what is your gain? You must die and rise as Jesus did, then you'll become Jesus. You must come to the fontanelle and become the universe. All is white snow; all of your body, and all that is, is white snow. Feel the pendulum within—this is Jesus." The master again held the hair of my head, pulling upward and I passed into a blissful state. Though my body was outwardly stiff and rigid, I inwardly felt I as though walking over clouds in an unfettered freedom. An eternity later, a brief memory of a passionate affair in Japan danced across my mind—Baba immediately perceived my inner dilemma and pounced with a bitter truth, "In India, a woman has only one husband. In your world, how do you know who the father is? Here a man knows his wife is with no other man. His mind is free." I opened my eyes and my bitterness melted in the solar love radiating from him.

> By alchemy you may learn your livelihood;
> You may wander through the universe incognito;
> Make vassals of the gods; be ever youthful;
> You can walk on water and live in fire;
> But control of the mind is better and more difficult.[3]

Days later at evening meditation, Baba told a story, "One day a small boy here in Puri was asked how to spell 'wolf' and the boy replied, 'W-I-F-E.' The teacher agreed, 'You are right!'" We laughed, and Baba continued, "You see, I am free because I have no wolf. My brother has a wolf, and it bites him. Every day he must go to his office far away to bring home money for his wolf and three cubs. His wife is a slave to their children." He grinned widely and pointed at me. "He has already had so many wives—and they bite, bite, bite!" I shrank a bit, and cringed. Baba shared the dog and bone story: "A dog cracks and chews a bone. The sharp shards of the bone cause bleeding in his gums, but the dog believes he is getting blood from the bone, so on he chews, drinking his own blood. You are like this dog—you believe you are enjoying sexually, but it is sex that is enjoying you." Before I left the room Baba warned, "Do not give in to moods and whims!" As said by Paramahansa Yogananda:

> "Moods are caused by past overindulgence in sense pleasures, and consequent over-satiety and disgust. If you indulge your moods," he added warningly, "you will reinforce the mind's swing back again toward sense pleasures. For that is how the law of duality works: it moves constantly back and forth, like a pendulum, between opposite states of awareness. If, by not giving in to moods, you remove energy from one end of the pendulum's swing, you will find the hold that the senses have on you at the opposite end will weaken as well."[4]

One very hot afternoon a week later, I went to rest in the cool meditation hall at Karar Ashram. Swami Yogeswarananda Giri entered, greeted me, and opened a cabinet packed with books and photographs. There he showed me a large, striking photograph of our teacher Hariharananda sitting with a blue statue of the Hindu Goddess Kali, complete with sword and decapitated head in her arms. He explained that Baba had created the artistic wonder while in isolation here in Karar Ashram, and this goddess was one of the primary deities he worked with in his younger years of intensive practice. Kali may have signaled to him his own personal deconstruction in order to be reborn a spiritual master. He achieved nirvikalpa samadhi in 1948.

Kali is a tantric goddess of time and change, and she emanates a series of deep meanings. She is a cosmic force of radical transformation. Kali destroys ignorance and stands upon a dead or defeated Shiva. My unwholesome relationships were a hinderance to my spiritual advancement (and theirs), but I had to go through this fire. An intelligence was attempting to communicate with me and I was, so far, incapable of hearing her message. A wandering sadhu described in Yogananda's autobiography had this to say about Kali:

Few there be who solve her mystery! Good and evil is the challenging riddle which life places sphinx-like before every intelligence. Attempting no solution, most men pay forfeit with their lives, penalty now even as in the days of Thebes. Here and there, a towering lonely figure never cries defeat. From the maya of duality he plucks the cleaveless truth of unity.[5]

Meditating on Kali, my dreams, and all that Baba had taught me, the purification process of dissolution and distillation continued. New inner alchemical stages were reached, and I now sat for hours with little discomfort. Dream lucidity became a nightly event, and I inwardly asked before sleep, *What is to be my service to the All?* Late one night I awoke within a dream . . .

Fig. 40.2. Paramahansa Hariharananda at Karar Ashram.
Photo permission courtesy of Karar Ashram,
Puri, Orissa, India

*. . . to find myself sitting atop a Mayan pyramid, looking out over a dense Central American jungle in the early morning twilight. Such was the lucidity that I clearly felt the warm humid wind, and the hard stone below me. "Hmmm, I thought I was in India . . . what am I doing here?" A huge jaguar emerges from the jungle far below, and I sit motionless hoping the great cat doesn't notice me high atop the pyramid. Just as this thought passes my mind, the jaguar looks up right at me and bounds straight up the pyramid at speed! While I'm frozen with dread, the beast places his jaws over my head and holds my skull in his fearsome grip. I accept my demise, but it does not occur. The jaguar melts into me, and I into him, and a message is understood, portending a return to the land of the Maya, a future call to shamanism.*

Days later Baba called me to his room. Raising his eyebrows, he looked deeply into my eyes, penetrating my brain and soul. "The mango is ripening." And so, in early 1995, Baba initiated me further into Kriya Yoga. Putting his hand on my head as I bowed low, he said, "Feeblest breath, subtlest breath, take a tiny breath and know he is above. You must abstract your senses to the third circuit [third ventricle between the right and left thalamus], above the pituitary. This is the true place to seek the experience of God. The Kundalini Shakti will rise. The milk has been churned and the cream will go up to the top." He removed his hand and as I sat up my brain was showered in light. He instructed me in the mantras needed to perform the new movements in the upper chakras and cranium, and I sat for long in silence. Later outside, Swami Brahmananda confirmed the finer details of third Kriya. Baba writes:

Through this technique you can always remain in the third circuit [the third ventricle of the brain], i.e., inside the cranium above the pituitary, which is the kingdom of God, the cave of Brahma. . . . A Kriyavan practicing third Kriya feels the triple divine qualities [vibration, light, sound] rotating inside the cranium, and it feels as though the soul is floating in the vacuum. Clearly the Kriyavan feels that the superpower of God is doing work through him. This samadhi is called *tanu-manasa* samadhi.[6]

Sitting early the next morning with the monks in the master's room, I had a passing intuition of a future family. Baba perceived my thoughts immediately and said, "Lahiri Baba was married and got realization, but this is rare. Sri Yuktewar was also married and had a family, but he reached realization only after they passed away early. You should get realization first; then if a family comes, so be it." After long sitting in near immobility due the power of his presence, my legs wobbled and I could only just stand. He took my arm. "Be in good company, but it's even better to be in isolation. For many years here in Puri, I did not go outside the ashram at all."

That evening, an Indian man asked in English about astrological karma. Baba replied, "A traditional astrological reading is useless for a Kriya yogi, as he is dispelling astrological influence every time he practices. Each day he changes his destiny." Yogananda wrote: "The starry inscription at one's birth, I came to understand, is not that man is a puppet of his past. . . . His freedom is final and immediate, if he so wills; it depends not on outer but inner victories." Sri Yukteswar said, "The wise man defeats his planets . . . by transferring his allegiance from the creation to the Creator. The more he realizes his unity with Spirit, the less he can be dominated by matter. The soul is ever-free . . . it cannot be regimented by stars."[7]

Baba often shared rich stories of the Hindu deities, each containing hidden spiritual teachings. I envied the Hindus of India who are still largely lived by the wisdom of their mythologies, capable of carrying them through intensive spiritual processes. Despite a long history of worldwide esoteric knowledge and tradition, most of us from industrialized countries have lost this connection to living lineages, and our cultural mythos no longer lives through us. As a Westerner, I wished for a rich spiritual heritage like that of India, and a rebirth of a Western esoteric heritage. On my departure day, Baba bid me to remain behind with him after morning meditation. He said, "Once we take a breath

Fig. 40.3. Time flies: here Saturn (lead) or Chronos (time) with a winged hourglass on his head and holding his scythe, attempts to cut human life short with the help of the negative influence of the other planets, to prevent completion of the alchemical process in a single lifetime. Note the planetary symbols on the limbs of the tricephalic dragon. Both Kriya and Hermetic practices mitigate and transform this negative planetary influence. Diagram from the *Thesaurus Thesaurorum* (1725), p. 10.

the pendulum swings from birth to death, but if we enter the breathless, pulseless state before we expire, then we have completed the great quest."

When I returned to Japan, I had changed. As Dr. Jung suggests, I didn't know the women in Kyoto; I knew only my *anima* projections upon them. In Jungian psychology, the anima is the man's internal other, his feminine soul. Once projected outward onto a woman, the anima typically attacks the man in his inferior function. As most men are thinking types, his feeling function will be less developed; it is here the anima manipulates his emotions. The anima can represent the divine aspect of the human being, a goddess that imbues everything with numinosity and mystery, but if the anima of a man falls into the unconscious, the dark aspect is projected out onto women who fascinate that man. Indeed, I had been bewitched countless times; I had to develop my weak feeling function before I could withdraw anima projections.

The anima became a bridge to my wholeness. I was still largely an emotional teenager with little understanding of the mature masculine mode of feeling, but I was slowly learning. I explored the emotions behind thought, and continued meditations with an almost Herculean effort. Now unable to see Dr. Kawai (his home in Kobe had been damaged by the earthquake), I kept at dream journaling with a new fervor.

> *To face the dragon is to seize life.*
> ALCHEMICAL AXIOM, IN HAUCK, *ALCHEMY*

Then came a dream of completion:

*I face a strikingly beautiful woman on a hilltop; she morphs between a red-lipped seductress and terrifying destroyer. I do not react. In frustration and resignation, she turns and walks away down the hill.*

When I awoke, the projection was withdrawn. I now knew and more importantly *felt* there was no longer a hook—the pendulum stopped.

Curiously, the woman I had been recently dating disappeared immediately without even a hint of sentimentality. I then understood there never had been a relationship or even a friendship with her, only a kind of interaction. Weeks later I learned that she was engaged to a German after a whirlwind romance, and they moved to Switzerland not long later. I marvelled at her new destination, recalling the astral holiday makers had a history there. The swinging *Dance of the Incarnationers* would continue without me, thankfully. Nevertheless, no progress for me had been possible without this *hellishness to wholeness* experience, and I felt both relief and gratitude.

The year 1995 came to a cool December's close, and I made the decision to leave Asia and return to my country of birth to start a new life. But first I would spend a last winter in India with the Master of Kriya. I gladly resigned from the universities and closed out January's final exams in a snowy Kyoto. I sold my motorcycle, car, furniture, and packed up my last belongings for shipping to Seattle for an indefinite storage. At the airport in Osaka I boarded a flight with a one-way ticket to India, and from that runway, reached for an infinite sky.

# 41

# With the Master

*The science of this Art [alchemy] has never been fully*
*revealed to anyone who has not approved himself worthy*
*by a good and noble life, and who has not shewn himself to*
*be deserving of this gracious gift by his love of truth, virtue,*
*and knowledge. From those who are otherwise minded this*
*knowledge must ever remain concealed. Nor can anyone*
*attain to this Art, unless there be some person sent by God*
*to instruct him in it. For the matter is so glorious and*
*wonderful that it cannot be fully delivered to anyone but*
*by word of mouth.*

THOMAS NORTON, *THE ORDINAL OF ALCHEMY*, 1477

*H*ome free in India! A decade has passed since my initial Kriya
Yoga initiation, and this time I'm here to receive everything
the master had to teach, if only I can be spiritually mature enough to
receive it. Baba stayed with a relative of his in Calcutta, so I checked
into a hotel a few metro stops away. The sprawling city, a living disas-
ter only a decade ago, now has a clean and well-operating subway, and
even the street traffic is manageable. I wondered if the great Bengali
poet Rabindranath Tagore might feel some of the charm of the old

city has been lost. Tagore shares the same first name with Swami Hariharananda Giri (before becoming a monk). I had heard mention that Bhupendranath Sanyal (the great disciple of Lahiri Mahasaya who initiated Hariharananda into the higher Kriyas) and Tagore, the *Bard of Bengal*, had known each other in the 1930s. Both being seekers I felt a kinship with, they reputedly often wrote to each other asking, "Have you reached samadhi yet?"

The cost of living in India is so reasonable that I pondered arranging some kind of early retirement here, but I was just thirty-five years old and had much life still ahead. I followed the directions to the address given and climbed the staircases to the third floor. I bowed low, and Baba put his hand on my head. "You can get samadhi just now—all you need do is die."

Naturally, Baba refers here to the inner, voluntary crucifixion, the sacrifice of the little ego that opens one to soul awakening and *enlightenment*, the transformation of a leaden personality into the light or the gold of the *Atma*, the eternal soul, the higher Self, closest to the *All That Is*. The master himself is a highly polished mirror, reflecting back to us what we needed to learn at any given time. I was rightfully suspicious of other status-seeking, money-grubbing swamis and sadhus, but Hariharananda never asked anything of me. He truly wished realization for all those who desired it. I made donations according to my means at the time, and as far as I know, he never coveted such donations. He lived in the ever-present now.

Each evening I travel to Baba, now tightly surrounded by disciples in his nephew's living room. Bengal is his province of origin, and even though he speaks fluent Hindi, Oriya, and English, his easy joy at speaking his native Bengali is a delight. I usually arrive early should he wish to see me. If we are alone, he often has me bow my head to the floor, while he presses the back of my cerebellum and gives further instructions. I'm immobile for long periods after this, with my tongue rolled back, glued to the roof of my mouth, scarcely breathing. By the time others come for the evening's meditation, I can move and speak again.

One evening Baba shared: "The physical body is full of delusion, illusion, and error. If you know that the powerful soul is abiding in you, then surely it is your greatest achievement. You'll be immortal. Kriya Yoga is not a religion; it is a technique, a spiritual methodology, not a theory. It is a universal, direct experience." He pointed to his cranium. "You'll get secretion from the pituitary—this is *amrita*, and you'll appear young for an extended time. You see this photo?" Baba took up an old photo of his younger self on the table and showed us. "I was fifty years old here." He looked barely thirty in the picture. How yogis live to the extremes of old age was now clear: *Kriya Yoga produces the hidden alchemical elixir!*

"The practice of Kriya Yoga reverses the current of power outward to the senses, back inward to the center of the brain. Similarly, the chakras also get change, turning each lotus [chakra] with their different petals upward toward the brain. Prana is directed toward our inner heavenly Father. Once life force is controlled, control of the breath follows. The current of kundalini supercharges and evolves the bodily cells of the yogi, so that he attains the breathless state. Breathlessness is deathlessness." Baba continued: "In Kriya Yoga, if you keep your attention in the vacuum four inches deepest inside the brain, your Kundalini Shakti will rise to the top and all delusion will disappear. You'll get the samadhi stage. Control of breath is a result of controlling the life force!" He lifted his finger to the sky. "In the state of breathlessness, the body is held in a kind of suspension, where the current both supercharges and changes the actual atomic composition of body cells. Yoganandaji's body did not decay for weeks after his death."

The highest level of Kriya Yoga, the breathless, pulseless state of samadhi, also involves a conservation of vital essence that for most men is lost to momentary pleasures. Eliade writes:

As for the exercises in rhythm-control culminating in the stoppage of breathing, these had for many centuries been part of the discipline of Chinese alchemy. Pao Pu'tzu writes that rejuvenation is obtained by halting respiration for a thousand heart-beats. "When an old man has reached that stage then he will be transformed into a young man." Under Indian influence, certain neo-Taoist sects, like the Tantrics of the "left hand," considered the stopping of respiration a means of immobilizing [for men] the semen and the psycho-mental flow. . . .

The symbiosis of tantric yoga and alchemy is also well attested in the literary tradition of the Sanskrit and vernacular texts. Nagarjuna . . . in his Sarva-darshana-samgraha, Madhava shows alchemy (*rase-shvara darshana*, lit., "the science of mercury"\*) to be a branch of Hatha-yoga.[1]

After two weeks in Calcutta, I noticed for the first time a television in my hotel room. I had been using it as a clothes rack, but today I was bored and felt drawn to distraction. *What has become of Indian television since I last watched years ago?* I cleared my clothes from the screen and turned the switch. Buxom women in tight saris burst from the screen, dancing and singing in high, piercing voices; then dancing men with wild eyes appeared, their eyebrows furiously pumping up and down at the undulating ladies. A fight broke out, which moved quickly into some kind of family drama scene. I gazed for only a few moments, *Hmmm, same old masala films.*

The master's presence was then viscerally felt, and I turned the machine off with a loud snap. I would sit for meditation. Unfortunately, any focus had been scattered by the televised extravaganza, so I took a walk to a crowded, bustling café for a pot of chai. I took a seat by the open door and gazed out at Calcutta walking by. Moments later, in the threshold of the door, a giant crow, one of the many great scavengers of Calcutta, suddenly dropped with a large rat in its beak. Its powerful maw tore the rat in half. The huge bird cawed proudly, stared at me with sharp, wild eyes, and picked the innards out of the split rat, tossing them back in his throat with greedy head jerks. I felt sickened and wished I'd just stayed in my room. I left half a pot of chai behind and returned through the chaos of the Calcutta streets to my hotel.

---

\*The mercury mentioned here is an alchemical metaphor for a spiritual principle. Please do not confuse the alchemical Mercury of the Philosophers with the highly toxic, ordinary liquid metal.

I felt scattered, but showered and left for the evening's meditation, arriving only just in time. The room was packed and I had to make my way to the back. Hariharananda immediately pointed at me, and shouted, "You must keep good company—turning on the television is NOT good company! There are so many dancing girls and boys there, no, no—this is not meditation." He looked over the crowd and then back at me again shouting fiercely, "Stay in isolation and do not go out—the busy world outside will eat you!" He grinned at me with wild, birdlike eyes, and I was stunned into silence. Such clairvoyance is almost incomprehensible for the average person. To be with a true master is to know that nothing is hidden from *Cosmic Mind.*

A few blissful days of isolation passed in both my hotel and in afternoons privately in his presence. He gave me more scoldings, gentle head bops, further instructions, and even rare morsels of praise—just enough so I would not become discouraged. One evening he held my shirt. "You have the seed of liberation within you; let it sprout and grow in good company."

The following evening while I rode the subway, my eyes led me to an Indian beauty in a scarlet red and gold sari. Though momentarily entranced by her poise and radiant elegance, I felt no base desire, no wish to speak with her. I only entertained a passing thought of good company: *Perhaps it might further one to marry a spiritual Hindu woman and stay in India indefinitely?* She stood, alighted at the next stop, and was quickly forgotten. When I arrived at the suburban home of his stay, Baba was again surrounded by a large number of visiting Indian disciples. He saw me enter, and immediately turned, pointed, and shouted at me over everyone, "He'll never catch an Indian girl!" Grinning with fiery eyes, he added, "Here, we have one wife or none!" I was so caught off guard I only nodded and did not even recall the woman on the subway until after I sat down. My flushed red face hid any inner gold, and I dropped into the silence of surrender for the evening's meditation.

After a long sit in the crowded room, I returned to my hotel in a dim mood. *How can anyone rise to this master's impossibly lofty stan-*

*dards, where even my slightest thought is known to his spirited mind?* I felt depressed that I would not likely be liberated in this life. I was just too much a product of my modern, materialistic culture. I lay back and concluded, *Well, perhaps I must slog through endless incarnations before I can purify myself enough.* With that I fell into a deep sleep. Only shortly before sunrise was this broken by a dream visitation:

*I stand alone in a void . . . Krishna appears. The skin upon his bald head is the most beautiful deep violet blue. He pushes a large standing mirror before me, and therein I see changing faces of how I appeared in other times and places. Some faces were vaguely known to me, while others become fresh re-memories. Krishna and I then merge and are now One, and I look down to see the blue skin of my hands, now our hands. Krishna's traditional consort, Radha then appears in all her glorious beauty. Like magnets we're drawn into merging, a loving play of sensual light and joy. . . .*

In the morning I could only stare at the ceiling for a long spell before I finally rolled over and noted down the blissful dream-vision. Sitting up into meditation in such a timeless elation, I missed breakfast and mysteriously found myself lying down again, sleeping. I stood up, dizzy. Dimensions again felt slippery and I sensed Baba wanted to see me early. After a quick *tiffin* (light afternoon snack) I left the hotel.

> *The subtle unity of the phenomenal world is not hidden from true Yogis. I instantly see and converse with my disciples in distant Calcutta.*
>
> YOGANANDA, *AUTOBIOGRAPHY OF A YOGI*, CHAP. 3

Baba is sipping chai on the third floor veranda with two sadhus in dusty ochre robes I had not met before. They stand and briefly introduce themselves as wandering disciples of Baba. "You won't see us often; we come only when inwardly summoned by the master." This summoning I now understand, and I only nod. We sit down and Baba turns to me. "Sri

Yukteswarji once said to Yogananda, 'I will put my head inside yours.'" Baba leans forward, his watery eyes unblinking, "I'm also telling—the moment you arrived, I am you, and you are Hariharananda."

Merging one's consciousness with a spiritual master is perhaps humankind's oldest method for raising one's vibrational rate and state of consciousness to cosmic consciousness. This is known as *guru yoga* in both India and Tibet. This is a voluntary merging with a transcendent consciousness, merging with the object of devotion, whoever that may be, a master in a thangka painting, a teacher of spiritual lineage, a saint, an angel, or a deity. Even the slightest intention of doing so causes one to resonate with that being's level of consciousness, at least up to one's capacity. Profound intention and focus bring progress, finally allowing deeper merging, accelerating one's soul evolution.

> *The real history of the world is the progressive incarnation*
> *of the deity.*
>
> C. G. JUNG, *LETTERS*, 2:436

More chai appears on the balcony table, courtesy of his hosts. The master sits staring out into the sky, like a central sun holding a galaxy in orbit. We all rest in complete silence; more passed in that hour than I could hope to process in a year. After a spacious eternity, someone appears and mumbles to Baba. He waves and turns to me, looking into my soul with an infinite love, and I know again the inner silent knowing I had known as a child, the contact with *the inner guru.*

Other local disciples noisily arrived in the receiving room, hoping for an audience with the master. I escaped down the stairs to the street for a short walk through this suburban neighborhood of Calcutta, now transformed into dancing light. Everyone now, even the roaming cows, seemed blessed representatives of the *Most High.* Feeling a bit overwhelmed by it all, I pondered returning to my hotel room, but an inner call bid me stay. I returned to his nephew's flat, wound my way through the seated crowd, and sat for meditation at the back while Baba held court, all eyes on him:

"I'm not seeing any of you. You are all the power of God, you are God in form—that is all I see, light above your heads." He stroked his bushy white beard, smiled, and leaned toward some Indian women and men sitting close to him. "You are married, yes?" And turning to others in the room. "And you are all married too, yes?" He took a deep breath. "Marriage is difficult, is it not?" They all smiled and sighed an embarrassed relief, as here we can be in truth. "So many are getting trouble with marriage. If you are married, remain so—know God through that. If you can avoid marriage, it is better to do so." Baba smiled to the nodding crowd, also nodding his head up and down.

Baba suddenly bellowed, "You are NOT you, no; you are the Infinite in form!" Baba's voice shook with power. "Your wife, your husband is God in form." He paused again, looking about with a fire in his eyes unusual even for him. "You are not getting sexual desire. God is giving you sexual desire, and you are God loving your spouse, who is God." The normally shy-to-discuss-such-topics Indians were held spellbound, almost breathless. "Know always that even in sex you are God loving God!"

Seeing the crowd trembling, Baba softened and explained, "The idea of sex enjoyment in Kriya is that the father nature, the non-manifest God as Soul, at the crown of the head, the fontanelle, is drawing breath up and down from the mother nature, the physical manifestation. Back and forth—this is spiritual copulation, done within each human being. No partner is needed. Feel this, know this."

A strange power emanated from him, and I now perceived him in silhouette with a glowing illumination about him reaching to the ceiling. Unable to move or even speak, indescribable Grace poured over us. Tears streamed down eyes unable to blink, as we *en masse* moved into *Shambhavi mudra*, the state of unblinking, eyes-open perception of the Divine Light over everyone and everything. He intoned, "Move up and down between the pituitary (jiva) and the fontanelle; this is making love to God. This is the true sexuality." I cannot recall how much time passed, but no formal meditation was done that evening. After a long while we could scarcely stand, and in the purest of silences, so rare in India, we departed.

# 42

# Fourth Kriya

Fig. 42.1. An angel guiding a couple through the labyrinth
of astrological obstacles to the alchemical marriage, cosmic union,
and the birth of the *alchemical divine child*.
Goossen van Vreeswyk, *De Groene Leeuw* (The Green Lion),
Amsterdam 1674, p. 123.

D ays later the crowds in the Calcutta home became wearisome.
Baba, two monks, and myself escaped to the Rourkela Ashram,
some 500 kilometers to the west, at the northern tip of Orissa State.
Swami Atmananda, a leading disciple who usually headed this ashram

at the time, was teaching overseas and few knew that Baba had arrived. Swami Brahmananda greeted us warmly and we settled in for a longer stay, one of those rare opportunities to spend daily time with the master in unhurried circumstances.

Hariharananda is an alchemical catalyst of great heat, cooking his disciples, purifying and refining us in the hermetically sealed vessels of our own skulls, preparing us for the conjunction of spirt, soul, and body. I meditate each morning and evening with Baba and the monks. In these small groups, Baba speaks casually and teaches spontaneously. The Kriya master is now eighty-eight years old, and he seems to also be preparing his ashrams in India for his eventual departure. Privately he says to me: "Remain with pinpoint attention at the fontanelle. You must become the atom point; you must pass the test—the breath will become feeble. Hariharananda may not always be here." He turns to sip a bit of chai and continues, "The secret fire will light up the center of your brain—some disciples fall into samadhi after a single long bow."

At evening meditation, another handful of seekers arrived. Baba again held the group spellbound. "Do not see anyone's face. See only snow-white light over everything. Know that he is all form, and yet beyond all form. This formlessness is your desert, your forest. Jesus went into the desert; Buddha went into the forest. Be your own best friend, not your own worst enemy. Why don't you get the samadhi stage? Because of attachment to the body sense. Let it go—be the whole universe. Right action, and right practice! Be absorbed in *paravastha*—formlessness. Take the feeblest breath from the pituitary, up to the fontanelle, and exhale into the universe, just as in Shiva's hair in the Nataraja dance. Do not miss a single breath. Only God is doing; you are free."

> *Only when the illusion of "self" has disappeared from my heart and mind, and my consciousness risen to that state in which there is no more personal self, then, will I not be the doer of works and will not that spirit of wisdom perform its wonders through my instrumentality?*
>
> Paracelsus, *Liber de Occulta Philosophia*, 1686

Baba knew and could easily perceive our commitment, and our readiness. The next evening, he told us: "One man came to Karar Ashram years ago, and asked what we did. We replied that we meditate daily and take care of the ashram and our guru. The man then said, 'Oh, yes, I want to join the ashram, but not as a *chela* (student)—I shall join as guru!'" We burst with laughter. "Similarly, all of you want to be guru, without being chela first."

Baba often quoted from his favorite Upanishad, the Mundanishad 2:2:4: "*Pranava dhanuh, sarahi esa atma Brahman tad lakhyam ucyate.* Om is the bow; the soul is the arrow; and Brahman is its target. One should become one with it just like an arrow. You are magnetizing your spine, bending it on the ground, and it is just like a bow. Then with a short breath, you release the arrow! The breath is going up just like that arrow, touching the Almighty Father in the fontanelle, then all your evils in your body will disappear. This is *pranava dhanuh*, and *sarahi esa atma.*" Baba continued, "In the Bible, Jesus said, 'Believest yet not that I am in my Father and the Father in me? The words that I speak unto you I speak not for myself: but the Father that dwelleth in me. He doeth the works.' This is *Kri*, work, and *ya*, the power of God. God breathes and acts through you."

Here in rural India, meditations deepened quickly. After a series of breakthroughs, Baba one early morning took me through the next initiation without explaining it was fourth Kriya. Over a cup of Indian chai that afternoon, Swami Brahmananda clarified the technique. In his book on Kriya Yoga, Hariharananda writes:

> By practicing the fourth Kriya you feel some special movement of the soul inside the forehead, pons, thalamus, hypothalamus, pineal gland, in front of the pituitary and in the mid brain.* You feel that the light is rotating around from the high heavens to the earth. This

---

*Important note: Haphazard stimulation of the kundalini fire and the glands within the brain is unadvisable. The full techniques cannot be given here; one must seek a qualified teacher (acharya) of Kriya Yoga for direct initiation and instruction.

fourth level is called *asamshakti samadhi*, it means you are roaming freely in superconsciousness and perceive the living presence of God in your whole body. . . . The body of the guru will appear dark, with illumination all around it.[1]

The sixteenth-century Spanish saint, Teresa of Avila, practiced and taught her advanced nuns a similar spiral path of meditation leading inward and rising to a crystal at the center of the upper cranium. Her book *The Interior Castle* (1577) is likely based on a similar inner journey she had herself made. She uses the image of seven Mansions, just like the seven chakras, from the first Mansion of the Inquirer-beginner to the seventh Mansion of the inner spiritual marriage in the cranium. This journey leads from the outside courtyard of a castle, spiralling inward and upward to the central room where the king lived, full of light. She, like a Kriya master, knew that we have this capacity to be the home of the triune God, Father, Son, and Holy Spirit. St. Teresa of Avila also manifested many documented *siddhi* (yogic powers) that Indian tantrikas still demonstrate to this day.

One morning over breakfast Swami Brahamanda asked, "When will Kevin-baba take *sannyas* (monk's vow of renunciation)?" I pondered this all day, but in the evening Hariharananda clearly answered this question, saying directly to me: "Do not join an ashram—that's not for you, as you will only grow busy and frustrated. Don't be a slave of an organization; instead, remain in solitude and isolation as much as possible. Don't go out talking and milling about—this will only impede your progress. Isolation is for your benefit; it is the price of greatness."

One afternoon Baba said to a small group of us, "In Kriya you should practice with extreme focus for shorter periods, several times a day. You'll obtain a single-minded meditative state throughout the day and even at night. Sitting for hours will only bring many thoughts; this is one of the old ways, but most cannot succeed in this. It isn't fruitful to sit with eyes closed thinking of the whole world." He took up a nearby book (*The Gospel of Sri Ramakrishna*) and said, "Ramakrishna once said, 'The ego can disappear only when one's mind ascends to the seventh plane, into samadhi.' Ramakrishna felt the world is a deep well, and that his spirit would drown in it. He looked upon his relatives as venomous snakes; he had great inward resolution."

> Man is like a puppet. The strings of his habits, emotions, whims, passions and sense make him dance to their bidding. He who is unwilling to or unable to cut himself free in order to know God, will not find him. I see myself apart from all these attachments. I gave up all physical necessities to prove to myself that I do not need them. . . . This is not your true home. Live in this world as a guest. It is only a wayside inn, a brief halt on the long journey home to God.[2]

The *Mahashivaratri* annual festival arrived in mid-February 1996, and most of India was singing praise to Shiva this evening. We tried to hold regular meditation, but we could not hear the master's words over the endless banging of cymbals, shouting, singing, and chanting outside. In exasperation, Baba shouted, "All this shouting, banging, and screaming all night . . . is God deaf?" We sat in silence while the great cacophony outside continued. An hour later, there was a brief reprieve and Baba said, "Singing and chanting may inspire us to go further within. But you have Kriya Yoga, the superhighway to God consciousness! Meditate deeply. Know that it is God outside singing and no one else." As soon as these words reached our ringing ears, *God* started up again and no one slept that night.

# 43

# Higher Kriyas

A week later while sitting in the main hall during evening meditation, I inwardly collapsed into a deep state and a channel opened far above my head. Baba leaned forward and said, "You have made some progress tonight." For the next two days the greater portion of my consciousness remained up in the sky while only a small portion stayed with my five bodily senses, just enough to slowly walk about, eat, wash, and speak softly. Unable to sleep much, I walked about the ashram garden at night, my head in the stars. I trembled the longer I held this state. After three days, I found myself back in normal bodily consciousness.

Baba and I walked in the garden the following morning. "You need continuous purification. The mango [cranium] isn't ripe enough; you cannot hold this state. When you can, you'll be ready to approach the inner samadhi." He paused before resting. "You have seen the Mahabharata paintings of Krishna with his head covering the sky?" I nodded, and he continued, "You are reaching for God. He will reach down and give you samadhi when you have been prepared. Sow the field now with fifth Kriya." Baba further writes:

In fifth Kriya the devotee mostly feels divine sensation in the cerebellum. You are gradually coming close to the pineal gland and are trying your utmost to enter into it. As lightning strikes, accompanied by

251

thunder and rain, so do sparks fly up from your coccyx to illuminate your whole world with powerful sound, light, and vibration. . . . You cannot stop crying, because you are in the living presence of God. This fifth level of samadhi is called *sattapatti samadhi*. *Satta* means soul. *Patti* means appearing. The soul is appearing and trying to enter into the pineal gland. That means you are near nirvikalpa samadhi.[1]

One evening a disciple asked about the tantras, and Baba responded, "Tantra is misunderstood. Tan-tatra means 'You are there.' When in every action you are feeling soul, this is tantra. If you know the indwelling soul is performing all actions through you, that is tantra." He gave the Sanskrit phrases for this, but I could not write them down quickly enough. Baba continued, "Pray and repent, 'Oh, Lord, I have been your foolish, naughty child. Help me to reach you once again, to attain God-consciousness.'" Baba often shared one of Sri Yukteswar's oft-told stories about a cat and a fox to illustrate the simplicity and directness of Kriya Yoga, compared to the complexities of other systems:

A cat and a fox meet in the forest. The cat said, "When trouble comes, I go straight up the tree. What do you do, oh fox, most sly of all the animals?" Fox replied, "Oh, I have this great bag of tricks here to escape danger." Just then a hunter and five dogs came. The cat shot straight up the tree, but the fox was still rummaging in his bag of tricks and was immediately pounced upon by the five hounds. So, I am telling, the cat went straight to the fontanelle, while the fox was caught by the five hounds, the five physical senses (or, in other versions, the five lower chakras).

Eventually, here too, word spread of Baba's arrival and a large crowd descended upon the Rourkela Ashram. Baba, two monks, and myself again made a clandestine escape, this time to Cuttack, to a newly constructed ashram, built by one of Baba's leading disciples, Swami Prajnanananda, who was currently in teaching in Europe. The two monks and I were alone with Baba for the first week in Cuttack. One

Fig. 43.1. Paramahansa Hariharananda and the author, India, 1996.
Author's personal photo

hot afternoon while the monks were out, Baba bid me sit in the main hall and told me privately, "Sri Yukteswar looks after his disciples, even now, decades after he has gone. Only yesterday, he told me to increase this medicine and decrease this other one, and it works! Practice with utmost sincerity, and Sri Yukteswar will look after you too." Privately and so casual like this, Baba no longer appeared superhuman as he often does before larger groups. This day he was like an amazed child, pure and innocent, exhibiting a humility so rare in this world.

Baba regularly guided us in long, predawn meditation sessions, focusing on minute details he didn't cover in the public meditations. My breath moved from feeble to almost nonexistent for lengthening periods of time. Baba laid on his sofa, his aging body now weak, clairvoyantly following our inner progress, giving instructions when we came upon obstacles to interiorization. Visions of practicing a similar technique in other times and places floated about in peripheral consciousness. That week, from the moment I sat for meditation, I was absorbed in brilliant inner light and intense upward pressure from the center of my skull. I recalled that Wolfram von Eschenbach implied that the real meaning of Parzival's name was "Pierce valley." *Perhaps this is the piercing of the cranium's Valley of the Holy Grail that lies between the two hemispheres of the brain?*

> *Where the skull divides, there lies the Gate of God.*
>
> THE TAITTIREEYA UPANISHAD

> *Our universal secret needs only the most Secret Fire of the philosophers. The Secret Fire therefore and the Azoth [spiritual mercury] are sufficient.*
>
> PARACELSUS, OF THE CHYMICAL TRANSMUTATION GENEALOGY AND GENERATION OF METALS AND MINERALS, 1657

Eliade writes of Indian alchemy:

The Rudrayamala Tantra calls Shiva the "god of mercury" (Ray, II, p. 19).* In the Kubjika Tantra, Shiva speaks of mercury as his generating principle and lauds its efficiency when it has been "fixed" (i.e., dead) "six" times. . . . In alchemical terms, to "fix" or to "kill" mercury is tantamount to attaining to the *cittavrttinirodha*, which is the ultimate aim of yoga. Hence the limitless efficiency of "fixed" mercury . . . the alchemical process of "killing" mercury was revealed by Shiva and secretly transmitted from One generation of adepts to another.[2]

On an auspicious day in early March 1996, Hariharananda beckoned me alone into a small room at the back of the new meditation hall. The building is unfinished, and the room is full of boards, cans of paint, stacked chairs, and building equipment. He sits in a chair and puts his

---

*Eliade references Praphulla Chandra Ray's *A History of Hindu Chemistry*, vol. II, p. 21. Cf. the myth of the "doctrinal transmission" among the tantric siddha in Eliade, *Le Yoga*, 305 sq.

hand atop my head for a long while and instructs me in sixth Kriya. Power, light, and bliss pour through me as I receive the vibrational upgrade, simultaneously listening and taking inner note of his new instructions. Baba ends thus, "When you have *fixed the mercury*, you will be in samadhi, the breathless, pulseless state of God-consciousness."

*In the depth of mercury . . . is nothing but pure fire occult.*
*. . . The bound Mercury is the greatest secret.*
GOLDSMITH, *THESAURUS THESAURORUM*, 123–24,
ROSICRUCIAN ALCHEMICAL TEXT, 1580

Immobile for a spell, breath returns to me and I open my eyes. Leaning toward me, Baba adds in a whisper with utmost gravity, "Sri Yukteswarji did not give this out, but this is the scientific age." Baba leaned back, gazed over my head, and added, "Pierce the mercury! Practice only this, and you'll reach samadhi soon. Don't worry if your breath stops—let it go. The Lord will not allow you to go into samadhi unless He wills it."*

*He who knows the Stone, is silent about it.*
HEINRICH KHUNRATH (1560–1605),
DRESDEN

Lahiri Mahasaya, Sri Yukteswar, Yogananda, and Hariharananda, among many others have demonstrated the breathless, pulseless states of savikalpa and nirvikalpa samadhi countless times; one can learn to "not live by bread alone but by every word that proceedeth out of the mouth of God" (Matthew 4:4). The breathless, pulseless, immobile state of savikalpa samadhi has been described by scores of adepts and witnesses across traditions, from forest shamans to Christian saints, the

---

*Kriya Yoga initiation must be received from a qualified yogacharya (teacher), and the quotes about mercury throughout this text always refer to spiritual mercury, never the ordinary, highly toxic metal.

Coptic yogis of Egypt, and further across Persia, India, Tibet, to the Taoist adepts of China. Hariharananda writes of sixth Kriya and the final stages:

> You are living your daily life, but you are always remaining near the door of God. At any moment you can enter nirvikalpa samadhi, the seventh level of samadhi. This means you are both in the world and not in the world. You may enter at will the breathless and pulseless state. This introvert stage is also known as turiya samadhi, which means to merge in God.[3]

The next day I was again privileged to be alone with Baba for an hour. He picked up where we left off yesterday, as though only a moment had passed, "Sri Yukteswarji said I could achieve the breathless, pulseless samadhi stage in just seven months of total isolation, but I required eleven months to reach it." I pondered, *The average between seven and eleven months would be nine months, the normal gestation of a human child.* I recalled the alchemical gestation time to give birth to

Fig. 43.2. Sri Yukteswar in shambhavi mudra. From Evans-Wentz, *Tibetan Yoga & Secret Doctrines*, 1935. Copyright Oxford University Press. Reproduced with permission of the Licensor through PLSclear.

the Alchemical Child, aka the Philosophers' Child, is often said to be forty weeks, just over nine months.

> *The matter of the Philosophers' Stone is none other than a*
> *fiery and perfect Mercury.*
>
> PARACELSUS, *The Aurora of the Philosophers*,
> FROM WAITE, *The Hermetic and*
> *Alchemical Writings*, 1:66

Hariharananda exemplified the humility of a true master and initiate, and never boasted of his spiritual stature, always deferring to his teachers as greater than he. Yet on occasion he let slip stories of his hidden spiritual powers: "When my father died, my mother almost went mad with emotion. All my family was there. I told them that I'd go into samadhi, and they would be able to see my body appear as my father's body, but no one must touch me, or it'll change the samadhi state. They agreed, and I entered samadhi. Soon they all saw my body as my father's, and they jumped to touch and hold me. They later brought two doctors, but they could not bring me out of the breathless, pulseless state for six hours."

Days later, after evening meditation Baba raised his eyebrows and looked deeply into me, penetrating my every thought. "Kriya Yoga gives you godly calmness, through which you can reach God at the true cross inside the brain, where the light of Christ consciousness is always shining." He leaned forward to me. "The more you practice in isolation, the more you'll perceive light in your whole brain. Gradually, you'll see light inside the thalamus and hypothalamus." I made note of this, and later discovered the meaning of *thalamus* in both Greek and Latin is "bridal chamber."

*Jesus said: "There are many standing at the door, but it is the solitary who will enter the bridal chamber."*

SAYING 75, FROM GRANT,
THE SECRET SAYINGS OF JESUS

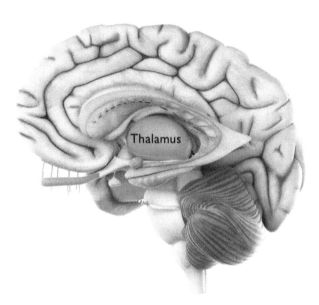

Fig. 43.3. Location of the thalamus, the *bridal chamber* or *alchemical* egg. From "Neuroimaging of acute and chronic unilateral and bilateral thalamic lesions" by C. Tuttle, J. Boto, S. Martin, I. Barnaure, A. M. Korchi, M. Scheffler, and M. I. Vargas. *Insights Into Imaging*, 10 (2019).

Thalamus

# 44

# The Alchemy of Kriya Yoga

*The highest mystery of the whole Work is the . . . dissolution into Mercury.*

BENEDICTUS FIGULUS, ALCHEMIST & ROSICRUCIAN,
*A GOLDEN AND BLESSED CASKET OF
NATURE'S MARVELS*, 1608

A great hidden mystery of alchemy came clear there in India that day in March 1996. In this plate from the Rosicrucian alchemical tradition, we can easily see the human cranium, the place of golgotha (the skull) where the spiritual crucifixion takes place. The solar-pineal and lunar-pituitary forces combine to give birth to the Alchemical Child at the center of the skull, shown as a child in the womb of an angel (bridal chamber). At right, we see the enclosed, limited cave of the left brain, the arena of measurement and analytical categorization; at left, we see the open chamber of the right brain, where the intuitive is directly connected to the limitless flow from the greater ocean of consciousness. At the fontanelle (top of the skull) reads CVM DEO, "With God." At top, in the tent of the upper chakras, we see the alchemist in his oratory with censer and anointing oil in a transcendent state of consciousness (probably borrowed from

Fig. 44.1. Alchemical emblem of the golgotha (skull).
Theophilus Schweighardt Constantiens, *Speculum Sophicum Rhodostauroticum*
("The Mirror of the Wisdom of the Rosy Cross"), 1618.

Khunrath). The very same spiritual technology, the same sacred key has been known across the ages.

> *In allegories and fables, the philosophers have given to this Secret Fire names such as the sword or knife.*
>
> ANTOINE JOSEPH PERNETY (1716–1796),
> *AN ALCHEMICAL TREATISE ON THE GREAT ART*, 1758

I focused intensive efforts in fifth and sixth Kriya. Breath was suspended for longer and longer periods, though the state is so timeless and filled with light that I cannot compare it to ordinary time. After another week, Baba pulled me close. "You will get the pulseless, breathless stage. You got it for a few minutes, yes?" I nodded. "You must take up Durga's spear with extreme concentration. You will get it—keep working, keep trying!"

> *All weaponry in alchemy, signifies the secret fire, the deathly active dissolvent which kills metals.*
>
> LYNDY ABRAHAM, *A DICTIONARY OF ALCHEMICAL IMAGERY*

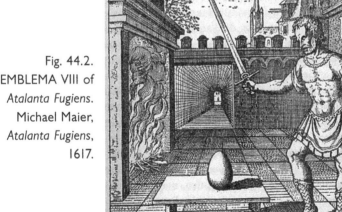

Fig. 44.2. EMBLEMA VIII of *Atalanta Fugiens*. Michael Maier, *Atalanta Fugiens*, 1617.

*Accipe ovum & igneo percute gladio.*
Take the egg and pierce it with a fiery sword.
Alternate version from Opus Mulierum:
*Accipe ovan, id est, vas, et ingeas percute gladio.*
Heat the egg in the vessel, and pierce it with a sword.[1]

One might imagine that with the divine technique of Kriya Yoga one would drop everything in pursuit of completing the million years of evolution in a short time, but I was then young and my worldly identity pushed back. Vague wishes to become a Kriya Yogacharya (teacher/initiator), live in one of the ashrams, and perhaps even marry a spiritual woman and have a family floated through my meditations. Reading my every thought like an open book, Baba again called me in. "I have given you everything. What more do you want?" He held a finger upward and pronounced, "I've told you many times—be free, gain your liberation! That is the best thing you can do for everyone, and for yourself. When you are fully liberated, then God will serve others through you. Until then, do not feel that you are a teacher, do not get puffed up, and never boast that you're practicing higher Kriyas."

Baba moved to Karar Ashram in nearby Puri, and by mid-April the Orissan heat and the crowds grew intense. Day by day, one had to arrive earlier and earlier to find a seat in the hall. Baba, with his great love of humanity, stood fast amid the pressures and gave his all, but between the ever-increasing heat, dust, and crowds I felt choked. Full to my spiritual brim, I could receive no more and I knew it. I went to offer my goodbyes to Baba. He asked me about my plans, and I explained that I would be relocating from Asia to America. "Will you come to New York next month?" I nodded. "Good. Then you also sit with Don Abrams there whenever you can—he is advanced. He is good company."

A month later in New York City, several new acharya (teachers empowered to give Kriya Yoga initiation) were publicly appointed by Hariharanada at the large program in Manhattan, including Don

Abrams and Swami Sarveshswarananda Giri.* Despite the crowds, I was able to briefly see Baba privately, but he made no mention to me of acharya-ship or living in ashrams. He saw a different destiny for me, and only said, "I'm so happy you are roaming all over the world, learning so many things." Thus far, my life's focus had been directed toward spirituality. I pondered, *What can worldly life hold for me now?*

Alchemists and Rosicrucians surely once held the secrets of liberation, of becoming a Philosophers' Stone, like Hariharananda, a catalyst for the transformation of souls from leaden into golden. Inwardly a debt I owed a pan-Eurasian esoteric tradition still compelled me to follow the trail of this sacred knowledge across traditions. I would soon journey to Vienna, once a nexus of alchemy, and now a home for the Kriya Yoga of Sri Yukteswar in Europe.

---

*Readers who wish to receive Kriya Yoga initiation are advised to seek it out from a qualified Kriya Yogacharya. While there are many Kriya lineages, the author recommends those stemming from Sri Yukteswar, Hariharananda, and Karar Ashram in Puri, Orissa, India.

# 45

# Vienna Exile

*The present is the only thing that has no end.*

ERWIN SCHRÖDINGER,
*MY VIEW OF THE WORLD*

A city of soaring spires and Cold War espionage, Vienna poked a deep dent east into the Iron Curtain for nearly four decades. It may still be the most multilingual city in Europe. The Berlin Wall fell in 1989, and one can now hear Czech, Hungarian, Polish, Slovak, Slovene, Serbian, Croatian, Ukrainian, Russian, as well as all the western European languages on a brief stroll within the Ringstrasse. The visiting Germans are still bold, while the Austrians themselves are circumspect, speaking far less directly.

A shadowy disquiet always surrounded Vienna for me. Avoiding the old capital of many empires, I passed through the main station twice by train just three years prior, but now upon my arrival in the warm months of 1996 I find it utterly charming. The beauty of Vienna is stunning, with its *Jugendstil* (Art Nouveau) architecture and the royal parks. Sublime classical music pours from even residential windows throughout the city. Vienna, so rich in cultural history, was, along with Prague, Leipzig, and Dresden, also a medieval locus of alchemy. A beguiling sense of an invisible circle's completion pervaded the atmo-sphere of my summer here.

Paramahansa Hariharananda decided to found his primary European ashram in Vienna, seconded by the one in Holland. The first temporary ashram at this time was a sprawling house in the ninth dis-trict, just north of the *Innere Stadt* (inner city) where I sublet a small flat for two months from a musician and tango instructor. Most of the buildings in this area are from the eighteenth or nineteenth century. By chance, the cozy, two-room flat was in an older building on Langegasse, just off the inner ring roads of Vienna, located in a direct line to the medical university where my grandfather had studied in 1938. I smiled and imagined Dr. Bailey walking the same streets; *he may have even stayed in this area?* Following Langegasse north only a few hundred meters, the road changes its name to Spitalgasse, and leads directly to the *Medizinische Universität Wien*, where Mesmer (the father of mod-ern hypnosis) studied in 1760 and my grandfather more recently. With the *Anschluss* (annexation of Austria by Nazi Germany) in March 1938, half of the university's medical professors and instructors were dis-missed. As tensions in Europe heated up, my grandfather left Vienna for Budapest where he continued his studies until the next world war appeared imminent.

Arriving at the ashram, Baba seemed surprised to see me. "Always I see Kevin-heaven-seven! In India, New York, and now here in Vienna. I have already given you everything. What is it you need?" He searched my mind and quickly knew that I still carried a concealed wish to be an acharya and to live in an ashram community. "I've already told you to be free and do your utmost to get samadhi. So why have you come here?" I was speechless and could only bow. Baba looked troubled for a moment, but softened and put his hand on my head. "Well, it is good that you have come. Do not talk too much and be at meditation every evening."

The following day, soaking in the ambience of the Café Landtmann, enjoying tea and a *Sachertorte*, the famed Viennese chocolate delicacy, I looked over the clientele, either in animated conversation or with their noses buried in newspapers, and wondered *what could be of such intense worldly interest?* Those first weeks in Vienna I meditated intently in my flat during the day and at the ashram each evening. Though I was invited out to cafés, galleries, and concerts, I declined, trying my best to follow Baba's directive for isolation. I sat in full lotus until my knees swelled, and this only intensified my inward drive. Within a few days, there was a profound deepening in my meditations. The secret fire had now become a mysterious glow of light at the upper cavity of my head. Baba appeared in dreams regularly, teaching mantras and other finer points in this *Night School.* Days later in the ashram Baba pulled me aside after meditation. "You're feeling advancement, are you not?" I nodded and bowed. Within a week came particular inner visions. While he probably knew of these already, I felt I had to tell Baba of these in ordinary words.

When I reached the Vienna ashram on the afternoon of September 9, 1996, Don Abrams had just arrived from New York. We greeted each other and both went in to see Baba, along with other monks and acharya. I wanted to report my experiences privately, so Baba asked me to come close. After whispering the inner visions, to my complete surprise he responded loudly for everyone in the room to hear, "This is an advanced stage. You should live in the ashram as a *brahmachari* monk, and become a Kriya Yoga acharya!" I prostrated on the floor. He went on, "You have deepest desire for God-realization. You should move around and make programs, giving initiation to many. You may live in the ashram here in Vienna or in Florida, as you wish."

I could scarcely stand—my dream had come true. I prostrated in silence while he talked with others. I was led out in a daze. *To become a renunciant and teacher, a yogacharya—it's finally real.* Baba knew what I wanted, and he granted it to me, very publicly. A goal had been reached, and now that it was here, I was terrified. My funeral had again been arranged. *Would I attend, and formally die to my little self?*

In India he had repeatedly told me to not join an ashram. Now he has gifted me with exactly what I want—*and yet the opposite of what he advises?* On the one hand, renunciation seemed freeing and divine, but on the other, austere—even imprisoning. Baba preferred his acharya to be either celibate monks or married, and I was neither at the time. *To give up my private life, to only serve others?* I felt frozen in time and numb in mind and heart. That evening I stumbled through the Vienna streets, back to the Innere Stadt.

I coddled a warm tea in a café and Schrödinger's Gedankenexperiment came to mind, as the famous physicist was himself from Vienna. Schrödinger was not only a genius but quite the character: he completed his doctorate in physics at the University of Vienna, eventually moving to the University of Zurich. He was finally promoted to Berlin where he succeeded Max Planck at the Friedrich Wilhelm University, while scandalously living with both his wife and mistress. Schrödinger left Germany in 1933 as the Nazis rose to power and returned to Vienna, but after the Anschluss he fled to Ireland.

I was not his cat but rather Schrödinger's Kriyavan, now in the *superposition*, with all possibilities existing at once. I stared out the window unblinking. I might not understand his thought experiment (1935) fully, but at this moment it seems the quantum possibilities are three: (1) live as a celibate monk and acharya; (2) become a married acharya; or (3) live freely in the world as a secret yogi. Schrödinger's famous thought experiment poses the question, "*When* does a quantum system stop existing as a superposition of states and become one or the others?" I sipped my tea, now cold, and left, aimlessly walking the darkening streets until it rained.

*The total number of minds in the universe is one, in fact, consciousness is a singularity phasing within all beings.*
ERWIN SCHRÖDINGER, GEIST UND MATERIE

The next day I again wandered the Vienna streets, muttering a mournful farewell to worldly life. At the ashram, before the evening meditation, Baba called me into his room and solemnly intoned, "You must pass the exam; only then will you be an acharya. The other acharya are not going out at all. You must end all extroversion."

Throughout the evening's meditation my mind flitted between quantum probabilities. On my way home I stopped to enjoy a *last* glass of wine before my renunciation.

In the morning, a boyish rebellion emerged. Instead of remaining in to meditate, I went out for breakfast at the Central Café on Herrengasse. Architecturally, it is a stunning café, patronized for over a hundred years by famed writers, philosophers, professors, and even revolutionaries. As I recall, I opted for the *Wiener Frühstück*, the only reasonably priced breakfast. I pulled a *Wiener Zeitung* newspaper from the old wooden rack and pretended to read it, laughing at myself as I was able to decipher only a few headlines and some phrases here and there. I gazed outside at passersby, and then inside around the café, feeling the life force of its patrons, sensing the atmosphere, and taking in the delicious aromas of coffees and sweets. All at once, I felt an intense love for the world and all it offered.

Instead of catching a tram to the ashram, I ignored Baba's advice and went straight to the nearby Hofburg Palace Museum, just down the street. *Before I become a monk and an "ashram slave" I simply must see this history-rich palace!* The palace and museum are impressive, but the *Weltliche Schatzkammer* (Imperial Treasury) is simply jaw-dropping, a collection of immeasurable value. The treasury is located in the oldest part of the palace, dating back to the thirteenth century. One must first pass through the narrow Swiss Court, named for the Swiss Guard who were responsible for the protection of the emperors and kings. Among the great array of treasures, I took special note of the Holy Lance, legendarily known as the spear that pierced Jesus's side as he hung on the cross.

Dazzled and dazed, I left the palace and the treasures, crossed the nearby Michaelerplatz, and found a table at the Café Grössenwahn. This café faces the Palace Museum and was historically known for the insatiable ambitions of its artistic clientele. While I imagine the heated debates of yesteryear among strong coffee and cigars, I notice no one is smoking today, a rarity in any Viennese coffeehouse. Many great artists, musicians, and writers of the last century had frequented this café, including the mystics Rudolf Steiner, W. J. Stein, Friedrich Eckstein, the composer Hugo Wolf, and the author Stefan Zweig. Perhaps even the most infamous Austrian megalomaniac of all, the amateur artist who lived in Vienna in the early 1910s, might have brooded over his *kampf* (struggle) with a coffee here. In fact, I later learned, the future dictators Hitler, Stalin, Tito, and Freud all lived in Vienna in the same year, 1913—the very same year that Rudolf Steiner laid out the site plain for his masterpiece of spiritual architecture in Dornach, Switzerland.

Coffee agitates me, so I took tea and pondered the symbol of that spear. According to scientific testing I read about in a brochure, this particular lancehead dates back to only the seventh century, so the "Holy Lance" may well be more a symbol or a metaphor for something else entirely, just like the Holy Grail isn't likely an ordinary stone or cup. Hariharananda often said Christ was first crucified in the "cup" of the cranium (*Golgotha* means "skull"), where the individual soul dissolves into God-consciousness through special processes in the brain— the essence of the higher Kriyas. Manly P. Hall writes, "The key to the Grail Mysteries will be apparent if the sacred spear is recognized as the pineal gland with its peculiar point-like projection and in the Holy Grail the pituitary body containing the mysterious Water of Life."[1]

*The lance and bowl, the spear of destiny, and the cranial bowl of the skull?* Outward legends often mirror inner processes. Charlemagne, among others, imagined possession of this metal-tipped spear would bring him worldly power, a typical externalized interpretation of what surely took place inwardly. I looked over the café patrons. Most read their newspapers quietly, but an animated debate broke out among a group of young men, and I felt it time to return to the ashram. *Enough of the world for today.* Evening meditation would offer a blissful respite from the illusory realm of mega-egos, including my own.

At the ashram that early evening I was greeted with smiling eyes from a number of persons I hadn't spoken with before—word had spread that I would be one of the new acharya. I cannot deny that I enjoyed this new respect and attention. Invitations to cafés and restaurants mysteriously increased, along with admiring glances. My self-confidence accepted the boost and I unknowingly exuded a self-assured charm. This did not go unnoticed by Baba, who warned me the next evening, "You must not be the blind leading the blind."

Café lounging and more reading soon replaced daytime meditations. Cozy dinner parties held by local students for visiting Kriyavan became regular events. Everyone wanted to hear my charismatic stories of India. Soon came visits to Gustave Klimt exhibitions, concerts, then a Chinese circus. We talked late into the evenings, often returning to my flat to listen to the cache of tango music in my sublet owner's collection. Days passed and I missed more evening meditations due to social engagements. I was rising later in the mornings, even skipping meditations for more sightseeing with new friends.

Following an inward summons, I arrived at the ashram early in the afternoon. Baba immediately laid into me: "Don't waste your time in idle talk, gossip, and chatter. Stay ninety-nine percent at the fontanelle; the moment you feel something pulling you down, remove it immediately. Is the mango ready to fall from the mother tree?" He gazed into the space above my head and added, "Too much socializing makes you a fool!"

Not only those seeking enlightenment come to ashrams and monasteries. Many of us desperately in need of healing often arrive at the feet of a master *believing* we seek spiritual liberation when in fact we only wish to be relieved of our pain. Once even a small amount of healing occurs, we so quickly return to worldly illusion. I failed to understand both my own suffering and that of other Kriyavan as a microcosm for the suffering of the world. Women with glowing, watery eyes, yearning for love and healing, pulled at me. Compassion is easily mistaken for romantic love, and even a renunciate is not immune to this.

> *Tear-filled eyes make sweet lips.*
>
> Wolfram von Eschenbach, *Parzival*,
> bk. 5, st. 272, line 12, circa 1200

Foolishly continuing my socializing and sightseeing, I felt a growing distance from the austere ashram. The spiritual heights I had touched in India earlier this year now felt ever more remote. I could no longer hold the spiritual power and was easily led back to apana, a downward flow. Days later, I walked a short distance north from my flat on Langegasse to explore a new part of the city, crossing over the large Waehringestrasse to a small street, continuing on toward the river. Strolling happily, I noticed a stone plaque on a building on my left, which read:

*In diesem Haus lebte und wirkte*
*PROFESSOR SIGMUND FREUD*
*in den Jahren 1891~1938*

*Freud's home and office right here, now a museum!* As I leaned to enter, I was overcome by a dark melancholy and found myself unable to move in or out of the door, frozen on the threshold. After a struggle I pulled away, slipping away down the street to the east. The shadowy despondence didn't lift until I reached a canal, where I sat on a bench gazing over the water to the city beyond. I never walked on Berggasse again.

Under a radiant sun I watched the waters of the Donaukanal flow past my bench and late summer flowers. I pondered my situation: *What happened to the householder yoga? Are the advanced stages of Kriya Yoga only for monks? Surely, advanced Kriyavan can still be married householders, as are a number of disciples?* Intense doubt regarding renunciation set in and I stewed in a dismal gloom. Shortly later, two lovely women from the ashram walked past by chance and greeted me with squeals and broad smiles. They joined me on the bench and we chatted for a spell with dancing eyes. Despite the brilliant sunshine, a sudden cool wind blew over the river, portending autumn. We felt chilled and were soon in a warm café nearby with *Kaffee und Torten* (tarts), enjoying each other's company.

*Only the misfortune of exile can provide the in-depth*
*understanding and overview into the realities of the world.*
STEFAN ZWEIG, *FOUCHÉ: PORTRAIT OF A POLITICIAN*

The afternoon grew late and the three of us left the café, going directly to the ashram together for evening meditation. Before I could sit in the hall, I was called to Baba's room by Swami Prajnanananda Giri, who wore a worried face. In his room Baba was as stern as I had ever seen him: "You're mixing too much with others here. You have divided interests, and you're not meditating deeply. This is not the behavior of an acharya. Get samadhi, and then you'll be a teacher. Until then, you must leave the ashram and purify yourself. You're not ready." I was so stunned that I could only drop my head against his chair. Baba stroked my hair, "You have the seed within you for Realization—this seed has only sprouted. You must become the tree—go!"

*When the student is ready, the teacher appears.*
*When the student is truly ready, the teacher disappears.*

Fig. 45.1. The Ouroboros, symbol of the eternal process of soul evolution, life and death, destruction and re-creation. Drawing from 1478 by Theodoros Pelecanos, in alchemical tract titled *Synosius*. Fol. 279 of Codex Parisinus graecus 2327.

*So, this is exile?* I lift my heavy head from the café counter and look out to the busy Vienna street outside. I had heard of disciples being sent away, but this was a surprise. It is said, "Truth gives strength to the strong, but wounds the weak." *Which am I?* I nibbled at my lunch and made the decision: *I choose to accept the truth with strength.* I could no longer rely upon refuge in an ashram indefinitely. *India is not an escape, and Baba is not a crutch; he is a catalyst and a bridge.* Parzival had been shown the Stone but had not yet become it. I knew that only by aligning with the *inner guru* would I cross the great water.

Baba's last words to me gave me a strange mixture of both painful desolation and quiet joy. There would be no holding to my spiritual father here in Vienna; I would not become a Kriya Yogacharya. I would walk another path, like his mysterious wandering disciples in India who are called to him only now and then. Readiness to teach, initiate, and pass the *Secret Fire* to others is a sacred measure and requires maturity at all levels. Oddly enough, since this time, Paramahansa Hariharananda's wisdom and influence have grown in me, such that I often feel he is more present with me now than when I was in his physical presence.

Vienna has a rich history of exiles. Just as Freud, Schrödinger, and even Bailey all left after the Anschluss in 1938, I too left Vienna for exile. Freud never returned, nor did my grandfather, and, so far, neither have I.

# 46

# Sovereignty

After a dozen years in Eurasia, the youthfulness of America struck me dumb and I felt sorely out of place. Fortunately, I met yogacharya Don Abrams soon after my return from Vienna, and he offered the wisest of words: "The goal isn't becoming an acharya, Kevin—the goal is liberation." The truth of this remained a vital support. Hariharananda had achieved nirvikalpa samadhi through being a monk; he knew no other way. The tremendous focus required to attain such a state was aided by his isolation in an ashram. But not all of us are suited to live as monks in cloisters, especially in the first half of our lives. Even Sri Yukteswar took monastic vows only after the untimely passing of his wife and daughter.

Seattle, my new home, greeted me with gray months of mild, drizzling rain. I unpacked all that I had shipped from Kyoto and settled in. I started a new business and a new life, but the disorientation resulting from my exile from the Kriyavan community brought to my attention an inner emotional immaturity. At thirty-five years of age, I felt in many ways still a boy. As mentioned before, I envied those from cultures who were still lived by their myths, as Hariharananda was lived by the richness of Hindu mythology. I lamented the loss of this in the industrialized nations of the world and had no idea how to regain it. *Where are the mature men of power in my culture?*

While waiting for the universe to respond to this request, the Project still called me and after years of studying Eastern esotericism, curiosity drove me to deepen my investigations into Western esoteric traditions. Inspired by Manly Hall's writings on alchemy, I entered an old bookstore in Seattle and asked for alchemical texts. "Seeking the Arcanum, are we?" said the bookkeeper with a raised eyebrow. After a short absence, he placed a large volume with a green cover before me, *The Hermetic Museum*. At first glance, it was again simply incomprehensible, but out of sheer stubbornness I purchased it and steadfastly poured over the nonsensical gibberish. I felt unsure I'd discover more secrets in this, but it was an interesting relic from antiquity, part of a widening puzzle of archaic sacred knowledge that might just reveal more on how to pierce the veil of samsara. The relationship of alchemy to the pursuit of the Holy Grail, Illumination, kundalini force, and the Philosophers' Stone slowly became more apparent. Meditation often brought memories of my painful failure. As healing, I built a second personal library to further bridge East and West and read more widely.

The legends of the Holy Grail are surely a hidden metaphor. Of the two primary authors of the earliest versions, Chretien considered the Grail a cup, but Wolfram insisted the Grail is a stone. Wolfram seemed to have more authority to me, as he got the story from the poet Kyot, who got it from a Moorish alchemist in Spain, who understood the Grail to be a stone that falls from heaven. This may be akin to the Indo-Tibetan *Cintamani* stone (wish-fulling gem), or the Islamic *Kaba* stone that fell from heaven. *Perhaps the Grail is both the cranial cup, and a metaphorical stone that falls to the center of the skull, thus "piercing the valley"?*

Life in Seattle took a new turn. By coincidence, my old friend Larry was offered a promotion to move here with his family for work in the burgeoning IT security arena, the neo-silicon valley in Pugent Sound. Not only had we gone to high school, a student exchange in Germany, and a portion of university together, he had even taken initiation into

Kriya Yoga after I introduced him to Hariharananda some years ago. We gladly met again and I saw a deep change in him, a different kind of change. A solidity of presence and a clarity in his eyes exuded from his being; I felt him to be rooted in the very soil. He had *power*.

Now it was Larry's turn to gift me with an important healing and next step. He informed me of an initiatory program, a rite of passage from boy to man, applicable to men of any age. Larry would not say what it was, but only cryptically intoned, "I didn't know that I'd been living as only half a man." He added with conviction, "That changes after initiation." I recalled the boy from the film *The Emerald Forest*, and asked if it was something like that, "Yes, but no fire ants. It's a challenging mythopoetic approach, condensed and modernized." His eyes held steady; no hidden shame or shadow averted his gaze.

Among the many anthropologists and psychologists, Moore and Gillette have perhaps best laid out the map of the masculine psyche in their remarkable book *King, Warrior, Magician, Lover*. The four archetypes of masculine psychology and the powers they exemplify are magnificently described therein, as well as the bipolar shadow elements of each. Even without an initiatory rite of passage into adulthood, the average male passes through the stages of Lover, Knight, King, and Magician to some degree throughout his life, though for most of us there are deficiencies or overcompensations due to the lack of the full, primordial rites of passage. Naturally, there are also very important female rites of passage for the journey from girl to woman, but that is not the discussion here.

Briefly, the Lover is an archetype that men are born with—the joyful, playful, curious boy who naturally loves his family, community, and life itself. The next stage appears in adolescence when the boy must learn to stand up and act in his world, even when he doesn't want to; thus, we have our chores, sports training, and disciplined studies. This "warrior" stage is not about making war, but about tempering the teenage boy's highly creative testosterone into a vehicle for action in service of the community. The Knight archetype, for me, is preferable to the term *warrior*, as it better connotes service. Unfortunately, due to the disappearing rites of passage from boy to man, most males in industrialized cultures don't have the opportunity to develop the Knight. They might seek it in sport, films, superhero comics, or even gang initiations, but these all fall short of fully throwing the switch from boy psychology to the mature masculine. Unfortunately, these boys grow into *older boys* who create wars and chaos in order to initiate themselves. The rite of passage is best performed for the adolescent by the initiated Knights, Kings in their own right, and the elder Magicians of the tribe.

The King archetype tends to appear when a male reaches his midthirties, or else life will force it upon him. This is the taking of full responsibility for his life. He can try to blame his parents, his culture, his schools, his government, but eventually he must create his own life, gain his own independence, make a living, and be prepared to be responsible for more than himself (i.e., family and community). The arrival of children often thrusts a man onto this stage, but there may remain hidden teenage shadows within. He remains underdeveloped, as we so often see in husbands and fathers today.

The Magician-Shaman archetype normally emerges later in life, if at all, after living decades in this world. The Elder/Magician becomes a conductor of cultural heritage, one who passes on the wisdom and myths of the tribe. On rare occasion, the Magician is overly developed in youth, prior to the development of the Knight and King archetypes, as in my case. I had dashed ahead into the spiritual realms of the Magician, but weakness in my personality structure remained. Even at my age I was in many ways living by whims, not yet fully responsible for my life, and I was learning the hard way. Only a balanced development of the four primary archetypes can bring the stability needed *to cross the great water.*

Just weeks prior to my thirty-sixth birthday, I undertook the ordeal of a forty-eight-hour rite of passage into the mature masculine. In Indigenous tribes this is normally done in adolescence, but if a male hasn't received this from his tribe then he is considered still a boy. Thus, my current age was irrelevant. There are at least four steps in the initiation rite from boy to man, and they vary in length and style from tribe to tribe.

The first stage is *Separation*: when a boy's time comes, he must be taken out of the mother's circle; the psychic umbilical cord of dependence must be cut. He will not grow up to be a woman; he will soon be a man, and after this rite he will never sleep in his mother's teepee again. If this doesn't occur, the boy-man will re-create his mother's circle with his girlfriend, wife, or future partners, leading to incomprehensible misery for both.

The second stage is the ritual *Ordeal*. This needn't be scarring or abusive, but it is a challenging introduction to the painful realities of adult life, with no mothers present to comfort the boy. One must feel that there is a risk of failure or even death to complete this stage. Next, the newly born man must be taught to *work with his shadow*, lest his unconscious fears and selfish desires derail his life. Finally, there is the *Vision Quest*—what is the new man's reason to be? This is the spiritual stage, where he may undergo another kind of ritual death-rebirth into a Knight who serves a higher purpose for the greater good of the community (unlike the uninitiated boy-men who run so much of the world now). Once the Knight archetype is activated, it is only a matter of time before he advances into the King archetype—full acceptance and responsibility for all aspects of one's life.

Initiations must always be secret; one cannot know what will happen in advance. Thus, I will not reveal more here, but to say this rite of passage was a missing piece in my life would be a great understatement. I emerged from that primordial experience a new and powerful being, perhaps an adult for the first time. If I had experienced this rite in my adolescence, a great deal of trouble for myself and others would likely have been unnecessary. This was the missing piece of maturity, groundedness, and power I needed. I no longer sought a boyish, flying-away kind of freedom. I was fully in my body, and I stood firmly on the earth.

The day after I returned there came a most interesting manifestation of this new power: I was driving out of a supermarket parking lot when a black-leather-jacketed gang type walked in front of my car and placed an empty beer bottle on the pavement in the middle of the car exit, dead in front of my car, as if to say, "I dare you to say a word to me about it." I immediately opened my car door, stood pointing at the bottle, and bellowed with a fearless authority I'd never heard in my voice before, "You pick up that bottle right now!" The guy was so stunned by the undaunted ferocity in my voice that he meekly turned, picked up the bottle, and slinked away. I got back in the car and drove out the exit. I had changed. I was present, fearless, nothing shook the inner conviction that I was indeed the sovereign of my life, even if I were to die from it.

A week later I learned that an accomplished professor of anthropology would offer a weekend shamanism workshop in Vancouver, Canada, in October. He had lived with Amazonian jungle tribes and had eventually become a fully initiated shaman. I simply knew to my core that I had to be there to meet him. I registered immediately and looked forward to attending.

Only days later a business colleague scheduled an event the same weekend in Oregon and insisted I attend. I informed her that I was not available that weekend, and after a short discussion it was clear that my attendance wasn't essential for this particular event. However, as senior to me in this field, she seemed to take my choice as a personal affront to her "authority." She strongly insisted I attend regardless. I stood my ground, explaining I was available for all other events on other weekends, except that one. That I dared say *No* to her was intolerable, and she actually hung up on me. Holding that buzzing receiver in my hand, I growled deeply with power and my very bones felt denser. I felt and knew I now had the fearless, grounded power to live a soul-directed life in this world. A structure to contain celestial influence was born. Weakness in character cannot be bypassed—I tried, I know. One must become a complete human being first; then celestial power can be contained and brought to the material plane for the benefit of all.

In the Grail story, Parzival finally removes his mother's garment, cutting the psychic umbilical cord that holds him in the child's circle.

Fig. 46.1. Emblem IX, *The Book of Lambspring*, Prague, 1599.
Barnaud, Nicholas. The Book of Lambspring, from *Triga chemica: de lapide philosophico tractatus tres*. Prague, 1599. Also published in Musaeum Hermeticum in 1625 by Lucas Jennis in Frankfurt, and republished by Waite (translator & editor) in London, 1893.

Only then could Parzival find the Grail, in order to heal the king, and heal the land—himself and the larger world he inhabits. "Whom does the Grail serve?" In a matter of months, I would be initiated on the healing path of the compassionate shaman, one where Parzival asks, "Friend, what ails thee?" I would become an inward renunciate and an outward healer. My spiritual circuitry had been upgraded by

Hariharananda, but my earthly, body-personality complex had been too weak to complete the alchemical process of Kriya Yoga. Now a new structure came into being, an essential step in the Magnum Opus. My personality configuration now bolstered and empowered, my eyes met the horizon. A new sovereign was born.

# 47

# The Mirror of Mercurius

*Mercurius is an invisible spirit like the reflection in a mirror, intangible, yet it is at the same time the root of all the substances necessary to the alchemical process.*

BASILIUS VALENTINUS, *THE TWELVE KEYS*, 1678

The birthday gathering with a circle of friends at the Port of Seattle is a gentle one. After sharing a meal, stories, laughter, and the warm summer views over the water, I return home. Another year older. Closing three twelve-year cycles of the Asian zodiac today I wondered with a sigh, *What next?* My brief foray into American life was coming to an end. I had already made a tentative decision to return to Asia early next year. I meditated on my bed late into the evening and did not recall when I laid down to sleep . . .

An ancient voice calls in a dream, and I awake. I turn on no lights, preferring the soft moonlight of the predawn morning. My face is reflected in the twilit mirror over my washroom sink. I pause and fall into an eternal present. In the shadowy, diffuse gray light, I see that my adult facial bone structure is now fully set, and my mouth drops open with astonishment. I recall the dream vision of fifteen years earlier. The elderly Teacher's face of light is—rather, will be in decades to come—none other than my own. I stagger back and chills run through me and I know: *linear time and linear incarnation are illusory.*

> *The stone which the philosophers do seek is an invisible and impalpable spirit.*
>
> MARSILIUS FICINUS, *BOOK OF THE CHEMICAL ART*, CHAP. 10, 1518

I feel dizzy and want to lie on the floor, but I'm held before the magic mirror by an invisible force. This is no dream—I'm awake and *I am.* Gazing in that mirror at the head of glowing light the face of another incarnation emerges, and then another just as quickly. In the eternal present, I, he, she—we are all a singular idea, the *Causal Spirit* from above, the source of my group of incarnations embodied in the time-bound forms below.

> You have read in the scriptures . . . that God encased the human soul successively in three bodies—the idea, or causal, body; the subtle astral body, seat of man's mental and emotional natures; and the gross physical body. On earth a man is equipped with his physical senses. An astral being works with his consciousness and feelings and a body made of lifetrons [prana]. A causal-bodied being remains in the blissful realm of ideas.
>
> SWAMI SRI YUKTESWAR GIRI[1]

> Three spirits, united in one, live and act in man; three worlds, united into one, throw their rays upon him . . . the first is the essence of the elements [physical]; the second the [astral] soul of the stars; the third the [causal] spirit—the life.
>
> PARACELSUS[2]

> *The true alchemist is one in whom the spiritual descends into the material, creating a unity, or vinculum, which has the power to hold all celestial influences.*
>
> ELIAS ASHMOLE, *THEATRICUM CHEMICUM BRITTANICUM*, PROLOGUE, JANUARY 26, 1652

*Samadhi* has been translated as a "collected state of being." Shamarpa Rinpoche's prophetic words that I would one day be able to *encompass* my incarnations returned with a new depth and meaning. Knowledge of linear reincarnation is a limited perspective; thus, I coin a third new term in this volume: *Multi-Incarnational Consciousness* (MINC), the living knowledge and real-time experience of the Overself, or Causal Soul's many emanations into astral and physical incarnations. This topic will be discussed further in a subsequent volume.

Mercurius, the invisible spirit, inspires remembrance of the Overself. I was never trapped on this planet; the life of the spirit can be both freedom and full engagement at the physical level. Heavenly compassion, power, and wisdom do embody on Earth.

*As above, so below.*

Fig. 47.1. Hermetic philosophy in the eye of the imagination: *Aurum Aurae* (Gold of the Air, sky, or Heavens). Upward (*sursum*) and downward (*deorsum*), fire and water, sun and moon merge in the mercurial world-soul, whose mirror image is the *lapis* (stone) in the water. *As above, so below.* Baldinus, *Aurum Hermeticum*, Amsterdam, 1675.

*The Cosmic Rose*, Christ-Cruciform or *Sigillum Dei* engraving.
Heinrich Khunrath, *Amphitheatrum Sapientiæ Æternæ* 1595.

# Notes

## CHAPTER 1. CAVE OF FIRE

1. St. Germain, *The Most Holy Trinosophia*, Section 2 (translating *La Très Sainte Trinosophie*, page 16).
2. St. Germain, *The Most Holy Trinosophia*, Section 4 (translating *La Très Sainte Trinosophie*, page 31).
3. Zosimos of Panopolis, *Concerning the True Book of Sophe, the Egyptian, and of the Divine Master of the Hebrews and the Sabaoth Powers*, in Jung, *Modern Psychology: November 1940–July 1941: Alchemy*, 44–45.

## CHAPTER 2. PINEAL PORTAL

1. Waite, *The Hermetic Museum*, vol. 1.
2. Fox, *Astral Projection*, 77.
3. Manly Hall, notes and commentaries to *The Trinosophia*, p. 100.
4. St. Germain, *The Most Holy Trinosophia*, sec. 4 (translating *La Très Sainte Trinosophie*, 34).

## CHAPTER 3. DOMINUS LIMINIS

1. Haggard, *She*, chap. 13.
2. Steiner, *Knowledge of the Higher Worlds*, chap. 10, "The Guardian of the Threshold."

## CHAPTER 4. TEMPLE

1. Forshaw, "Curious Knowledge and Wonder-Working Wisdom in the Occult Works of Heinrich Khunrath," 114, quoting Khunrath's *Amphitheatre*, 168.

## CHAPTER 6. ZWEI SEELEN

1. Novak, "Edgar Cayce and the Binary Soul Doctrine."
2. Anderson, "Encountering the Sacred," 1.

## CHAPTER 8. SPIRITUAL SCIENCE

1. Fox, *Astral Projection*, 97.
2. Fox, *Astral Projection*, 128.
3. Adam and Tannery, *Oeuvres de Descartes*, 11:120; Cottingham, Stoothoff, and Murdoch, *The Philosophical Writings of Descartes*, 1:99.

## CHAPTER 9. KUNDALINI FIRE

1. Woodroffe, *Sakti and Sakta*, chap. 29.
2. Woodroffe, *Sakti and Sakta*, chap. 29.

## CHAPTER 11. THE QUEST

1. Lati Rinpoche, *Death, Intermediate States, and Rebirth*, 36–37.
2. Freemantle and Trungpa, *The Tibetan Book of the Dead*, 71.
3. Gray, *Goethe, the Alchemist*, 7–29.

## CHAPTER 12. GREATER GUARDIAN

1. Steiner, *Knowledge of the Higher Worlds*, chap. 10.

## CHAPTER 14. MANDALA

1. Thrangpu Rinpoche, *A Song for the King*, 64n37.

## CHAPTER 22. ATMAN EQUALS BRAHMAN

1. O'Neill, "The Sun Invincible," 14.
2. Hauck, "The Philosophers' Stone," 26.

## CHAPTER 23. MASTER OF KRIYA

1. Waite, *The Secret Tradition in Alchemy*, 7, quoting Jacob Boehme.
2. Yogananda, *Autobiography of a Yogi*, 142.
3. Yogananda, *Autobiography of a Yogi*, 142.

## CHAPTER 24. ORISSA

1. Yogananda, *Autobiography of a Yogi*, 143.
2. Bacon, *The Root of the World*, 2.
3. Yogananda, *Autobiography of a Yogi*, 144.
4. Yogananda, *Autobiography of a Yogi*, 144.
5. Waite, *The Secret Tradition in Alchemy*, 39.

## CHAPTER 25. LAMA

1. Evans-Wentz, *The Tibetan Book of the Dead*, Commentary by Jung, xliii, xlviii, and xlix.

## CHAPTER 27. VAJRAYANA

1. Samuels, *Civilized Shamans*, 8.
2. Govinda, *Way of the White Clouds*, 153.
3. Sangharakshita and Mallander, *In the Realm of the Lotus*, 37.
4. Kriyananda, *The New Path*, 317.
5. Boehme, *Mysterium Magnum*, chap. 11, stanzas 28–29.

## CHAPTER 31. TAOIST ALCHEMY

1. Lu, *Taoist Yoga*, chap. 1.
2. Lu, *Taoist Yoga*, chap. 1.
3. Lu, *Taoist Yoga*, chap. 12.

4. Krishna, *Kundalini*, 126.
5. Wilhelm, *The Secret of the Golden Flower*, 59.

## CHAPTER 36. PANTHEON PIGNA

1. Griffiths, "Abaris," 1.

## CHAPTER 37. SWISS SYNCHRONICITIES

1. Kriyananda, *The New Path*, 400.

## CHAPTER 38. SECOND KRIYA

1. Yogananda, *Autobiography of a Yogi*, 225, 231, 227, 232.
2. Yogananda, *Autobiography of a Yogi*, chap. 26.
3. Hariharananda, *Kriya Yoga*, 101.

## CHAPTER 39. MUNICH TO DRESDEN

1. Forshaw, "Curious Knowledge and Wonder-Working Wisdom in the Occult Works of Heinrich Khunrath," 107.
2. Forshaw, "Curious Knowledge and Wonder-Working Wisdom," 124.

## CHAPTER 40. PENDULUM

1. Fradon, *The Gnostic Faustus*, introduction.
2. Kriyananda, *Conversations with Yogananda*, 427.
3. Yogananda, *Autobiography of a Yogi*, 367.
4. Kriyananda, *The New Path*, 278.
5. Yogananda, *Autobiography of a Yogi*, chap. 5.
6. Hariharananda, *Kriya Yoga*, 101.
7. Yogananda, *Autobiography of a Yogi*, chap. 16, "Outwitting the Stars."

## CHAPTER 41. WITH THE MASTER

1. Eliade, *The Forge and the Crucible*, 125, 128.

## CHAPTER 42. FOURTH KRIYA

1. Hariharananda, *Kriya Yoga*, 102.
2. Yogananda, *Man's Eternal Quest*, 26.

## CHAPTER 43. HIGHER KRIYAS

1. Hariharananda, *Kriya Yoga*, 102.
2. Eliade, *The Forge and the Crucible*, 133.
3. Hariharananda, *Kriya Yoga*, 102.

## CHAPTER 44. THE ALCHEMY OF KRIYA YOGA

1. De Jong, *Michael Maier's Atalanta Fugiens*, 96.

## CHAPTER 45. VIENNA EXILE

1. Hall, *The Secret Teachings of All Ages*, clxxvii.

## CHAPTER 47. THE MIRROR OF MERCURIUS

1. Yogananda, *Autobiography of a Yogi*, chap. 43, quoting Sri Yukteswar.
2. Hartmann, *The Life and the Doctrines*, 263–64, quoting Paracelsus.

# Bibliography

Adam, C., and P. Tannery, eds. *Oeuvres de Descartes*. 11 vols. 1897–1913. Paris: Vrin/CNRS, 1964–1974.

Anderson, Adrian. "Encountering the Sacred: Rudolf Steiner's Discovery of Spiritual Wisdom in Goethe's Poem, 'Elegy.'" Ebooklet available at Rudolf Steiner Studies website. Accessed April 10, 2024.

Artephius. *The Secret Book of Artephius* (Fr: *Livre de Artephius*). *Bibliotheque des Philosophes Chimiques*, Paris, 1741. Originally published in the twelfth century. Republished by Global Grey ebooks, 2018.

Ashmole, Elias. *Theatricum chemicum Brittanicum*. London, 1652.

Bacon, Roger. *The Root of the World*. Originally published in the fifteenth century. Republished by Global Grey ebooks, 2018.

Baker, I. A. *The Dalai Lama's Secret Temple: Tantric Wall Paintings from Tibet*. Photographs by Thomas Laird. London: Thames & Hudson, 2000.

Ball, Philip. *The Devil's Doctor: Paracelsus and the World of Renaissance Magic and Science*. New York: Farrar, Straus, and Giroux, ebook, 2011.

Barnaud, Nicholas. The Book of Lambspring, from *Triga chemica: de lapide philosophico tractatus tres*. Prague, 1599. Also published in Musaeum Hermeticum in 1625 by Lucas Jennis in Frankfurt, and republished by Waite (translator & editor). London, 1893.

Boehme, Jacob. *Mysterium Magnum*. Originally published 1623. Amsterdam: Theosophische Werke, 1682. Republished London: G. Robinson, 1772.

Bonus, Petrus. *The New Pearl of Great Price*. Originally published in 1338. London: James Elliott, 1894.

Carus, C. G. *Psyche: On the Development of the Soul*. Originally published in German in 1846. Thompson, CT: Spring Publications, 1970.

Cleary, Thomas. *Dogen Zenji Goroku: Record of Sayings of Zen Master Dogen.* 2015. Kindle.

Comenius, John Amos. *Orbis Pictus.* Nuremberg, 1658.

Cottingham, J., R. Stoothoff, and D. Murdoch. *The Philosophical Writings of Descartes.* 2 vols. Cambridge: Cambridge University Press, 1984.

De Jong, H. M. E. *Michael Maier's Atalanta Fugiens.* York Beach, ME: Nicolas-Hays, 2002.

de Saint Didier, Limojon, and Alexandre Toussaint. *Le Triomphe Hermetique.* Amsterdam: H. Wetstein, 1689 (In French). London: P. Hanet, 1723.

Descartes, R. L'Homme. Paris: Charles Angot, 1664 (In French). Translation in T. S. Hall, *Treatise of Man.* Cambridge, MA: Harvard University Press, 1972.

Dorneus (Gerhard Dorn). *Theatrum Chemicum.* Vol. 1. Oberuzel: Lazarus Zetzner, 1602.

Eckhart, Meister. *Sermons of Meister Eckhart.* Translated by Claud Field. London: H. R. Allenson, 1909.

Eliade, Mircea. *Le yoga: Immortalité et liberté.* Payot, 1975.

Eliade, Mircea. *The Forge and the Crucible.* Chicago: University of Chicago Press, 1978.

Evans-Wentz, W. Y. *The Tibetan Book of the Dead, or The After-Death Experience on the Bardo Plane.* 3rd ed. With Commentary by C. G. Jung. London: Oxford University Press, 1957.

——. *Tibet's Great Yogi Milarepa.* London: Oxford University Press, 1971.

Ficinus, Marsilius. *Book of the Chemical Art.* 1518. Item 7 from British Library MS Sloane 3638. Transcribed by Justin von Budjoss from a Latin text, *Liber de Arte Chemica*, in *Bibliotheca Chemica Curiosa*, vol 2, p. 172–83, edited by Jean-Jacques Manget. Geneva: Chouet, 1702.

Figulus, Benedictus. *An Epigram Concerning the Philosophers' Stone* (Alexander de S. to Guliemus Blancus) from *Pandora magnalium naturalium aurea et benedicta de Paracelse.* Strasbourg: Lazare Zetzner, 1608.

Flaherty, Gloria. *Shamanism and the Eighteenth Century.* Princeton, NJ: Princeton University Press, 1992.

Forshaw, Peter. "Curious Knowledge and Wonder-Working Wisdom in the Occult Works of Heinrich Khunrath." Chapter 6 of *Curiosity and Wonder from the Renaissance to the Enlightenment*, edited by R. J. W. Evans and A. Marr. London: Routledge, 2016.

Fox, Oliver. *Astral Projection*. Secaucus, NJ: Citadel Press, 1962.

———. "The Pineal Doorway." *Occult Review* 31, no. 4 (April 1920), 190–98.

Fradon, Ramona. *The Gnostic Faustus: The Teachings behind the Classic Text*. Rochester, VT: Inner Traditions, 2007.

Freemantle, Francesca, and Chögyam Trungpa. *The Tibetan Book of the Dead: The Great Liberation through Hearing in the Bardo*. Boston: Shambhala Publications, 1975.

Fuller, Jean O. *The Comte de Saint Germain: Last Scion of the House of Rakoczy*. UK: East-West Publications, 1988.

Gibson, Morgan, and Hiroshi Murakami. *Tantric Poetry of Kukai*. New York: White Wine Press, 1987.

Goddard, David. *The Tower of Alchemy*. York Beach, ME: Red Wheel/Weiser, 1999.

Goethe, Johann Wolfgang von. *Goethe: The Collected Works*. Vol. 2, *Faust I & II*, edited and translated by Stuart Atkins. Princeton, NJ: Princeton University Press, 1984.

———. *Maxims and Reflections*. Originally published 1833. London: Penguin, 1998.

Goldsmith, Adam, trans. *The Thesaurus Thesaurorum: The Treasure of Treasures of the Brotherhood of the Golden & Rosy Cross, 1580*. USA: Vitriol Publishing, 2012.

Govinda, Lama Anagarika. *The Way of the White Clouds*. Berkeley, CA: Shambhala, 1970.

Grant, Robert M. *The Secret Sayings of Jesus According to the Gospel of Thomas*. Originally published by Fontana Books, 1960. Republished by Barnes & Noble Books, 1993.

Gray, Ronald. *Goethe, the Alchemist*. Cambridge: Cambridge University Press, 1952.

Green, John. *Will Grayson, Will Grayson*. London: Penguin, 2012.

Griffiths, Alan H. "Abaris." In *The Oxford Classical Dictionary*, 3rd ed., edited by Simon Hornblower and Anthony Spawforth, 1. Oxford: Oxford University Press, 2003.

Haggard, H. Rider. *She*. London: Longmans, Green, 1887.

Halevi, Z'Ev. *Kabbalah: The Divine Plan*. New York: Harper Collins, 1996.

Hall, Manly P. *Man: The Grand Symbol of the Mysteries*. Los Angeles: Philosophers Press, 1937.

——. *The Most Holy Trinosophia of the Comte St. Germain.* Los Angeles: Philosophical Research Society, 1983.

——. *The Secret Teachings of All Ages.* San Francisco: H.S. Crocker, 1928.

Hariharananda, Paramahansa. *Kriya Yoga: The Scientific Process of Soul-Culture and the Essence of All Religions.* Delhi: Motilal Banarsidass Publishers, 1988.

Hartmann, Franz. *Alchemy.* Sequim, WA: Holmes Publishing Group, 1984

——. *The Life and the Doctrines of Philippus Theophrastus, Bombast of Hohenheim, known by the name of Paracelsus.* New York: Macoy Publishing, 1945.

Hauck, Dennis. *Alchemy.* Penguin Random House. Digital edition, 2021.

——. "Materia Prima: The Nature of the First Matter in the Esoteric and Scientific Traditions." Presented at the Hidden In Plain Sight Conference at the Rosicrucian Order AMORC, San Jose, California, July 23, 2010.

——. "The Philosophers' Stone." *Rosicrucian Digest: Alchemy* 91, no. 1 (2013): 22–30.

——. "The Roots of a Science of Consciousness in Hermetic Alchemy." *Rose+Croix Journal* 11 (2016): 34–51.

Helmond, Johannes. *Alchemy Unveiled.* Canada: Merker Publishing, 1996.

Hillman, James. *Anima: An Anatomy of a Personified Notion.* New York: Spring Publications, 1985.

Jung, C. G. *The Archetypes and the Collective Unconscious.* Vol. 9, part 1 of *Collected Works of C. G. Jung,* edited and translated by Gerhard Adler and R. F. C. Hull. Bollingen Series XX. Princeton, NJ: Princeton University Press, 1970.

——. *C. G. Jung Letters.* Vol. 2: 1951–1961. Edited by G. Adler. Bollingen Series. Princeton, NJ: Princeton University Press, 1976.

——. *Modern Psychology: November 1940–July 1941: Alchemy.* Vols. 1–2. Edited by Elizabeth Welsh and Barbara Hannah. Switzerland: K. Schippert, 1960.

——. *Mysterium Coniunctionis: An Inquiry into the Separation and Synthesis of Psychic Opposites in Alchemy.* Vol. 14 of *Collected Works of C. G. Jung,* edited and translated by Gerhard Adler and R. F. C. Hull. Princeton, NJ: Princeton University Press, 1977.

——. *Synchronicity: An Acausal Connecting Principle.* In *The Structure and Dynamics of the Psyche,* vol. 8 of *Collected Works of C. G. Jung,* edited and translated by Gerhard Adler and R. F. C. Hull. Princeton, NJ: Princeton University Press, 1960.

Kelly, Edward. *Stone of the Philosophers*. From *Tractatus duo egregii, de Lapide Philosophorum, una cum Theatro astronomiæ terrestri, cum Figuris, in gratiam filiorum Hermetis nunc primum in lucem editi, curante J. L. M. C.* [Johanne Lange Medicin Candidato]. Hamburg, 1676. Department of Special Collections, Memorial Library, University of Wisconsin–Madison.

Khunrath, Heinrich. *Amphitheatrum Sapientiæ Æternæ*. Hamburg, 1595. Duveen Collection, Department of Special Collections, Memorial Library, University of Wisconsin–Madison.

Kluckhohn, Paul, Richard Samuel, Gerhard Schulz, and Hans-Joachim Mähl, eds. *Novalis Schriften. Die Werke Friedrich von Hardenbergs*. 6 vols. Historische-kritische Ausgabe. Stuttgart: Kohlhammer Verlag, 1960–2006.

Krishna, Gopi. *Kundalini: The Evolutionary Energy in Man*. London: Stuart & Watkins, 1970.

Kriyananda, Swami [J. Donald Walters]. *Conversations with Yogananda*. Nevada City, CA: Crystal Clarity Publishers, 2004.

———. *The New Path: My Life with Paramahansa Yogananda*. Nevada City, CA: Crystal Clarity Publishers, 2009.

Lati Rinpoche, Lama. *Death, Intermediate States, and Rebirth in Tibetan Buddhism*. Ithaca, NY: Snow Lion Publications, 1981.

Lu, K'uan Yu (Charles Luk). *Taoist Yoga: Alchemy and Immortality*. York Beach, ME: Samuel Weiser, 1970.

Mather, Mathew. *The Alchemical Mercurius: Esoteric Symbol of Jung's Life and Works*. Research in Analytical Psychology and Jungian Studies. London: Routledge, 2014.

McLean, Adam. *The Alchemical Mandala: A Survey of the Mandala in the Western Esoteric Traditions*. 2nd ed. Grand Rapids, MI: Phanes Press, 2002.

———. "The Alchemical Vessel as Symbol of the Soul." *Hermetic Journal*. 1986. Available at The Alchemy Website. Accessed April 2024.

Meffert, Ekkehard. "C. G. Carus und J. W. von Goethe—Geheimer Gleichklang zweier Seelen." *Der Europäer: Symptomatisches aus Politik, Kultur und Wirtschaft, Monatsschrift auf Grundlage der Geisteswissenschaft* 3, no. 12 (Oct. 1999): 3–6.

Monroe, Robert A. *Journeys Out of the Body*. New York: Broadway Books, 1977.

Nietzsche, Friedrich. *Thus Spoke Zarathrustra*. New York: Modern Library, 1917.

Norton, Thomas. *The Ordinal of Alchemy*. England, ca. 1477. Mellon MS 46,

Beineke Rare Book and Manuscript Library, Yale University, New Haven CT.

Novak, Peter. "Edgar Cayce and the Binary Soul Doctrine." Graham Hancock website, October 21, 2003. Accessed April 10, 2024.

Novalis (Georg Philipp Friedrich Freiherr von Hardenberg). *Novalis: Philosophical Writings*. Translated and edited by Margaret Mahony Stoljar. Albany: State University of New York Press, 1997.

O'Neill, T. J. "The Sun Invincible." *Rosicrucian Digest: Alchemy* 91, no. 1 (2013): 13–16.

Paracelsus. *Of the Chymical Transmutation: Genealogy and Generation of Metals and Minerals*. London, 1657. Translated by Robert Turner. Montana: Kessinger Publishing, 2010.

———. *Liber de Occulta Philosophia*. Munich, 1686.

Philoponus, P. A. B. *Thesaurus Thesaurorum*. Bologna, 1725. MS 4775 in the Wellcome Collection, London.

Prajnanananda, Paramahansa. *Sanyal Mahashaya: A Life of Humility*. Kolkata: Prajna Publications, 2017.

Raphael, Alice. *Goethe and the Philosophers' Stone: Symbolical Patterns in "The Parable" and the Second Part of "Faust."* New York: Helix Press/Garrett Publications, 1965.

Ray, Prafulla Chadra. *A History of Hindu Chemistry*. 2nd ed. Calcutta, 1904–09, 2 vols.

Robinson, Samuel. "Secret Temples of the Rosicrucians." Nov. 2015. Pansophy Website. Accessed April 2024.

Roob, Alexander. *The Hermetic Museum: Alchemy & Mysticism*. Cologne: Taschen GmbH, 2001.

Samuels, Geoffrey. *Civilized Shamans: Buddhism in Tibetan Societies*. Washington, DC: Smithsonian Institute Press, 1993.

Sangharakshita and J. O. Mallander. *In the Realm of the Lotus: A Conversation About Art, Beauty, and the Spiritual Life*. Birmingham, UK: Windhorse Publications, 1995.

St. Germain, Comte de. *The Most Holy Trinosophia, or The Most Holy Threefold Wisdom*. Introduction & Commentary by Manly Hall. Los Angeles: Phoenix Press, 1933. Based on the original French version, *La Très Sainte Trinosophie*, MS 2400 in the Library at Troyes, published in the late eighteenth century.

———. *The Most Holy Trinosophia*. Edited by Manly P. Hall. Los Angeles: Philosophical Research Society, 1983.

St. Teresa of Avila. *The Interior Castle*. Originally published in 1577. London: Thomas Baker, 1921.

Steiner, Rudolf. *Goethe's Secret Revelation*. Originally published 1908, and by R. Steiner Publ., 1932. Ferndale, MI: Trismegistus Press, 1980.

———. *Knowledge of Higher Worlds and Its Attainment*. New York: Anthroposophic Press, 1994.

Stolzenberg, D. Stolzius von. *Viridarium chymicum*. Frankfurt, 1624.

Szepes, Maria. *The Red Lion: The Elixer of Eternal Life*. Originally published as *A Vörös Oroszlán* (Hungary, 1946). Yelm, WA: Horus Publishing, 1997.

Tagore, Rabindranath. *Rabindranath Tagore Collected Works*. N.p.: Delphi Poets Series, 2017.

Thrangpu Rinpoche, Kenchen. *A Song for the King: Saraha on Mahamudra Meditation*. Boston: Wisdom Publications. 2006.

Turner, Kevin B. "Ibu Jero Gambuh: The Resurrected Healer of Bali." *Journal for the Foundation for Shamanic Studies*, Issue 29 (December 2016): 6–11.

———. *Sky Shamans of Mongolia: Meetings with Remarkable Healers*. Berkeley, CA: North Atlantic Books, 2016.

Turner, Kevin B., and C. W. Yang. "Decoding Toni's Stone: C. G. Jung's Memorial for Toni Wolff." *Jung Journal: Culture & Psyche*. Vol. 15, Issue 3 (2021): 90–102.

Vaughan, Thomas. *The Works of Thomas Vaughan, Eugenius Philalethes*. Edited, annotated, and introduced by Arthur E. Waite. London: Theosophical Publishing House, 1919.

Waite, Arthur Edward, trans. and ed. *The Hermetic and Alchemical Writings of Paracelsus Aureolus Philippus Theophrastus Bombast of Hohenheim, called Paracelsus the Great*. 2 vols. Reproduced from Dr. L. W. de Laurence edition (London: James Elliot, 1894). Berkeley, CA: Shambhala Publications 1976.

———, ed. *The Hermetic Museum*. Boston: Red Wheel Weiser, 1990.

———. *The Secret Tradition in Alchemy*. First published in 1926. New York: Routledge, 2013.

White, David Gordon. *The Alchemical Body: Siddha Traditions in Medieval India*. Chicago: University of Chicago University Press, 1996.

Wilhelm, Richard. *The Secret of the Golden Flower: A Chinese Book of Life*. London: Kegan Paul, Trench, Trubner, 1947.

Woodroffe, Sir John [Arthur Avalon, pseud.]. *Sakti and Sakta*. London: Luzac, 1918.

Yogananda, Paramahansa. *Man's Eternal Quest*. Los Angeles: Self-Realization Fellowship, 1982.

———. *Autobiography of a Yogi*. Los Angeles, CA: Self-Realization Fellowship, 1981.

Yogananda, Paramhansa. *Autobiography of a Yogi*. Nevada City, CA: Crystal Clarity Publishers, 1995. Reprint of the 1946 original edition.

———. *Revelations of Christ*. Nevada City, CA: Crystal Clarity Publishers, 2010.

Zosimos of Panopolis. *The Book of the Keys of the Work*. Edited by Theodor Abt and translated by Salwa Fuad and Theodor Abt. Zurich: Living Human Human Heritage Publications, 2016.

———. *The Book of Pictures: Mushaf as-suwar*. Edited by Theodor Abt and translated by Salwa Fuad. Zurich: Living Human Human Heritage Publications, 2011.

# Index

Page references in *italics* refer to illustrations.

# About the Author

Kevin B. Turner is the Director for Asia, a senior teaching faculty member, and a field research associate at the Foundation for Shamanic Studies (FSS). He was also a residential facilitator at the Monroe Institute (TMI) for more than twelve years.

Kevin has been a Kriya yogi since 1986 and was personally initiated by Swami Hariharananda Giri, the last living disciple of Sri Yukteswar, at Karar Ashram in Orissa, India. He has also received initiations and training in the Karma Kagyu School of Tibetan Buddhism and has studied esoteric traditions across Eurasia.

Born in Arizona, Kevin has lived in Asia for more than thirty years and is now based in Bali, Indonesia. His website is **shamanism-asia.com**.

# BOOKS OF RELATED INTEREST

**Dark Light Consciousness**
Melanin, Serpent Power, and the Luminous Matrix of Reality
*by Edward Bruce Bynum, Ph.D., ABPP*

**Kriya Yoga for Self-Discovery**
Practices for Deep States of Meditation
*by Keith G. Lowenstein, M.D.*
*with Andrea J. Lett, M.A.*

**Vipassana Meditation and Ayahuasca**
Skillful Means for Transcending the Ego and
Opening to Spiritual Growth
*by C. Clinton Sidle*

**Thai Tattoo Magick**
The Initiatory Practices of the Thai Buddhist Magicians
*by Sheer Zed*

**Searching for the Philosophers' Stone**
Encounters with Mystics, Scientists, and Healers
*by Ralph Metzner, Ph.D.*

**Jung, Buddhism, and the Incarnation of Sophia**
Unpublished Writings from the Philosopher of the Soul
*by Henry Corbin*

**Psychedelic Buddhism**
A User's Guide to Traditions, Symbols, and Ceremonies
*by Lama Mike Crowley*
*Forewords by Dr. Ben Sessa and Gwyllm Llwydd*

**The Alchemical Search for the Unified Field**
Pythagorean, Hermetic, and Shamanic Journeys into
Invisible and Ethereal Realms
*by R. E. Kretz*

INNER TRADITIONS • BEAR & COMPANY
P.O. Box 388 • Rochester, VT 05767
1-800-246-8648 • www.InnerTraditions.com

Or contact your local bookseller